A Midnight Dark & Golden

Books by Holly Race

Midnight's Twins
A Gathering Midnight
A Midnight Dark and Golden

A MIDNIGHT DARK & GOLDEN

HOLLY RACE

HOT KEY BOOKS

First published in Great Britain in 2022 by
HOT KEY BOOKS
4th Floor, Victoria House
Bloomsbury Square
London WC1B 4DA
Owned by Bonnier Books
Sveavägen 56, Stockholm, Sweden
www.hotkeybooks.com

A CIP catalogue record for this book is available from the British Library.

ISBN: 978-1-4714-1119-9
Also available as an ebook and in audio

2

This book is typeset using Atomik ePublisher
Printed and bound in Great Britain by Clays Ltd, Elcograf S.p.A.

FSC www.fsc.org
MIX
Paper from responsible sources
FSC® C018072

Hot Key Books is an imprint of Bonnier Books UK
www.bonnierbooks.co.uk

For Alex
Love is easy, belief is hard
We have both, and that's our concrete

'And one can, at all events, show one's own little light here, one's own poor little trembling flame, with the knowledge that it's not the only light that is shining in the darkness, and not the only one which the darkness doesn't comprehend.'

— E. M. Forster, 'What I Believe'

'Surely something resides in this heart that is not perishable – and life is more than a dream.'

— Mary Wollstonecraft

'But who can turn the Stream of Destiny,
Or break the Chain of strong Necessity?'

— Edmund Spenser, *The Faerie Queene*

Prologue

In the wake of the Great Betrayal . . .

The devastation of Annwn was almost complete. King Arthur had not waged war on the dreams and nightmares and Fay – he had tricked them as the Trojans had once been tricked. Andraste had watched her kin crumble into inspyre, then into nothingness. The only thing holding her together was a memory of an affection. A mutual desire that she knew, from her continued existence, Arthur could not quite shake off.

She would use it against him, even as her skin flaked away and her movements slowed. She could smell the desperation of some of his followers, not far from the cave where she helped to forge the instrument of her own downfall.

There had once been a forest on this mountain, and in the forest a clearing. She could feel the memory of roots and moss beneath her sore fingers as she climbed. All was now bare rock, and even that fell away beneath her feet and hands, making little avalanches. The barren landscape was dangerous. If Arthur saw her, then he would try to obliterate her. She had to hope that he was too caught up in the success of his treachery to mind a single, helpless woman.

It took many suns to reach the top of the mountain, for Andraste was weary. Her bones cracked. The strength that once flowed through her body was deserting her. Every breath was an expulsion of her life force. At the top, she allowed herself to stop and rest, and she looked back over the landscape of the world which she once ruled. Nothing could be seen but grey. The towers and encampments that used to litter the countryside were gone. So were the beasts and creatures that had roamed there. She looked out over the sea and saw that the empires beyond were crumbling too, beneath the onslaught of Arthur's power. His reach stretched south, to the ancestral homeland where all stories began. It stretched to the west and to the east, where the stories told in distant cultures were kith to the stories told here, their common threads woven into her sinews. All was dying.

It was time to move, but Andraste's limbs had lost their strength. Arthur was killing her last – a final cruelty to the goddess he had promised to worship for a lifetime and beyond. She closed her eyes and sent out a plea to the people nearby. They heard her, thin though her call was.

The knights Lancelot, Bedevere, Palomides, Gawain and Dagonet crested the top of the mountain. They had discarded their helmets and their faces were worn and worried. Palomides was the oldest of the knights, but Lancelot looked the weariest. Andraste could feel the threads of Nimue inside him, winding around those of her brother Lugh – the muse and the warrior, united. Lancelot had come to Annwn an ingenue, delighting in all that it had to offer, loving the nightmares even though he fought them. Andraste saw him as a young boy – his mind not set in the patterns that had taken hold of Palomides and that were even now taking hold of young Bedevere. She felt his grief over what had happened here as a bolster to her fading existence. He had made the choice, though he didn't know it yet . . .

'My lady.' Bedevere knelt before her. 'We did not know. I am sorry for what has happened.'

'You summoned us, my lady, did you not?' Palomides said, his voice deep and urgent. 'Is there something that we can do? Some way of reversing this?'

Dagonet laughed bitterly. 'Reverse it? How? How can we remake a world when he has such power? We may as well throw ourselves off these rocks and dash our brains out on that grey stuff below.'

'If he can destroy it in an instant, then surely it can be remade?' Gawain said. 'The other knights may have followed Arthur, but we remain true to our oaths. We swore to protect this land, and we do not see its destruction as protecting it. We remain true to Annwn, not to *him*.'

Andraste smiled weakly. 'I know. That is why I called you. My love betrayed me and the Fay, but there is a way back. Not in your living memory, but there have been other times when Annwn has been on the brink of destruction. Always there are people, Immral or not, who seek the death of imagination. And often they come close. But there is always hope.'

'How?' Lancelot said.

'Tell us and we will do it,' Dagonet promised.

'Not do it, find it,' Andraste said. 'The font of inspyre that will bring Annwn back. Kill the king, and then find it.'

She groaned. The pain coursing through her spiked. Arthur had become aware of her continued existence. She could feel the focus of his intent bent upon her now.

'Find what, my lady? Find what?'

Andraste felt her bones give way, twirling into inspyre inside her body. Her muscles and her veins would follow soon. She sank back, and Lancelot caught her in his arms. His youthful face stared in desperation into her eyes, a child witnessing the passing of an elder and understanding death for the first time. As she felt the voice and the life blood leave her body, she croaked out her final words, whispering the clues that would lead them to what they needed.

'The Grail. Find the Grail.'

Chapter 1

I can't get used to fighting without my Immral. Three months on and I still call on my power in the middle of battle.

My scimitar is moving faster than ever before, almost beyond my control – running on survival instinct. But nothing I do makes a difference. If I had time to think clearly, I'd curse my own lack of skill – my short-sightedness in not practising with my weapon more, back when I didn't really need it. Then I might stand a chance. But back then I had Immral, and I relied on it to get me out of scrapes like this.

'Help!' Nerizan shouts from the other side of the street, as overwhelmed as I am. There's a weak flash of blue light. My brother has freed her. He is the only one of us with Immral now – and the part of the power that was once mine is now his. I won't ask him for help. I won't. I double my efforts, swinging my scimitar back and forth, cutting down dreamer after dreamer, but they still push forward. They know no fear, no emotion but the desire to eradicate me and my kind from existence.

Gone are the times when we protected dreamers from their nightmares. Now it's all we can do to keep ourselves alive. It's not like there are any nightmares left to combat. Dreams – both good and bad – have fled Annwn, leaving nothing but the focused malice of Medraut's dreamer army in their place. And it's defeating us, slowly but certainly, like an ocean eroding a cliff.

A blade I didn't spot flashes down on my right, cutting deep into my shoulder.

'You little –' I swear, and reach a hand towards the dreamer, still expecting the old pull of Immral to run through my brain and arms and erupt in an explosion of inspyre. But nothing happens. I am forced to use the less elegent tactic of slashing my scimitar across his chest instead. He falls, and two more leap to take his place.

A dreamer at the back of the crowd attacking me drops with a muted cry. Another thud and two more go down, speared on the same arrow.

Samson.

Soon his face appears above the scrum, determined and fierce, as he uses handheld arrows to stab and slash at my assailants. In a few swipes he's at my side.

He grins. 'Thought you looked lonely.'

'Bored, too,' I pant, wishing I looked as calm as he does.

'What do you think?' he says. 'Time to get the rest of the regiment involved?'

What he means is: time to ask Ollie to finish this. I can't bring myself to say yes, but I don't say no either. Samson talks into his helmet and a moment later another blue flash has scattered the remaining dreamers. They are unconscious; not a threat for now. My brother stands in the middle of the street, his chakrams still hanging at his belt, his arms outstretched and his ears bleeding with the effort of using my Immral. No, not mine. *His*, now.

He and Samson had only been waiting for me to say the word. They could have stepped in at any time, and they didn't because they didn't want to injure my pride.

'Thanks for thinning them out.' Ollie smiles at me. 'I couldn't have done that with all of them.'

He's lying. We both know it. It would be so easy to fall back into my old surliness; to take refuge in thinking badly of my brother, and to imagine that Samson is pleased that I no longer have Immral, so he can play the saviour. It's a huge effort not to make a sarcastic comment about damsels in distress. I nod my thanks, which is all I can manage. Ollie can tell that this was the best I can offer, because he virtually sags in relief.

Samson is less aware of how close he just came to having his head bitten off. 'You okay?' he says, touching me lightly. I think he wants to grip my waist, but we're technically still on patrol, so his hand lingers on my arm instead.

The veneurs and apothecaries who've been holed up in a nearby medical unit swarm the street, checking for casualties. Jin, an apothecary and a friend, dearly won – nods at the cut on my shoulder. 'If I bandage that up you're not going to snap at me, are you?'

I pout and turn around in reply, pulling at my tunic to reveal the wound.

'Bloody hell,' Nerizan says, 'you kept fighting through that, Fern?'

'She's tough, that's for sure,' Jin says, probing the wound. I wince. There's a tingling in my shoulder, deeper than the cut, that makes me want to scream and lash out. I shake my head to clear it.

'You dizzy?' Jin asks.

'No,' I reply. 'You cleaning it just feels weird.'

'I'm being as gentle as I can,' she says, with a hint of her old irritation.

'I'm not saying you're not.'

I bite my lip and shake my head again. *Must not go back to the old Fern*. I don't want to be bitter. I have to hold on to the person I had become, even if I can feel her slipping away a little more each day.

'There, all patched up,' Jin says, slapping me on the back in an atta-girl kind of way.

'Cheers. Feel good as new.'

The rest of Bedevere haul themselves onto their horses. There aren't many of us left. Samson, Ollie, Nerizan and I are the remnants of the regiment that rode out of Tintagel's gates nearly two years ago. We had no idea that we were about to endure the first of many attacks machinated by Sebastien Medraut that would kill our friends and comrades.

'Can we call it a day?' Nerizan asks Samson.

'Do you want to?' Ollie replies.

'What I really want is to find an actual nightmare. Or a good dreamer to protect – one of us,' she replies.

'Ah, a palate cleanser,' I say.

'Yes, a sorbet, if you will,' she says, putting on an affected accent that reminds me of my peers at Bosco, 'to follow the main course of complete and total depression.'

Samson smiles. 'Let's see what we can do.' He relays Nerizan's request to Rachel through his helmet.

A moment later, she responds. 'It's slim pickings tonight, I'm afraid, Bedevere. But I *can* offer you a two for one on some trickster nightmares down by Parliament.'

'Done and done,' Nerizan says, but Samson and I exchange an uneasy glance. No one should be going close to Parliament unless they have to these days – not in Annwn *or* Ithr. Still, none of the other patrols are taking the job, so it's up for grabs. Nerizan looks at us desperately. She needs the hit. I understand. We all do.

'Off to Parliament we go, then,' I say.

'Bring it,' Ollie says, but he can't mask the tiredness in his voice. I know exactly how he must be feeling – the pounding headache in the back of the head. The burst of pain in the sinuses, followed by the warm rush of blood. I know it's ridiculous, but I can't help but feel jealous of Ollie. I hated the pain at the time, but it was proof that I was worth something. That I was exceptional. It turns out, though, that I wasn't exceptional enough. When my Immral was truly tested, I wasn't equal to it, and Excalibur punished me by draining me of my power.

As we draw closer to Parliament, the dreamers become more populous. Crowds of them mill around the streets, waiting for a command from their leader. It's now normal to see dreamers without mouths, and it's a growing occurrence to see them with trepanned skulls, the brain inside extracted – all thought removed. But here, as we approach Medraut's seat of power, I see not one who still has their skull intact. Coming here was a bad idea.

Lamb's haunches jostle a stray dreamer, and the dreamer twitches towards me, their face stretched in a grimace, their arms flailing wildly. I nudge Lamb out of their reach, pulling closer to Samson until our legs rub together. In any other circumstance I'd take comfort in being so close to him, but there is no comfort to be found here. The grey landscape crowds in on us just as much as the dreamers.

Then we see it – up ahead, a wall of people, blocking our path to the Houses of Parliament.

'I don't think this is going to happen, Nerizan,' Ollie says.

'I think you might be right,' she replies. Some of the nearby dreamers are eyeing the hijab beneath her helmet, inching closer to her.

'Humiliating retreat?' Samson says. We all nod.

We back the horses up, unable to find space enough to turn them. The wall of dreamers advances on us. Behind, they close in.

'Might need your help, bro,' I say out of the corner of my mouth.

'God, I wish this was still you,' Ollie says, but he closes his eyes and draws upon his Immral. With a cry of pain, he unleashes a jet of burning inspyre upon the dreamers blocking our way out. They fall back, their skin blistering beneath all that imagination.

'Go!' Samson says, and we wheel the horses round and gallop through the opening. It's not just the dreamers who reach for us as we pass. The buildings press in on us too, narrowing the streets. I curl my legs around Lamb's sides, steadying her as she weaves. Beside me, Ollie urges his horse, Balius, to leap over a group of dreamers wielding weapons, using his Immral to lift man and horse above the outstretched knives.

Nerizan's leg takes a cut that leaves a vicious, bloody mark on her horse's flank. She leans back to shove the dreamer. 'Hurt me all you like,' she says, 'but don't you touch my horse.'

It's several miles, when we're back in a relatively safe part of London, before we allow ourselves to slow to a walk and give the horses their heads. On our right, the Thames froths and roils. A sea monster rears up out of the water, great chunks of its flesh falling from its bones as it thrashes in its death throes. The blue inspyre that held it together dissipates, like an unheard whisper, and it finally bursts apart. Another creature lost to the drought of imagination.

'Remind me not to ask for stupid things again,' Nerizan says, then adds, 'Sorry.'

'Don't be,' Samson says. 'We get it, Nez.'

I nod at Nerizan. The need to fight nightmares instead of people is like a compulsion. She just said it out loud.

We round a corner, moving into narrower lanes. In Ithr, we'd be approaching St Paul's Cathedral. In Annwn, the cathedral has been replaced by a different building. Tintagel's familiar turrets rise above its neighbours, its central dome reaching for the heavens. The sight is accompanied by the low sound of war.

'Here we go again,' Ollie says.

As the castle comes into view, the source of the noise is revealed. Tintagel, my only haven in Annwn, is under siege.

Chapter 2

It began a few weeks after Medraut's coup. A steady stream of dreamers that flocked towards the moat and outer walls of the castle. They stayed there, forming a fortress of mindless, voiceless bodies, waiting for a command from their leader. It made getting in and out of the castle almost impossible for several days – if the dreamers saw us they had a tendency to attack. We took to flying out of the castle, but the extra strain on Ollie's Immral as he helped our horses over the dreamers was too great. It left him without enough energy to help us on the rest of patrol.

Lord Allenby didn't take long to come up with a solution. It came from a place that, this time last year, I'd have thought of as exceedingly unlikely – the remaining Fay. Merlin and Nimue, weakened though they are, still cling to existence. Since I brought Merlin back to life and proved my loyalty to Annwn, they have both been our allies; hiding Excalibur, bringing us news from other parts of the world and, in this case, creating a route into the castle: a moving portal that pops up when we need it a few streets away, emerging beyond Tintagel's walls.

As we ride through the portal, white light engulfs me. The sensation is akin to the gradual pull of sleep – the drawing of a soul from one realm to another. A moment later, we're inside the castle's grounds. The portal closes behind us with a sigh. We untack the horses in a busy, silent stable; the other regiments have returned at the same time, but no one speaks. Heart-deep exhaustion makes it difficult to talk. What would we talk about anyway? In the stables, our losses are too obvious for us to think about much else. The long, low building that houses the horses is only half full. Some stalls contain horses whose riders have disappeared, either because they're in trouble in Ithr, or because they've decided it's not worth the risk to keep fighting. Two lie empty in between Lamb and Natasha's horse, Domino. They used to house the horses of my friends, Sachi and Phoebe. Phoebe's death feels so long ago now that the wound should be a faded scar, but if it is, it's one that still burns. Every day, I force myself to remember her final seconds. The way her eyes caught mine as a monster raked knife-claws deep into her chest. I clutch the pain of that moment inside my heart, constantly checking it's still there, because if it is it means I'm still human. I can still feel. I'm still me.

Sachi's death is something else altogether. It's tied up with the death of her brother, Ramesh, so tangled that I can no longer work out where the guilt ends and the grief begins. I failed them both. I promised Sachi that we'd avenge her brother's death together. I painted her a heroic portrait of the two of us versus Sebastien Medraut. I brought her on board my regiment, thinking that I could protect her when all I did was put her in more danger. She was the one who realised that I could never save her anyway. It was never my place.

I used to visit Ramesh's grave in Ithr – it had become a refuge, where I could confide in my old friend even if he couldn't reply. My visits are rarer now. Seeing his grave next to Sachi's is too much of a reproach – I can almost feel Ramesh's accusatory stare from his coffin – *Why didn't you save her? Why didn't you stop her? Why couldn't you catch her before she fell?*

'Stop brooding,' Ollie says, leaning over the stable door, blood oozing from one nostril from his earlier Immral use. 'Come on, we've still got patrol notes to do *and* the castle meet.'

'I was not brooding,' I lie. 'Also, you've got a blood bogey. Might want to deal with that.'

Ollie curses, cleaning himself up as I strut past him and return to the castle.

Tintagel itself is little more comforting than the rest of Annwn. Laid out on the footprint of St Paul's Cathedral, the castle is made up of a series of rooms and wings that lead off from a central, circular hall that sits beneath a huge dome.

What used to be a bustling place full of energy has become more sombre. The will is still there to fight Medraut, but his desire to wipe the world of independent thought is finding purchase even here. The tapestries that line the wooden panels of the knights' chamber are now leeched of their once vibrant colours. Maybe it's just my eyes playing tricks on me, but sometimes I feel sure that the blue of my tunic turns grey from time to time.

Still, I try to keep my spirits up, in public at least. I may no longer be the Chosen One, but I'm still a beacon. My role is different now – I'm the mascot. I've been through more than most of the survivors, and if I can keep smiling through all of it, then others take their cue from me. Their reactions are rooted in pity for what I've lost, but I'll wear the mantle they've assigned me for now. My fixed smile only becomes genuine when I pass our harker, Rachel, who's hunched over her desk in the cloisters that line the main hall.

'Sorry about the tricksters,' she says, trying to read my expression.

'Eh, it was worth a try,' I reply. 'Thanks for finding them – can't have been easy to spot.'

'Not me, it was one of the sentinels,' she says.

'When *are* you going to get that promotion?' I comment. 'You should've moved up ages ago. You're the best harker in our year.'

She blushes and looks down at her paperwork. 'Oh, I don't mind about that . . .' she says, but I know she's lying. She's told me many times how she'd love to be one of the elite harkers who man the Round Table, and she can't do that until she's a sentinel first. I was sure that Maisie would promote her after the work she did last year in helping me alter the Round Tables. I bite back a comment – I don't want to make Rachel feel bad about it.

A familiar hand slips into mine. Samson. 'We're not off duty yet, are we?' I smile, squeezing his hand to let him know I'm not telling him off. 'We've got another . . . twenty seconds to go?'

He looks down at me with the rakish smile I've come to love. 'You know me, always breaking the rules.'

Easa, a reeve I've come to rely on for his calm ability to gather knowledge, whistles quietly as he passes, shooting us a mischievous smile. I stick my tongue out at him. Great, Fern, very mature for a seventeen-year-old. Really acting your age there.

The knights' chamber is as full as it's going to get, and even that is half empty. When I was first recruited, I'd come back from patrol and struggle to find a chair to collapse into. I only managed to get 'my' armchair because no one wanted to face the grump of Fern. But these days empty seats are everywhere. It's not just that so many of our numbers have been killed off – it's that some are deserting us.

'Katie didn't turn up again today,' I hear Natasha tell Niamh and Amina from the captains and lieutenants' table.

'Our Lucas hasn't been in for a week either,' Niamh replies. 'The little birds are flying the nest, huh?'

None of them say what we're all thinking: that there are only three reasons our knights have stopped coming, and none of them are good ones. Either they've been turned against us by Medraut, or they're too scared, or they're dead. The temptation to search for them in Ithr is strong, but even if looking for each other in Ithr was permitted, none of us have the energy or willpower to do it. It could only bring us grief.

I grab a mug of hot chocolate, but before I can sit down a reeve pops her head round the door and beckons to me. 'She wants to talk to you.' I look desolately at my drink.

'I can keep it warm for you, if you like?' Niamh grins.

'Bugger that, I'm taking it with me.'

I trudge back through the main hall and wend my way towards a staircase in the east wing of the castle. It's set back from the cloisters, and easy to miss unless you know it's there.

This is entirely intentional. Last year it was used to hide something of Medraut's. This year it is housing something else that Medraut thought was his. Rapunzel pops into my head – a damsel in distress locked at the top of a tower. But this time it's for her own good.

The reeve unlocks several doors on the way up, then one final door right at the top. 'I'll wait outside,' she says, letting me squeeze pass her. Once I'm in, she locks the door behind me. The room is more spacious than it looks from the outside. A single window points towards the river. A light draught wends its way in through a gap in the glass, and the smell of distant sea air catches in my throat. A dog – a silly-looking black and white mongrel – lopes my way and drools over my boots.

'Hi, Loco,' I say, scratching his ears. Then I look at the girl sitting by the window, her legs drawn up to her chest. 'Hi, Charlie.'

I am still getting used to calling them by these names. I spent many months calling the dog Cavall – a name given to him by the knights he attached himself to when in search of his true owner. And in Ithr, Charlie is known across the country as Lottie, the daughter of Prime Minister Sebastien Medraut. We've been keeping her in the tower for her own safety, and ours. We can't risk Medraut getting his hands on her again. The last time he did, he experimented on her in the most vile ways possible. And she's seen enough of me and Tintagel that she would undoubtedly be able to give Medraut far more information than we would like. Better for *her* to stay within the castle grounds; the only place in Annwn that Medraut can't enter.

'You wanted to talk to me?' I say.

Charlie looks up at me, and everything her father's put her through is etched across her face, so painfully I catch my breath. She struggles to focus on anything for long. Even now her eyes wander back towards the window, drawn to the only view she's had in Annwn for years. I long to be able to let her out but we can't – not until Medraut is dead. As if that will ever happen.

'I want to try again,' she says.

'I should get my brother . . .'

'No. I want it to be you.'

'Lot– Charlie, I can't. I lost my power, remember? And Ollie's always been able to read emotions and memories – I've never been able to do that.'

'No,' she frets, rubbing at her knees and elbows, 'no, it has to be you. I don't want a man in my head. I can't . . .'

'Okay,' I say, as her movements become more erratic. 'Okay, Charlie, let's see what –'

But my reassurances are too late. She emits a low whining sound that grows in volume, and starts ripping at her clothes. I try to hug her, to hold her arms down, but she's too quick for me. Then what always happens begins. Threads materialise from nowhere and loop through her eyelids, sewing them shut again. Needles appear from the air and stab into her skin. The nightmare of her past torments, brought into the present.

Feeling utterly useless, I bang on the door. 'Get Jin!' I shout, hoping the reeve can hear me.

Loco the dog is leaping up at his mistress, barking frantically. 'That's not going to help, is it?' I tell him, trying to grab Charlie's arms, to stop her from hurting herself as she pulls at the needles and claws at her eyelids. 'Please, Charlie, let me . . .'

The next moment, the door opens and Jin scoots in. Charlie makes a dash for the opening, but behind Jin, Lord Allenby appears, and he's a bear enough of a man to block any escape. Charlie shrinks back from him, seeing him through her one open eye, terrified of his presence. Jin takes the opportunity to crush a handful of herbs against the stone walls, then hold them up to Charlie's nose. The whole room is filled with the fragrance of chamomile and lavender, and something subtler – an aroma only found in Annwn – a wholesome scent that speaks of warm fires and blankets and a full stomach. All of my anxiety and alarm disappears instantly, but Charlie takes longer to calm. She continues to stim quietly from her corner, Jin murmuring platitudes into her ear and Loco nuzzling her chest. When she gathers the dog into her arms, I know she's feeling herself once more.

Jin snips at the threads and delicately pulls the needles out. They fragment in her hands.

'She's getting worse,' I tell the others.

'Yes,' Lord Allenby says from his place in the doorway, 'and we're running out of time.'

Chapter 3

We had hoped that Charlie would provide us with some way of finding out what Medraut's plans were, but perhaps it was always a fruitless endeavour. Medraut had set his own daughter up as a trap, after all. He'd known how we were going to use her: he had arranged her just so, a perfect way for me to rescue Charlie and turn her against her father. All so that I could find Excalibur, only to have him take it from me at the last moment. Of course he won't have intentionally placed any information in Charlie that we could use against him. But there might be something unintentional in there – something that might give us the key to bringing him down.

Charlie herself is willing, in theory. She asks for me nearly every night, desperate to help, but the trauma she's experienced always bubbles to the surface. If I had my brother's power, then maybe we could make some headway, but I'm useless now. Ollie's the only one who can look inside her head, and she won't – she can't – be in the same room as him or anyone else who reminds her of her father.

'It's not fair on her,' I say to Jin as we walk back down to the hall after she's patched Charlie up. 'We've got to get her to stop trying.'

'She thinks that she's the only one who can fight her dad.'

'Did I do that?' I didn't use my Immral on her a few months ago, when we first rescued her and I asked for her help, but perhaps what I said was enough to get inside her poor, broken mind.

'Don't even start,' Jin says, fixing me with one of her glares. 'You are not taking *that* guilt on as well.'

'Okay, okay,' I say, 'but bear in mind that feeling guilty is pretty much all I'm good for –'

'Nope,' Jin says. 'Not listening to the self-pity either. Shut it. Zip it. Get over yourself, King.'

'Aye, aye, Captain.' I salute and we part ways. This is why I need Jin – she doesn't let me get away with the stuff that Ollie and Samson do. This time last year I never thought I'd *need* Jin for anything, but here we are. I pop my head back into the knights' chamber and wave down one of the newer knights, Bandile. 'Have they all gone?' I ask him.

'Yeah, they said they'd wait for you before starting.'

I back out of the chamber and trot down the corridor to one of the larger rooms that line the edge of the castle. Ducking inside, I find myself at the back of a sloped lecture theatre. Rows of pews face towards a chalkboard. Most of the seats are occupied with a range of the more experienced thanes from every lore. Samson, Natasha and Ollie wave at me from the back, and I push my way over, settling myself between Natasha and Samson and leaning into his embrace.

'Missed you,' he says into my hair.

‘I should hope so. We were apart for a whole thirty minutes.’

‘Bleurgh.’ Ollie grins.

‘Sickening,’ Natasha sing-songs.

‘Jealous,’ I reply.

Something flashes across Ollie’s face. Of course he’s jealous. He may have a boyfriend in Ithr, but Kieran knows nothing about Annwn or the thanes. Ollie has to keep half of his life a secret from the person he’s supposed to be able to confide in. Sometimes I defend myself in my head, thinking that Samson doesn’t know about my Ithr life, but that’s not true. Now that I look pretty much the same in Ithr and Annwn, my burn scar visible, there’s very little left to keep secret from Samson.

I’m about to apologise when Lord Allenby enters, followed by Easa and Niamh. As usual, Easa is clutching a sheaf of papers. We have been having weekly castle-wide meetings ever since Medraut became prime minister, and the level of importance of the meeting usually correlates to how much paper Easa is carrying.

I lean forward in my seat, hope blossoming, as it always does when we’re due some news. One of the reeves’ priorities is combing through the archives to see if there’s anything in there about how to kick start my Immral. Otherwise it could be years – maybe even decades – before I regain any semblance of my former power. We don’t have that kind of time.

‘Do you think they’ve found something?’ I whisper.

‘Maybe,’ Samson says, ‘but it doesn’t matter. We’ll be fine either way.’

I bite back a retort. It’s alright for him to say that when

he's the same fighter he's always been. I'm the one who's lost part of myself.

Niamh wheels around the theatre to join us. Before I can ask her anything, she shakes her head. 'Nothing for you, Fern. Sorry.'

I bite my lip in shame. I can feel a dozen eyes on me. They're all pitying me, and not one of them knows what to say.

'Well, it's not like we don't have an Immral already,' I joke. 'Two was a crowd anyway, right, Ollie?'

Ollie doesn't reply, still annoyed with me. Some of the others exchange looks, and for once I know it's not because of me. Ollie has been getting more and more ratty lately.

'You're a superhero already,' Samson says. 'You don't need Immral to be amazing.'

It does help, though, I think.

Lord Allenby coughs significantly, and the room falls silent.

'This,' he says, taking a long list from Easa's hand and holding it up to us, 'is a list of the knights across the country who have disappeared in the last week.'

I can see, even from this distance, that the names cover the page. That in itself doesn't surprise me – of course knights in the other thaneships will be having the same fears as those from Tintagel. Niamh, who is still in contact with her former colleagues in the Cambridge branch, has told us as much. What does surprise me is what Lord Allenby says next.

'We have reason to believe that Medraut is kidnapping these knights.'

'*What?*' Natasha whispers, leaning forward.

'I *knew* it,' says Samson, who always defended those who went missing.

Something settles in my stomach – guilt over my own anger towards the knights who'd disappeared. I had thought they were either cowards or too weak to withstand Medraut's influence. I think of Charlie in her turret prison – is Medraut experimenting on them? Is he taking them because we have removed his previous victim – his daughter?

Lord Allenby holds up a hand to silence the exclamations. 'Earlier tonight, a pair of knights – two brothers – entered Annwn at the same time in the Cornish thaneship. As soon as they arrived, they were ambushed. One was taken; the other escaped.'

'Medraut took them?' Ollie asks.

'Yes and no. The brother who escaped said that he didn't see anything except for . . . this.'

Easa pins a rough sketch to a board, and the drawing grows to fill the frame. The hairs on my arms rise. Two snake-like forms wind their way across the paper. I understand immediately why they think Medraut is behind this. Instead of heads, there are sharp, eyeless mouths that remind me of the golden treitre I defeated two years ago. It's like an homage to that monster. And the snakes' bodies are covered in spikes.

'They look like Medraut's rope of thorns,' I say.

'Exactly,' Lord Allenby says, 'except that these are bigger – larger than a human. And apparently they snatched this knight's brother clean out of Annwn.'

'But he's still alive in Ithr?' Samson says. I can tell that he's as frightened as me – he presses the side of his body into me like a great tree trying to stay upright.

'That's right. But a shadow of himself, apparently. He's got no memory of the thanes, or Annwn. He barely recognises his brother.'

'And you don't know where they're coming from, these creatures? Or where they're taking our people?' Maisie, the head harker, asks from the front row.

'No,' Easa says.

'They must have come from somewhere,' Maisie says. 'Have they looked properly? Maybe if I took a team –'

'They've looked, Maisie,' Lord Allenby says warningly. 'They've all looked.'

'If you want to tell Cambridge and Oxford that they're not doing their jobs properly, though, be my guest.' Easa raises an eyebrow. There are snickers from those of us who've met the Cambridge lot and an outright snort from Niamh.

Lord Allenby looks at each of us in turn. 'It's clear that we have a new mission: find out what these things are, find out where they are coming from and, most importantly, find out what they're doing with our knights.'

If only it were as simple as that.

Chapter 4

As soon as we're dismissed, a low rumble of conversation flows around the room. No one is entirely satisfied with the decision to simply gather information. Usually it's the knights who want to run headfirst into trouble and leave the planning for later, but this time everyone is eager to do something to stem the tide of abductions, now that we suspect that's what they are.

'They weren't just flaking,' Natasha says. 'They weren't scared, or depressed. I was so angry with them all.'

'I know, it could have been any of us. But don't beat yourself up about it, okay?' Niamh says.

I turn away from them and go against the tide of people leaving the room to study the drawing up close. There's something strange about it – something I can't put my finger on. I trace the snake-creature's lithe body, from its eyeless head all the way down the horned body to . . .

'Where's the tail?' I say to no one in particular.

Easa, who had been conferring privately with Lord Allenby and Ollie nearby, looks over. 'What was that, Fern?'

'Did the knight who saw it describe the tail?'

'I think it's just a representative sketch,' Easa replies. 'I can check, though.'

'No, no it's fine.' I've done enough drawings in my time to know that sometimes you only sketch the relevant parts of a body or face, fading out when it gets less interesting. It doesn't necessarily mean anything more than that. Medraut's influence must be getting to me too – making me read things literally instead of using my imagination.

That doesn't stop me thinking about the creature, and its seeming lack of tail, when we return to Ithr. Kieran comes over for the day, so I can hang out downstairs at the dining table with my artwork, while he and my brother lie entwined on the sofa in front of a film. Kieran's over more often of late. I assumed Ollie would be happy about that, but nothing much seems to make him happy these days. He lies with his head on Kieran's lap, watching the screen listlessly.

I start a new sketch – my own version of the snake-creature, and play around with finishing it. *Does* it have a tail? Are the two heads at opposite ends of the same creature? Nothing I try feels quite right. Why can't I let this go?

'I'm so sorry,' Ollie says to Kieran, which makes me look up.

'Sorry about what?' I ask.

Kieran shrugs. 'My parents. I guess my sister's death made them realise they didn't want to lose me too, but now enough time has passed and they're not grieving as much, they're back to thinking I'm just "going through a phase".'

'Speaking of bigots,' I say, 'do we think Clemmie's going to pop in tonight?'

Dad's on night shift at the fancy apartment block where he

works as a concierge. Clemmie, his long-term girlfriend, would usually check on us, but that's been happening less and less lately. It's no mystery to us as to why that is. Ollie snorts. 'Without Dad at home she won't want to be tainted by us freaks.'

'We're not freaks,' Kieran says hotly. There was a time when I'd be as spiteful about Clemmie's change as Ollie, but mostly I just feel sad. It must be doubly hard for my brother, though – Clemmie used to adore him. Clemmie tried with me, but I made things hard for her. I'm not sure if I regret that now – I was protecting myself from being hurt. Was it worth it? Did it push Clemmie to Medraut's side more quickly? These are the questions I can't help but ask myself.

'You're coming with me to the protest, right?' Kieran asks Ollie.

'Shout Louder?' I ask.

'Course. We're not giving up, Fern. You can always rejoin, you know.'

I shake my head.

'I don't know,' Ollie says, 'I'm so tired . . .'

'Come *on*.' Kieran jiggles Ollie's head. 'That's what they want – to wear us out. It'll be fun.'

Ollie eventually agrees, but there's no enthusiasm to it. Not for the first time, I worry that my wonderful, popular, vibrant brother is . . . fading away.

Kieran stays the night, so I don't get a chance to raise the matter with Ollie until the next day. We meet up on our way back from school, as usual. It's safety in numbers. Medraut's followers are less likely to start something when we're together – if I'd been walking home alone I'd have been spat on or shoved at least twice already.

'What's going on with you?' I ask.

'What are you talking about?'

I look at him pointedly.

'You're imagining things, Fern. I'm fine.'

'I'm not blind. Are you okay? Is anything else the matter besides . . . ?' I gesture vaguely around us, as if to say, *the general state of the world*.

'Don't think you know me so well,' Ollie snaps.

'This is what I mean,' I push. 'The way you're acting . . .'

'Piss off, Fern,' Ollie says, and storms away. I don't try to catch up with him and I'm not going to apologise. Something *is* wrong, and if I don't work out what it is, I'm scared that it will consume my brother. But as soon as I've decided not to pursue him, I regret it. I'm alone on the street now, and even though this part of London is more accepting than most, Medraut's influence is still potent. A group of men loiter outside a takeaway, swigging beer and jeering at passers-by. Then one of them fixes on me – and on my burn scar – and I know that I'm in trouble. He swaggers into my path. I sidestep. He blocks me. I move the other way. He mirrors. His friends catch on to the game now, cheering him on.

'Don't be unfriendly, love.'

'She's playing hard to get.'

'I just want to get past,' I say, as firmly as I can.

'Aww, don't you want to talk? You're hurting my feelings,' the man sneers.

'Get away from my sister.'

Ollie is there, pushing the man aside and dragging me past. He radiates . . . not rage, although that's some of it. Power.

He radiates power. It's the Ithr version of his Immral, I realise suddenly. This is the kind of power Medraut wields here: the ability to command others, to dominate or light up a room. It's the kind I had started to wield before my Immral was taken from me.

'We were just playing,' the man says.

'Let's go,' I mutter, pulling at Ollie's arm. All I want to do is get home.

'Like we'd be interested in a face like that anyway,' one of the other men mutters.

Ollie starts back, but I am quicker. I might not have my Immral any more, but I still have a right hook. And I use it, putting all my anger behind it, feeling for the first time since I lost my power that I am strong again.

The man reels back, more out of shock than pain. His friends crowd round him and I pull Ollie away, the two of us running as fast as we can down side streets until we're sure we're not being followed.

'That was awesome,' he pants as we slow. Adrenalin is still surging through me. My knuckles are raw, making me think I might regret this later. But months – *years* – of pent-up anger at the injustice of what Medraut, Jenny, Clemmie, my dad and even Ollie have put me through, all came out in that one moment.

'I wouldn't have been brave enough if you hadn't come back to help,' I say.

'Yeah, well, it wouldn't have happened in the first place if I hadn't stormed off like a brat,' he replies.

Neither of us mention our argument. A truce has been called.

The truth of the matter will accumulate like sediment at the bottom of a pool, and eventually, when enough has gathered, it will push up into the light. For now, though, I will have to let it fester.

At home, I nurse my knuckles. As we always do after school now, Ollie puts on the news and we sit on the sofa, homework on our laps, with one eye on what's being said. Not a day goes by that Medraut isn't given airtime, the news reporters barely concealing their adoration.

'You've got to be kidding me,' Ollie snaps. I look up from my chemistry textbook. On the screen, a headline slides past: *Day of Remembrance Will Mark the Deaths of the Sleeping*. The reporter reads a statement from Medraut – something about holding our lost closer to us and remembering what they died for.

'They died for *you*!' Ollie says tearfully. But the screen has changed now – a grid of faces, just a handful of those who were lost in their sleep – appear. All of them killed either by the treitres or more recently Medraut's dreamers in Annwn.

I point at the screen. 'Notice anything?'

We stare at the grid. The faces are so similar that they might as well be the same person. They look eerily like Medraut or Charlie: cookie cutter acceptable. They are deliberately leaving out anyone who doesn't fit his ideal.

Just as I can't pinpoint why the snakelike monsters not having a tail bothers me so much, there's something about Medraut's eradication with that grid, and Kieran's parents' regression that feels inexplicably linked.

I have the same niggle when Ollie and I visit our friends'

resting places. Sachi and Ramesh's graves are two of the few that are still surrounded by flowers. Their family hasn't forgotten them, but from the look of the many other new graves, a lot of families have. This part of the cemetery used to be a riot of colours, celebrating lives that were cut short unfairly and suddenly. Now most graves lie bare. I bite back anger at the people who are moving on so quickly from their loved ones. What right have I to be angry at them when I'm, in part, responsible for some of these deaths? Sachi, closing her eyes, pulling away from me (or did I let her drop, to save Ollie? Which one is the truth?). Brandon, Medraut's leech-like creature feeding on his throat. Phoebe, her eyes pleading with me, willing me to reach her when I was too slow. Vien, Milosz, Linnea, who sacrificed themselves so that I could survive to become . . . what? The girl who lost Excalibur and lost her Immral in the process.

As Ollie arranges our supermarket-bought flowers, a cold wind passes through the trees around us, rustling the plastic wrapping. If I hadn't known that true ghosts have no ability to control the weather, I could have imagined this was the siblings, trying to tell me something.

Ollie sits back on his heels. 'There. I think we're done. Yellow for Sachi.'

'She'd have hated that,' I say. 'Swap hers with Ramesh's.'

Ollie is about to retort, when his eyes land on something behind me. He stands up quickly, links arms with me, and walks me along a narrow path that skirts the cemetery. I look back.

Two figures are hunched over the siblings' resting place now.

I recognise them from Ramesh's funeral – their parents. I often think about the Helliers. I sent them a letter a few months ago, just after Sachi's death, telling them the truth about the knights, Annwn and Sebastien Medraut. No one else knows that I did it. Quite apart from it being against the rules of the thanes, I knew what Ollie would say: 'They'll think you're mad. You might have upset them even more, Fern, you idiot.' He's probably right, but if there's the smallest chance that they believe me, it will be worth it. I can't imagine the truth upsetting them any more than having two dead children will.

As we leave the cemetery, I look back at Mr and Mrs Hellier one last time. He is kneeling before his children's graves, saying a prayer. She is looking straight at me.

Chapter 5

On the surface, nothing much changes after Lord Allenby's revelation that Medraut might have something to do with the disappearances of the knights. Underneath, though, there is a shift in the currents that steer the castle. The reeves, who had been spending all their time in the archives, now divide their efforts between research and tracking knight activity with the other thaneships. A huge map of the country is erected in one of the side rooms, and I often catch Easa adding pins to it – the places where missing knights were last seen.

Jin leads a small team of apothecaries who study the thorned ropes we found inside dreamers' heads last year, to see if they can offer us any clues to their larger counterpart's purpose. Others peek into the knights' chamber and the stables before we head out on patrol, offering handmade pendants containing herbs. 'There's shamrock and speedwell in this one,' someone tells me, trying to tie it round my neck as I fit Lamb's bridle. 'That's for luck and protection.'

'Sounds like something people used to ward off the plague,' I comment, and at the first opportunity I let Lamb eat the thing. Plants might genuinely have magical powers in Annwn, but none of us know what these creatures are or how to stop them. I highly doubt that a few dried leaves will do the trick.

The biggest change, though, is that *everyone* is on edge. I don't need Immral to feel the guilt, anxiety and fear flying round the castle like tornadoes.

One night, Natasha storms into Tintagel in a rage. It's not like her – she normally wears her calmness like a mask. She snaps at her regiment in the stables, and when her horse Domino nuzzles her a little too hard she says, 'Oh cut it *out*, Dom, for God's sake,' in a way that makes him flick his ears and stare at her in hurt. After patrol she stomps into the knights' chamber and throws herself into a chair. I eye her warily, and keep my distance. Ollie ambles over and bears the brunt of her wrath instead.

'Just sit down already. Why is everyone so *slow* today?' she says.

He raises his eyebrows at me in silence, refusing to engage with her.

'There's no need to be like that,' I say.

'I'm not being like anything,' she huffs.

'You're being a bitch,' Niamh says, approaching. 'What's happened? Tell me – you know I'll get it out of you eventually.'

Natasha grumbles, but gives in to Niamh's demands. 'It's my housemates. We . . . we lost one of them back when the treitres attacked Tintagel.'

Instinctively, I reach for Natasha's hand. She's never mentioned this before. She's been dealing with an Ithr loss on top of everything else and she never said. Samson joins us silently, a grave expression on his face.

Natasha continues. 'Anyway, he had this mug. One of those cheap ones with this slogan on it. *I'm a ray of fucking sunshine*. Kind of tacky, but it was his thing. He wouldn't drink from anything else, even wine had to be poured into this stupid mug. After he died we kept it in the kitchen, like in memory of him, so he'd always be with us. It was the only thing his family let us keep.'

Natasha takes a deep breath, holding back tears. 'I came home this afternoon and the others – they'd thrown it away. I'd never even have known if I hadn't needed to tidy up the kitchen and seen it in the bin, just lying there on top of some old fruit.'

'Are you sure it was them?' Samson says. 'It might have been a mistake – a cleaner . . . ?'

'It was them,' Natasha says harshly. 'You know what their excuse was?' She looks up at all of us, ranged around the table. 'They'd forgotten it was his. The *one thing* we always teased him about. That mug was basically attached to him and they'd forgotten? And they looked confused when I reminded them, like all three of them had just –' she clicks her fingers – 'erased him from their memories.'

Ollie startles. 'Oh my God, it's not them, Natasha. It's Medraut.'

'That's a bit of a reach,' Niamh says.

'No, it's happened to me,' Ollie says. 'Or, well, not to me – to my friend.' He glances at me, and I know he means Kieran. 'He lost his sister, and I was around at his house the other day and mentioned her, and his parents just got this totally blank look on their faces, like they'd forgotten her for a moment. It sounds like the same thing, right?'

'And you think it's because of Medraut?' Natasha sounds hopeful – she doesn't want to believe that her friends could be so heartless.

'It might not be something he's purposefully instigated,' Samson says, 'more like a side effect of everything that he's doing. The more we remember the actual people who've died, the more we might seek a reason for their deaths, right? We might get angry. I guess he doesn't have much use for anger any more – he just wants us brainwashed.'

We look at each other, the pain of our losses still raw enough to show on our faces, and we appreciate the truth of it. Ghosts are powerful. In Ithr, they are sources of fear. In Annwn, they are memories, signs of love everlasting. And Medraut is killing those memories as surely as he's killing imagination. Without our ghosts, we are nothing but empty shells. I think of how tired Ollie looks whenever Kieran persuades him to go to a protest, of the soul-sucking stillness in the stables now, and the truth of Samson's words sinks in. We are approaching Medraut's endgame: exhaustion comes before surrender.

'We should –' Natasha begins, but she is cut off by a distant scream. We rush out of the chambers in search of its origin. The sound is coming from Charlie's turret. An apothecary storms down the stairs from her room just as Lord Allenby strides out from his office to see what's going on.

'She's impossible!' the apothecary sputters.

'What were you doing up there?' Lord Allenby demands.

'I was trying to get her to open up . . .'

'Did you have authorisation?'

'We don't have time! We need her information *now*.'

I spot Jin slipping up the stairs to comfort Charlie, but my eyes are drawn back to Lord Allenby who has grown very still. The apothecary shrinks before his quiet rage.

'That young woman has endured endless torture from one of the people who should be protecting her. And you think that finding out what her father is up to is worth torturing her more, do you?'

'No, but –'

'Get out.'

'Sir?' The apothecary is disbelieving.

'I don't want any apothecary who re-traumatises someone in my castle.'

As the apothecary walks, shame-faced, to hand in their portal to the reeves, I watch Lord Allenby. He is staring up through the open door of the turret. I didn't think it was possible to admire him more, but in this moment I do. How can we stand against Medraut in good conscience if we're willing to stoop to his level?

'Do you think she'll be okay, sir?' I ask him.

'I don't know, Fern. What she needs is to feel safe, but how can she with so many people around who remind her of her father?'

Last year, Charlie was becoming increasingly cruel towards me. That was how I knew she was under her father's influence – her erratic behaviour convinced me that something was very wrong. I was right – Medraut was experimenting on his own daughter, and even though he can't reach her while she's in Tintagel, the scars run deep. In Ithr she is mellower than she was last year, but still a shell of her former self.

At Bosco she sits by herself. Once she would have been surrounded by a gaggle of friends. I don't know whether it's her father's lack of 'protection' now, but they have finally drifted away from her, no longer seeking her orbit. I've avoided her too, assuming she wouldn't want to be close to an enemy of her family. She might not like her dad, but people have complicated feelings when it comes to blood ties.

But the day after her latest meltdown, I am drawn to her. There's something about the way she sits so neatly, her legs crossed at the ankles, her gaze unfocused, that makes me want to comfort her. Then I realise what it is: she is moving her arms, softly mechanical. It's the same way she strokes Loco, the memory of her dog, in her little tower cell. I find myself sitting next to her. I think she's aware of my presence, because she angles her body towards me, accepting my company. I remain quietly next to her until her movements slow and finally still.

'I see you a lot. In my dreams,' she says. It's almost a question – wanting to make sure she's not going mad.

'Yes,' I whisper.

'There's you, and a woman called Jin. And a man. Tall . . .' She begins the stroking again. If Loco were really there he would be on his back, blissful.

'His name's Lord Allenby. He's nice. I promise he's there to help you.'

She looks at me for the first time, her eyes wide.

'He reminds me . . .' She peters out.

'Of your dad?' I finish. She nods. 'I get that,' I say, 'but he's about as different from Medraut as it's possible to be. He's been working against your dad for decades. He's sacrificed so much . . .' I can't go on. Only I know that Lord Allenby is homeless in Ithr. He would hate for anyone else to realise what Medraut's attacks more than fifteen years ago did to him.

'You told me you were going to kill him, didn't you?' she asks mildly.

'Your dad?'

She nods.

I check we're not being overheard before replying, 'Yeah.'

'Why is he not dead then?'

There's no malice or complaint in her voice – only curiosity.

'Do you still want him to be . . . dead, I mean?'

'Yes, please.'

The simplicity of her statement, coloured with a desperate sadness, shakes me.

'He's really safe? Lord Allenby?' she asks again.

'He is,' I say. 'You can trust him. I swear.'

She nods and turns away. I get up to leave, but her hand shoots out and grasps my wrist.

'Stay with me until the bell rings?' she says. I nod, and there we sit in silence, her hand resting on my arm as though I'm her anchor, until the bell sweeps us into our separate classes.

Chapter 6

Dad considered pulling me out of Bosco, after Medraut became prime minister. Even my purposefully ignorant father could no longer ignore the fact that I was being targeted by people who can't stand what I look like. I may no longer have red irises, but my burn scar is noticeable enough to mark me as different. And who knows, maybe Medraut has put some kind of 'bullseye' on me in people's minds in Annwn, so that they are drawn to hate me in Ithr.

'We could look at putting you into a different local,' Dad said. 'Maybe you and Ollie could move there together, now you . . .' *Don't hate each other's guts* was the unspoken end to the sentence. 'Or there's other scholarships we could put you up for? At a public school closer to home?' he said.

I shook my head. It still messes with my head that the only reason I'm at Bosco is because the person who murdered my mother arranged it. I can't work out how I feel about that, because Ellen herself didn't seem to know why she did it. Pity? To keep an eye on me? Remorse? Could someone who felt no fear feel any of those things? Or was I an offering to Medraut – an ironic gift presented for his daughter to bully?

For him to laugh at my misfortune?

But the events of the other day – the men blocking my path – have shaken me more than I'd like to let on. Instead of meeting Ollie at Stratford station for a gentle stroll back home, I half-jog, half-pelt along any road that feels too busy, or not busy enough. I get up even earlier to try to avoid the morning rush. If I'm in place before my fellow students arrive at Bosco, it's easier to melt into the background of the classroom.

Even though I don't tell anyone that's what I'm doing, my efforts have been noticed. Kieran turns up a few days later, clutching a make-up bag. He opens it on our dining table, brushes and powder spilling out across the wood.

'Am I performing in a musical?' I say, my voice sharp with warning.

'The opposite, actually. You're going to put on a disguise,' he says.

I shake my head.

'See?' Kieran says to Ollie. 'I told you she was way too brave.'

Ollie scowls. Suddenly, I understand that this is a bone of contention between them: Ollie is the one who wants me to do this, not Kieran.

'Please, Fern, will you stop being such a martyr?' my brother says.

'I'm not. I just don't think I should have to hide who I am.'

'You shouldn't. But what's the point in putting yourself in harm's way? What does anyone get out of you doing that?'

'You can talk. How was the Shout Louder protest yesterday?'

'That's different. We're in a group. You're mostly on your

own. I can't be around all the time, and you're going to break your hand if you punch everyone who tries to mess with you.'

I do see his point. Haven't I given enough to the cause already, even if no one in Ithr knows it? So, with an appropriate amount of grumbling so they know I'm still me, I let Kieran show me how to use foundation to cover up the worst of my burn scar. I obediently stroke the brush across my cheek until the shadows and hollows of my puckered skin pass for a case of old acne. Anyone getting up close will spot the deception, but it will allow me to get to school and back in peace.

'Keep it,' Kieran says, waving a hand airily when I try to return the make-up and brush. He knows I couldn't afford to buy this brand myself. I try to stifle the jealousy that flares up whenever I'm confronted by Kieran's wealth.

Jealousy is something I'm having to stifle a lot now. I'm an old hand at it, in fact. In Ithr, I'm jealous of Kieran, and in Annwn, I'm jealous of Ollie. It still hurts to see him wielding the Immral that should have been mine. I thought the pain would fade, but it is as tender as ever. I am even, to my shame, sometimes jealous of Samson, and his ability to see the best in anyone, even the dreamers who are attacking us. It comes so easily to him.

There is only one person towards whom I harbour only good wishes: Charlie Medraut.

It's been a few days since I spoke to her. She's been quiet in Annwn, insisting that only Loco be allowed inside her tower. But tonight, she asks to see Lord Allenby. Jin goes up with him, herbs in hand, but something tells me that tonight she won't have to use them. Despite his bulk, he moves up those stairs like a stranger approaching an injured animal, trying to communicate that they're there only to help.

I go out on patrol with a lighter heart. Perhaps what I said in Bosco has got through to Charlie – maybe this is the start of her healing. My good mood doesn't last for long, though. Tonight's route takes us through Richmond Park – a swathe of woods and fields in south-west London. The foliage and trees that once reached right up into the clouds in Annwn now crumble if you even brush a leaf as you pass. Dinosaurs and unicorns used to graze alongside the deer, but they are long gone. Few dreamers venture into the park now. The result is a melancholy, dying expanse of parkland.

'How's Gawain doing, Rachel?' Samson asks through his helmet. Amina wasn't looking forward to her Soho route, which has been increasingly dangerous of late.

'They're okay at the moment,' Rachel's voice comes back. 'They'll let you know if they need help.'

Nerizan and I exchange relieved glances.

'Oh!' Rachel says, so quietly I almost don't hear it.

'What is it?' Samson asks.

'The Round Table. It's . . . something's wrong with it.'

No one says anything. Rachel ended her sentence on the kind of note that makes you hold your breath. Sure enough, a few seconds later she speaks again. 'Bedevere, the Round Table is blurred at a place not far from you.'

'Violet inspyre?' I ask. Violet would mean Immral use, and has done ever since I changed the Round Tables earlier this year – our way of keeping track of Medraut's activity.

'No,' Rachel says. 'No inspyre. I can't explain it.'

'Tell us where to go,' Samson says, and a moment later we're galloping through the park, over ground that turns from lush grass to thick, stumpy tufts and then fades into dry soil. We should be in the thickest part of the woods now, but the trees falter. Some have toppled, some are mere stumps. Eventually, they disappear entirely. The earth is bumpy. Root systems that should be deep underground have risen to the surface in search of sustenance. It's as though some great storm has ravaged the landscape. I think of the tornado of Immral that appeared above the Royal Albert Hall earlier this year – Medraut's show of strength. The Hall had eventually reappeared, although it has an empty, abandoned feel to it now rather than the sparkling energy that once used to race through its galleries and stages. If a similar storm has occurred here, the trees show no signs of reappearing. Anger bubbles in me. Medraut *has* to be stopped. In this moment, looking at the devastation he has wreaked on Annwn, I realise in my bones that I am willing to do, to sacrifice, *anything* to bring him down and restore this world. *My* world. That knowledge settles inside me with a strange rush of warmth. Purpose. I may not have Immral any more but that doesn't matter. There are other ways of helping a cause. Having Immral gave me a chance of surviving, but survival no longer feels important.

Then we move on out into a clear space, and my eyes refuse to adjust to what they're seeing. An expansive clearing of grey soil and sky that shimmers as I move. I can see no end to it, and no beginning. It is at once substance-less and crushing, like grief. Once when I was much younger, maybe five or six, I had a fever overnight. I remember waking up and feeling as though my bedroom had expanded – the walls were both claustrophobic and frighteningly far away. Every logic of space had evaporated to my heat-soaked, dream-bordered mind. This gives me that same sensation.

Ollie slides off Balius's back and moves into the space, his hands outstretched. I can tell that he's trying to feel the inspyre there, and suddenly the empty feeling that was outside is inside too. *I should be doing that*. All I say is, 'Find anything?'

He shakes his head, then draws back as though stung.

'Come and see this,' he says.

We all dismount. Most of the horses are spooked by whatever is happening, fidgeting and stamping their hooves. Lamb follows me, though, her muzzle pressing against my back.

'Stand where I'm standing,' Ollie says, marking the ground with a scuff of his boot and moving to one side. Samson looks first, and his sharp intake of breath tells me nothing. Then he guides me to the right angle.

The view changes like a mirage. What was desolation morphs to a familiar sight: Richmond Park, full of trees and lush grass. It is night-time, though; a sliver of moonshine battling through the foliage. I shift slightly and I'm back in the cold sunlight and bare earth of Annwn. It takes me a moment to work out what has happened. As I move away to let Nerizan see, I voice it: 'That was Ithr.'

'I think so too,' Samson says.

'Are we sure?' Ollie asks. 'Couldn't it just be . . . I don't know, a portal to a different part of Annwn?'

Nerizan shakes her head. 'I can feel it, can't you?'

Now that she's said that, I *did* feel something different

when I was looking into the other Richmond Park. A pull at my eyes, like that moment between waking and sleep. Lamb nudges me out of the way and approaches the spot.

'Lamb, don't,' I warn, but she sniffs at the portal – or whatever it is – before thrusting her muzzle through.

'No!' I say. But Lamb doesn't seem to be in pain. The part of her in Annwn is my normal Lamb – brown, scraggy fur with one black sock. Her head, the part of her in Ithr, is outlined in blue – a remnant of the inspyre of which she's made. She is translucent – I can see leaves through her cheek. In Ithr, she is a ghost.

She draws back, and her muzzle becomes solid and coloured again.

'That settles it then,' Nerizan says. 'Definitely Ithr.'

'How, though?' Samson says. 'This isn't any normal portal.'

'Medraut,' I say grimly. 'He's done this. Look around us. He's drained this part of Annwn of inspyre.'

'You think the borders between the worlds are tearing?' Ollie says.

I look at the sliver again. 'I think that's exactly what's happening.' This is no portal: it's a rip.

Chapter 7

Lamb whickers mournfully as the rest of us look at each other, dumbfounded. The truth of my words is sinking in. It feels like the culmination of everything that Medraut has done – sucking Annwn so dry that he breaks it, like a brittle leaf. Inspyre is the glue, the very substance of Annwn – without it the world cannot hold together. We've seen something like this already, with dreams trying to escape Medraut's onslaught by running into Ithr through portals of their own creation. But now I wonder – *were* they of their own creation? Or were those portals the beginning of this rip?

On impulse, I reach my own hand towards the gap between the worlds.

'What are you doing?' Ollie hisses. But I am beyond caring. Samson grabs my wrist, but I shake him off and, knowing how reckless I'm being, I step through the sliver into Ithr.

The strangest feeling takes hold of me. In Annwn I always felt corporeal. I suppose I was technically still inside my own body in Ithr. But now, beneath Ithr's moon, I am only spirit. I can feel that somewhere across the other side of London, my soul has left my earthly form. I look down at my hands and arms. Like Lamb when she pushed through to this side, they are translucent. The rich blue of my tunic is faded, and my fingers and palms are mere outlines. I am a ghost. I almost laugh. A few years ago, this is how I felt – people ignored me, not wanting to feel uncomfortable by looking at my eyes and burn scar. So now I have been two different ghosts – one real, one metaphorical.

'Fern, come back now,' Samson says.

'Is that an order, Captain?' I say. I look at him through the doorway between the worlds. Compared to the rich, midnight darkness of Ithr, Annwn looks grey. That's never happened before – in my mind Annwn has always been bursting with colour and excitement. Seeing the two side by side, Medraut's ravaging of Annwn has never been more apparent.

'Yes, it's an order,' Samson says. He's furious with me, and my challenge to his authority. I can't really blame him.

'I'm fine,' I say, 'look.' I wave at him, but Nerizan gasps in shock. The inspyre that was holding my form together in Ithr is scattering like a dandelion head. My fingers are dissipating. I try to control my panic as I hurry back towards the gateway. Ollie is reaching through, his eyes closed and his arms outstretched. Something tenses inside me involuntarily, and the scattered inspyre flocks back to my fingers. Ollie's Immral has made me whole again.

I step back through the gateway, already ashamed. Ollie's nose is bleeding. It must have cost him a lot to put me back together.

'It's okay,' I say, holding up both hands and twirling for the others. My little display is meant to apologise for my recklessness. In the old days, when I had Immral as well, this schtick made the others smile. Now, they stare at me in disappointment. Ollie is nursing the hand he had been using to hold me together – blisters rise on his skin. That never happened to me when I used Immral.

'I'm sorry,' I say, 'I didn't think –'

'You thought we didn't need you now you don't have Immral?' Ollie says, wiping the blood from his nose. He spits some more onto the ground, away from the rest of us. The scarlet splatter is stark against the grey soil. Ollie stalks back to Balius. Samson follows him. I don't dare look at him. I don't need Immral to feel the rage rolling off him.

Behind us, the tear between the worlds shimmers. One end, deep in the trees, contracts. The rip is closing, or maybe healing itself. I shudder at the thought of being stuck on the other side, a ghost in Ithr, knowing I couldn't survive for long without Annwn nearby, waiting to disintegrate. Maybe it feels like drowning.

'Want to ride with me?' Nerizan says as I climb into Lamb's saddle. 'The ones who feel useless have got to stick together.'

An echo of her words – *Gotta keep the Immrals together, right?* – jolts me. Linnea, sacrificing herself for me. And for what? I climb onto Lamb's back and join Nerizan as we trot silently back to our patrol route. Samson tells Rachel over the helmets what has happened, although he glosses over what I did. I suppose I should feel grateful to him, but when he's signed off, I comment quietly, 'Oh look, he's saving me again.'

As soon as the words are said, I regret them, but there's no taking them back. I cannot will the others to forget what I've said. No one reacts, so I wonder for a long time whether they even heard me. As we wind our way back towards Tintagel, I make myself believe that I was even quieter than I'd thought, that I've got away with it. As we ride across the drawbridge, I tell myself that I'm imagining the tension that sits inside the long silence between the four of us. Because to admit that I'm not imagining it would be to face the possibility that I've just messed up my relationship with Samson, my friendship with Ollie, and the final bonds between what remains of my regiment.

My delusion is shattered as soon as we get to the stables. Ollie throws me a look of such contempt I almost wither into ash on the spot. He and Nerizan stalk back to the castle. Samson is still moving around in his horse's stable, his back to me. I give Lamb a final rub down then make my way over to him. The apology is on the tip of my tongue, when he turns to me and says, 'Can I speak to you in private before we take patrol notes, knight?'

He has never spoken to me so coldly before. I've cried on him, I've shouted at him, I've been helpless with him and he's absorbed it. As I follow him towards a secluded corner of the castle grounds, I realise suddenly that even though I've been trying to mask my bitterness, I've been wanting him to lose it with me for months. My success is not as satisfying as I'd anticipated.

When he's sure no one is going to interrupt us or listen in, he speaks again. 'Do you want to be in the thanes?'

I wasn't expecting this question. 'What? Yes.'

'Because it doesn't seem like you do. If you want out, then I can talk to Lord Allenby about transferring you to a different lore, or we can remove you altogether. Wipe your memories with the morrigans and send you back to Ithr.'

I'm totally wrong-footed. I feel desolate at the very thought of being turfed out of the thanes, or being moved to something like the reeves, even if that is all I'm good for now. I hadn't thought that my bitterness was so apparent, though. 'If that's what you want,' I say.

Samson smiles, but it's not the warm, inviting, sexy smile I've come to take as a sign to reach up and kiss him. It's a smile of frustration, of anger.

'Are we really playing these games?' he says.

I don't reply. He stares at me for what feels like the longest time. Then, at last, 'Fine. I'll tell Lord Allenby that I'm requesting you have a transfer. He can talk to you about whether that means leaving the regiment or the thanes.'

And he stalks off. I watch him go, utterly lost. 'Are we breaking up?' I say stupidly.

'You tell me,' he snaps, not looking back.

My first instinct is to run away. To hide in Ithr and never come back to Annwn. I want to curl up in my bed and spend the next year feeling sorry for myself. But that isn't an option. I know I've behaved badly. But I also know that something had to shift. If Samson's broken up with me because of it, well . . . the thought shatters me, but I'd deserve it.

I make my way towards the castle, tracing his footsteps. Something tells me that for all his justified anger at me, Samson won't have gone straight to Lord Allenby. Maybe there's a chance to salvage something, even if I've lost the man I love in the process.

They're all sitting around the largest table in the knights' chamber when I enter. Neither Samson nor Ollie look up, and Natasha's uneasy smile tells me that everyone knows that something's wrong. But there is still my seat between Natasha and Ollie. More unsure of myself than I have been in years, I sit, feeling the wall looming between my brother and me.

'Right, now we're all here, shall we start?' Samson says crisply.

'Sorry I'm late –' I begin, but Ollie cuts me off.

'The thing we've got to talk about is this break between the worlds, right?'

There's another awkward pause. Niamh, who would usually throw in a light-hearted remark, flicks her gaze between Ollie, Samson and I. Amina and Natasha exchange glances. As Samson and Ollie fill in the others on what we saw in Richmond Park, I note that they still skirt around me passing through to Ithr. I don't know whether to be grateful or resentful.

'Has anyone told Lord Allenby?' Amina asks.

'Rachel was going to fill him in, but we should follow up,' Samson says.

'Why don't I go with Fern?' Niamh offers. 'You lot can talk strategy.'

I can feel Samson's eyes on me as I follow Niamh out of the knights' chamber. Once we're out in the hallway, Niamh wastes no time. 'You went through to Ithr, didn't you?'

I stare at her. 'Did Ollie –?'

'Oh come on, it's what I'd do too. Is that why they're pissed at you?'

'No,' I say. 'Well, not just that. I said something I shouldn't have.'

Niamh huffs. 'Haven't we all, lately.'

We're about to knock on Lord Allenby's door when a passing reeve comments, 'He's not in there. He's at the Round Table.'

We wheel around and make our way back up to the front of the castle.

'Would you really have gone through as well?' I ask, side-eyeing Niamh.

'Of course. What did it feel like? You'd have turned into a ghost, right?'

I think about her question for some time. The memory is already hazy – perhaps some side effect of becoming a ghost.

'I felt invisible but also really aware of the body I wasn't inhabiting. Does that make sense?'

'So basically like normal life in Ithr?' Niamh says. The way her words mirror the exact comparison I made when I was a ghost make me laugh. It's the first time I've laughed in weeks.

A group of harkers is gathered around the Round Table – more than there normally are. Rachel hovers at the edges. Maisie and Lord Allenby lean over the table, heads close.

'Sir?' Niamh says, and Lord Allenby beckons to us without looking over.

'You should see this.'

I step up to the Round Table. The last time I was this close to it, I was altering it to show where Medraut's Immral was at work. Now the table sparks with nothing but violet inspyre, and there is none of the blue that signals imagination. It is all mind control. Maisie points to the part of the table that constitutes Richmond Park.

‘Is this where the tear was, Fern?’

I nod and run my hands over the table where she’s pointing. I had expected that area to be crackling with violet inspyre, but it isn’t. Rachel had said that the map on the Round Table was blurred at that point, but it’s more than that. I run my hand over the area, and my fingers find a crack in the wood. A crack that shouldn’t be there, and one that, beneath my touch, begins to splinter and fracture across more of the table. It’s as though the table is mirroring my own heartbreak. It’s not only Annwn that’s crumbling: the Round Table is dying too.

Chapter 8

I can't shake my fear when I wake up in Ithr the next morning. The memories of the cracks glancing across the Round Table; the way Samson and Ollie had looked at me in disgust and disappointment after my little adventure as a ghost . . . Everything is falling apart. Just a few months ago I had felt broken but capable. I may not have had Immral any more, but I had Samson's affection, Ollie's comradeship, and a solid group of friends. I had felt hopeful. But all that is crumbling. I should have known it would. The foundations of my relationships have been switched since I lost my power: instead of brick they are built on sand. How could I have expected them to remain upright? How could I expect them to stay the same when I no longer know who I am?

I'm frightened to go downstairs, frightened of Ollie's continued anger. So I hide in my room until the last minute, like I used to before we became friends again. I can hear him and Dad getting ready. At one point, I think my brother pauses outside my door on his way back from the bathroom. If he had knocked, I'd have answered, but he doesn't. At last, I hear him and Dad leaving for school and work, and hurry to get my stuff together. On the train, I briefly consider messaging Ollie an apology, but I don't. The petty part of me says that Ollie wouldn't have had to use Immral to save me when I went through to Ithr if he had been the one to wield Excalibur. Then he would have been drained of the power and I would still have it. I would still be me. If I should be apologising to anyone it's Samson, for disobeying his orders and then sniping at him.

But I can't message Samson. We have never met in Ithr, despite all of the kissing and confiding we have done in Annwn. I had asked Samson if we were breaking up last night, but what was there to break up? We were never really together. Does a relationship in Annwn even count?

Charlie asks me to sit with her again at break time today. I can't find it in my heart to say no even though I had planned on spending my break in the art room, where I can be sure of being alone. The art teacher, Mr Nolan, is there less and less nowadays. There are rumours that he's been asked to resign. After all, no one's interested in art any more. At least Charlie doesn't say anything. She grips my wrist as though it's the only thing keeping her from disintegrating. Her old friends are beginning to notice. They throw me suspicious glances, whisper amongst themselves, no doubt theorising that I'm manipulating her.

Eventually, one of them – Victoria Von Gellert, who used to be Charlie's closest confidante, approaches us. 'Are you okay, Lottie?' she asks.

'Mmm,' Charlie says vacantly.

'What's she doing to you?' Victoria spits. 'C'mon, Lots, let's go somewhere else. *That* –' she nods in my direction – 'stinks.'

'No, that would be the perfume you've drenched yourself in,' I say calmly. I won't be insulted to my face. They can do it behind my back instead, like normal people.

'Did you hear what it said to me?' Victoria says to Charlie.

'I heard that you deserved it,' Charlie says. 'Leave me alone, Victoria. I want to stay here with Fern.'

Victoria gapes, then stalks back to her friends. They put their heads together, whispering furiously as they move away from my 'stench'.

'That's going to come back to bite us,' I remark.

'Maybe,' Charlie says. She doesn't speak again for the rest of the day.

But actually, Charlie standing up for me sparks something. Gratitude towards her, but it also makes me think differently about Samson and Ollie. I had been interpreting their attempts to soften my loss of Immral as pity. But maybe it wasn't pity at all? Charlie standing up for me was done out of companionship, of understanding what was right. Could Samson and Ollie be acting in the same way? Could Ollie have got the morals this time, as well as the looks?

I know that I need to fundamentally change the way I see myself. I did it once before, exorcising my victimhood, becoming more open. Losing my Immral has threatened to turn me into . . . not a victim again, but into someone resentful, someone lacking any kind of hope. I've been so used to being the leader in one form or another. The saviour, the Chosen One. My grievance with Medraut is personal: he had my mother killed. He has tried to kill me and my brother many times over. To my mind, our fates have been intertwined ever since I discovered my Immral. I don't know who I am any more if I'm not at the centre of this story.

When evening comes, I wait downstairs only long enough to see Ollie return from his latest Shout Louder protest. Kieran is with him, and I wonder briefly whether he's brought him home as protection against any argument with me.

'What's up, gorgeous?' Kieran says cheerily as he comes into the sitting room. I am always amazed at the way he takes ownership of a space that isn't his – he belongs here far more than I do.

I shrug in response, willing Ollie to meet my eyes. Kieran looks between us. 'Oh, sibling quarrel, is it? I thought Ols was a bit off.'

'Don't act like you know me so well,' Ollie says. He's smiling, but there's a tension to his expression that Kieran doesn't pick up on.

'I'm right, though, aren't I?'

'I was a dick last night,' I tell Kieran. It's easier to talk to him than it is to Ollie. 'My head's a total mess right now.'

'Because of Medraut? Clemmie and your dad?'

'Kind of. Anyway, I keep taking it out on the people I love.'

Kieran shuffles, suddenly unsure of himself, and I wonder whether I've pushed things too far, made it all uncomfortable. Then Ollie speaks from the doorway. 'I know a bit about doing that. Taking out your own head mess on the ones who can't escape you. And I did it *way* worse than you.'

I am struck, as he smiles ruefully at me, by how tired my brother looks. And even as I smile in reply, I can't shake a knot of worry.

I enter Annwn earlier than usual, hoping that Samson will be his normal organised self. There's never been a time when I've arrived and he hasn't already been in the knights' chamber, or talking to one of the other lore captains, or Lord Allenby. A quick trip to the stables for a morale nuzzle from Lamb, and I go searching for him. It takes me a long time to find him – so long that I'm starting to wonder whether he's late for once. I do know he's not with Lord Allenby at least, because I pass Tintagel's commander on his way up to Charlie's tower, accompanied by Jin. Lord Allenby does nothing more than nod and smile at me. A spark of hope ignites in my chest – surely if Samson *had* told Lord Allenby that I no longer wanted to be in Bedevere, I'd have been called in for a serious conversation instead of being gently acknowledged and dismissed.

At last, I find Samson at the top of the dome, on the parapets that look out over the city. They are manned by a handful of sentinels, each one taking a corner of the compass. Samson is not at the edges with the harkers; he's in the centre, looking up at the dome that squats in the middle of the tower, apparently trying to work something out. His features cloud over as I approach.

'Can we talk?' I say.

'Now's not a great time –' he begins, but he's interrupted by Easa appearing from the other side of the dome.

'I can't see what they mean –' Easa says, and halts abruptly as he spots me. 'Oh. Sorry.'

'No, I'm the one who's interrupting,' I say. 'I just . . .'

I look desperately at Samson, hoping he'll understand what I need.

‘Give me a minute. I’ll see you downstairs,’ he tells me. I nod, feeling foolish, feeling banished, and climb back down the stairs to wait in the place I always wait for Samson – in the gardens, where the apothecaries tend to herbs and the scents of rosemary and eucalyptus combine in a heady aroma.

I don’t have to wait long. I want to ask Samson what he and Easa were doing up there, but there’s something more important to discuss first.

‘I’m sorry,’ I blurt out. ‘Please don’t make me leave.’

Samson comes to me, folding his arms around me, resting his head on mine. ‘I should never have threatened you with that.’

I stumble through my explanation for my behaviour, thinking all the while that it was so much easier doing it through a proxy like I did with Ollie and Kieran, and I wonder briefly if it would be too weird to ask Jin to join us to translate my ramblings.

‘You *know* I get it, don’t you?’ Samson says when I finally stop. ‘I can’t imagine exactly what it’s like for you, but I can guess, and I can guess how I’d feel too. But you’re doing exactly what I did when I walked into that house of vampires – you’re trying to prove a point you don’t have to prove.’

A few years ago, Samson admitted to me that the feat of bravery that put him on the thanes’ map was a heroic, foolish, against-the-rules attempt to save his then-girlfriend from depression.

‘But I *do* have something to prove,’ I say heatedly. ‘You can’t understand properly because you were chosen to be in the thanes. I wasn’t, remember? Andraste –’ my breath hitches on the name of my dead mentor – ‘she had to bring me here.

She and my mum had to blackmail Lord Allenby into letting me take the tournament.'

'And the tournament proved that you should be a knight,' Samson finishes. 'If you really hadn't belonged, your necklace wouldn't have changed. You wouldn't have your scimitar. You've got to let go of this idea that you don't belong, Fern.'

I try to believe him. There was a brief moment – a few months – where I could have truly accepted it, when I had my Immral and was really making a difference. When I felt valued by my fellow thanes.

'I don't know how to be useful,' I whisper. 'I don't know why any of you want me around now I don't have my power.'

Samson is silent for a long time. Long enough that I start to wonder whether he's going to admit that he doesn't know either, and would rather I jog on after all. Then he says, 'What do you want me to say, Fern? I can't make you believe that you're wanted here. No one here can. The only person who can really understand why we might want you to stay is *you*. Until you realise how amazing you are, Immral or not, no one else can do anything for you. Not properly.'

'I'm not trying to make you feel sorry for me or stroke my ego,' I say. 'I genuinely don't know myself.'

Samson sighs and sits down on the wood of a raised bed. I sink down next to him. He takes my hand in his, his skin deep umber against my pale sand.

'I've never told anyone this,' he says, 'not even Lord Allenby. When I was in Medraut's headquarters in the Royal Arsenal a few years ago, something happened.'

Samson has never spoken to me about exactly what he

experienced during his time undercover, just before I met him. I've raised it occasionally, but he's never wanted to talk about it and I haven't pushed him. There are some experiences you don't want to share, because once you do there's no changing how a person sees you. It colours everything they know about you. It's why I've only given him the briefest details of my burn scar. It's no secret that I'm bullied in Ithr – I don't think he'd think less of me for that – but I haven't told him about Ollie's part in it. I want to protect my brother from the way I think Samson would see him, if he knew.

I swallow my own fear over what he's about to reveal, and how it might make me feel. Instead, I cocoon his hand in mine, to let him know that he's safe. And he begins.

Chapter 9

Samson takes a long time to find the right words. I have never known him so uncertain. When he eventually starts talking, his voice is low, quiet, so I have to lean in to him to hear.

'Quite soon after I went in – this would have been about six months before you and Ollie joined the thanes – I made a friend in there.'

'Another spy?'

Samson shakes his head. He isn't looking at me, his eyes now fixed on our joined hands. I study his face. He's usually so strong, his cheekbones defined, his jaw hard. But now I can see the boy in him, the one whose parents like to coddle, much to his chagrin.

'He was a guard, like me. He'd been completely taken in by Medraut, but he was young. Well, my age. His older sister worked for Medraut, much higher up, and he worshipped her.'

'You changed his mind?'

'No.' Samson smiled. 'No, I never tried to. That would have risked my mission. But I did like him, and I think he liked me. Even for those who believed in Medraut, that place could be draining. It was hard being there night after night, seeing some of the things we had to see. I think he didn't much enjoy watching some of the experiments, but he kept telling me that it was for the best. It would end up making us all better.'

Samson shrugs. 'Anyway, we became friends, I guess, or as friendly as we could be considering I was keeping this huge secret . . . and then one day I was spotted with my knights' helmet. I thought I'd found a good hiding spot for it, and I was sure I hadn't been followed. But I was seen.'

'By your friend?'

'No. Someone else, but they didn't see my face. They went back to their superiors and given the placement and witnesses, they worked out it was either me or my friend.'

'Oh God,' I whisper. Had Samson accused his friend of being the spy?

'They took us both into separate cells for interrogation,' Samson says shakily, 'and the next thing I know, my friend . . . he confessed.'

'What?'

'He told them it was him, that I had nothing to do with it. He gave them proof as well – he told them where I had hidden the helmet. He must have known what I was doing all along.'

'What happened to him?'

Samson leans over our hands as though he's going to kiss them, then I feel his tears on my knuckles. I fold myself over him as he sobs, murmuring reassurances. *It wasn't your fault. He decided to help you. You couldn't have done anything – you'd only have got yourself killed* . . . None of it matters. None of it makes any difference. I know this because I still blame myself for all the deaths that have happened over the last few years. If only

I'd been quicker. If only I'd been stronger. Eventually, I stop saying anything at all, and Samson and I just hold each other.

Then something else occurs to me. 'That's why you won't kill dreamers,' I say softly. Over the last year, we've spent so many nights battling dreamers rather than dreams: those corrupted by Medraut's bigotry and manipulation. At the battle in Trafalgar Square, Samson nearly died because he fought off the hordes of dreamers who were attacking us, but he refused to ever kill them. I had always understood his reasons in a philosophical sense – it chimed with his moral nature. But now I understand that there's a personal reason for it as well.

'He was supposed to be on Medraut's side, but when it came down to it, he came through for me,' Samson says. 'Who knows which one of those dreamers might do the same, if they had the chance to save someone they loved?'

Personally, I think he might be giving too much credit to people, but the thought is comforting. That no dreamer is beyond redemption, if the right reason came along. That our fight to survive is worth something, that if we do come through the other side of this, we might be able to forgive those who turned on us. Or that they might be able to seek forgiveness from us.

When he pulls away to look into my eyes, something has shifted between us. We've explored each other's bodies in ways that make me buck and melt. But we haven't confided in each other, not like this. This is true intimacy.

'I promise I had a point to make about you.' Samson smiles weakly. 'I didn't just want to confess.'

I press my lips to his, acknowledging what he has just done

to try to make me feel better. Because I understand. I know that he would have felt helpless in that situation – helpless and at fault, even though he was working for the good of the thanes and couldn't give up his identity. And in the wake of that helplessness, he has had to forge himself a fresh identity, even while walking amongst friends who knew the old Samson. What he's trying to say is, *It can be done.* What I need to do is to strip myself back. Who am I, without my Immral? What did I think of myself before I knew I had that power, and how can I reconcile that with who I am now? I don't have the answers to these questions yet, but for the first time, I feel as though I might get there.

Samson and I cleave together as we return to the castle, both of us feeling raw. 'What *were* you doing up at the top of the castle with Easa?' I ask him.

He smiles ruefully. 'Trying to help you.'

'What do you mean?'

'We know how much you want to get your Immral back, so Easa and I have been doing our own research. We found a reference to transference, or transportation. We thought it might have something to do with the dome, but it didn't come to anything.'

I stop, pulling him to face me, speechless. Neither Samson nor Easa has the time to be doing that research either. They're already so overloaded.

'Don't give me that look, Fern. I know we didn't have to. We wanted to.'

I launch myself at him in a most undignified fashion. Several passing veneurs snigger. Any residual doubts I might have had about Samson being pleased that I am no longer stronger than him dissipate in a cloud of passing guilt.

'Do I take it you'd like us to carry on looking then?' Samson says when I eventually pull away.

'Yes. But only if I can join you.'

Easa appears behind Samson, smiling tightly. 'If you two are done, I've been asked to fetch Fern urgently.'

Samson squeezes my hand and goes on to the stables, while I match Easa's long strides back towards the castle.

'There's a meeting of all the Head Thanes,' Easa explains.

'Why do they want me?'

'Because you went through the rip. They want you to tell them what happened.'

We go to Lord Allenby's office, where he and Ollie are waiting. Lord Allenby is picking a doorknob from several that sit in a hidden wooden panel on one wall. He selects one that looks as though it's made of coal. A gold vein runs across a surface that's been rubbed smooth by centuries of use. He fits the doorknob into the door at the back of his office; a door that hides limitless destinations. A blue light emanates from the frame, and when Lord Allenby pulls it open, we are staring into a large, round room that's dominated by a series of windows and a huge, circular table in its centre.

It's only when I step through that I realise that we're in a tower. Each window offers a different vista. In the stone above each one is a different engraving. One, which looks out on a city draped in night, is titled *The Land of Promise*. A sunset over a peaceful ocean is labelled *The Dark Place*. Another window looks out over rolling hills where sheep graze alongside llamas and another animal I'm not sure exists in Ithr. Above the window the words *The Multi-Coloured Plain* are engraved. The final window, through which I spot snowy cliffs whipped by a tremendous wind, is called *The Silver-Cloud Plain*.

'Where is this place?' I ask, taking it all in.

'Somewhere you won't find on any map,' Lord Allenby answers. 'This is Avalon.'

Chapter 10

Easa whistles. 'I've read about this place, but never been here. The descriptions don't do it justice.'

The door that we came through opens again, and a weather-beaten woman wearing a horn at her hip and a storm in her eyes enters. Behind her, I spot a cave-like room whose walls are encrusted with gemstones.

'Finally we're going to figure out what to do about my missing knights,' she says.

'Lady Kaur.' Lord Allenby shakes her hand. 'I'm glad you could make it.'

They move to one side of the room to talk in low voices, and Easa, Ollie and I move to the other side. I look out at the snowy cliffs, absorbing their beauty, their danger. I imagine tearing my soul from my body and tossing it like ash on a wind from the window, urging it to explore Annwn as I'll never get to explore it as a mortal. My skin prickles.

'Wasn't Avalon supposed to be where King Arthur's buried?' Ollie asks.

'Come on now, Ollie, you know better than to believe everything you read.' Easa smiles. Ollie looks at him blankly, and once again worry for my brother sparks in me. Easa says softly, 'It's okay to smile, Ollie. You don't always have to be fighting, you know.'

My brother doesn't smile, but something shifts in him. He gazes at Easa as though he's seeing him properly for the first time. Then the door to the room opens once more, the spell is broken, and we turn our focus to the new arrivals.

As the tower fills, the conversation becomes more muted. Each time the door opens, it reveals a different castle – some spacious and cold, some cosy and richly tapestried. Some I recognise all too well, like Lady Carys's office in Cambridge. I take a seat between Ollie and a reeve from Oxford called Asher, who has a shock of ginger hair styled to stick straight up. Asher is cordial but tense, tapping their fingers on the table until everyone is ready to start.

When all the chairs are full, Lord Allenby stands and the room falls silent.

'Thank you for coming to this emergency meeting,' he begins. 'We all know why we're here. Something is happening to our knights, and we need to find out what. Only one thing is certain: I think we can all guess who is behind it.'

There are nods and hisses and muttering. Asher's hands are fists.

'We have some new information that might be related to these disappearances,' Lord Allenby says. 'Fern? Could you?'

I stand, feeling the curious glances directed my way. I recognise many of these lords, ladies and lieges from my tour of Annwn last year. They have all, I'm sure, heard that I've lost the Immral that helped to change the Round Tables, but that doesn't stop their eyes lingering on my newly hazel irises. I can't help but wonder if they're dismissing me already. *Just a knight*, are they thinking? Are they thinking, *Why is she here when she has nothing to offer us any more?*

Nevertheless, I tell them what I saw and felt when I stepped through that rip between Annwn and Ithr. The way I nearly came apart, like a ghost – perhaps would have entirely if it hadn't been for Ollie keeping me in one piece.

'Since your message last night, we've found similar rips in Yorkshire,' the lord from Suffolk says, 'and like yours, they heal themselves eventually.'

'What has this got to do with my missing knights?' Lady Kaur, the head thane of Cornwall, pipes up. Her thaneship had even fewer knights than us to begin with: Medraut's treitres wiped all of them out in their attacks two Ostaras ago.

'If I may?' Easa says, and he unfurls the map from the room in Tintagel – the one where he's been recording the disappearances. Lord Allenby points to the pins dotted across the map. 'These mark the last sightings of some of our missing knights,' he tells us.

His hand moves to a series of flags that I haven't seen before. 'And these,' he says, 'are where some of you have found rips.'

The flags stretch in short lines across the paper, like stab marks. I spot the correlation at the same time as the others. 'They're in the same places as the missing knights?' Ollie says.

Lord Allenby nods. 'Exactly. Now we don't know for sure, but what we do have here is a possibility. A possibility that the rips are related to those snakes that we think may have taken our knights.'

'You think a dozen of my knights were pulled into Ithr?' Lady Kaur says.

The others volley questions and theories.

'But those snake-creatures can't have come from Ithr, can they?'

'It's a diversion.'

'Even if it is true, what use is it to us?'

Lord Allenby raises a hand. 'I know it's not much to go on, but it's worth exploring, isn't it? But we have to work together on this. It's a countrywide problem and we must address it as a country.'

Lady Carys raises her own hand. 'Agreed, Lionel. I'd be willing to volunteer whoever you need from Cambridge. But I think we need to consider something longer term too.'

'What do you mean, longer term?' the lord from Suffolk asks.

'We have a bigger problem than missing knights. Shouldn't we be considering what to do about Annwn?'

'*Do* about it?'

'How to restore it? Fern and Ollie have described the decimation of Annwn around the rip they found. We have similar cases in Cambridgeshire. I'm sure we're not alone.'

Several heads nod.

'Well then. Annwn is dying, just as it did at the end of Arthur's reign. Do any records show what happened after that? Do we know how Annwn was restored?'

'Don't you have that in your archives?' the Oxford lord smirks.

'We focus on the science of Annwn, not the history, as you well know, Robin,' Carys says.

'Our archives do say something about it,' Asher speaks up. 'Annwn was stripped of inspyre.'

'Surely it was his death that restored Annwn?' Lady Kaur says. 'Kill Medraut, save Annwn.'

'Not quite,' Asher replies. 'Killing Arthur didn't bring back Annwn, although some speculate that it may have happened very slowly anyway.'

'But something helped?' Lord Allenby says.

'The Grail,' Asher answers. 'They found the Grail, but the records say that they destroyed it in the process of restoring Annwn.'

'Records can be deceptive,' Lord Allenby says. 'Look at what happened with Excalibur.'

'With all due respect, my lord, the Excalibur records were missing, but what we did have was consistent. The Grail legend is far more nebulous.'

'What do you mean?' I ask.

Asher looks to Robin, the lord of Oxford, and Robin nods silently. 'One moment, please,' Asher says, and slips from the room back to Oxford's castle. I dimly remember their castle as a huge, round library with vast underground offices and chambers. A few moments later, they return carrying a thick sheaf of papers, and spread them out across the table. I pull one towards me: an illustration of a medieval banquet.

'I fail to see how this is connected to the Grail,' one of the lords says, holding up another piece of paper. 'This is a picture of a cauldron.'

'That's rather the point,' Asher replies. 'There's really no saying *what* the Grail is, for a start. Some records show it as a food platter, some as a cauldron, some as a cup. It's very disparate, and I'm afraid to say that that suggests it doesn't exist as an object at all.'

'If it doesn't exist as an object, what *does* it exist as?' Carys asks.

'An idea,' Asher says, to frustrated murmurings around the table. I understand why: Excalibur was a tangible object of hope – a lighthouse telling us that if we could just find it, we'd be safe. An idea is no good to us at all.

'The only thing in common with all of the Grail stories is that they result in enlightenment of some kind. Plenty and restoration. Creation. A sick land healed by the sudden harvest, and prosperity brought about by the Grail.'

'But it must exist, surely,' Lady Carys says, 'because we know that it was used to restore Annwn after Arthur's death.'

'Here's our record of that time,' Asher says, pushing another piece of paper into the middle of the table. The lettering is strong – it's been read recently, and many times – but I can't make sense of the language.

'It's in Old English,' Asher explains. 'It translates roughly as follows. *With the land laid waste, and a great Dark Age upon Ithr, the surviving knights gathered at the remains of the Round Table for a council. Excalibur was laid in the centre of the table, whereupon a great debate was held about how to replenish the land of Annwn. The council raged for three days and three nights, and at its conclusion the one surviving fay, the Lady Guinevere –'*

'Guinevere?' someone whispers. 'I don't know a Fay called Guinevere.'

'They mean the Lady Andraste,' Lady Kaur responds. My heart reels. Andraste was Guinevere?

'*The Lady Guinevere,*' Asher repeats pointedly, '*strode into the room and told them that one amongst them had the power to restore Annwn, although it would come at a great cost. It was decided between them that Lancelot would take up the Grail quest, and in doing so, the Grail was broken apart, and in doing so, inspyre was restored to Annwn and a great age of science and art was begun in Ithr.*'

'I assume the writer means the Renaissance,' Carys says, 'but that came centuries after Arthur, didn't it?'

'That's how I read it too,' Asher replies, 'that the Grail has the power to influence imagination for centuries after it's used.'

'But it's been destroyed,' Lord Allenby says, 'so for our purposes, it's useless. May I suggest that we turn our attention back to the matter at hand – how to bring down Medraut and how to find out what he's done to our missing knights?'

The room erupts in objections and agreements.

'We need a long-term strategy, though –'

'If we get him, we won't need to worry about fictional relics –'

'Why can't we do both?'

I look over at Asher, who is one of the few not arguing. 'Do you think the Grail could be mended and used again, if we found it?' I ask them.

They study me, their eyes guarded. 'I'm not sure it's a matter of mending and recycling it,' they say. 'Like I said, I'm not sure the Grail ever existed in a tangible form to begin with.'

'But if it was destroyed, surely it had to be real?'

'Not necessarily. If the Grail is an *idea*, then it can still be broken, can't it? Look at what's happening now under Medraut – all the ideas we might have had about ourselves being open-minded, good people are being destroyed, aren't they? Look at what's happening to Annwn, or how people are behaving towards anyone who seems different, and tell me that isn't tangible.'

I think about the devastation that Medraut's single idea has wrought. It has taken form, wormed its way into people's heads and laid waste to the land.

'So you think that the Grail was Arthur's "idea" of the world? And that's what they broke?'

Asher shrugs. 'Maybe. Maybe not. I'm only theorising. But we've got to stop applying the physics of Ithr to what's possible in Annwn.'

I nod. 'Imagination, that's the key, isn't it? The key to all of this.' A strange feeling settles in my stomach, as though my gut is trying to tell me something that I'm not yet ready to hear. *A great cost*. That's what Guinevere – Andraste – had told the founding knights. No one else has mentioned that part of the text, but it seems to reverberate through my body, like a premonition.

Lord Allenby raises a hand to quell the commotion. 'I understand what you're all saying,' he growls. 'I propose that a delegation of reeves investigates the Grail legend further, so we have a plan in place should the worst happen. But in the meantime, do we have an agreement on what to do about the missing knights?'

Around the table, the lords and ladies and lieges nod their assent. That's when the bargaining begins: the how manys and the who. One thing alone is clear: Tintagel's population is about to get a lot bigger.

Chapter 11

It isn't long before teams of harkers, veneurs, apothecaries and reeves descend. They seem to arrive en masse, even though they come from every castle in the country. Some of them are even retired, but have been persuaded to return to duty by the desperation of the Head Thanes. The one lore we don't see any more of is the knights.

'It's not that they're not willing,' Niamh tells us. 'It's that the Head Thanes and knight captains won't let them go. They've already lost a load of their people and they're worried they'll lose the best of the rest.'

She's indignant that the knights aren't being given the chance to transfer to Tintagel, but I can understand the Head Thanes' perspective: they're already low on knights thanks to all the deaths over the last few years, the recent disappearances and the lack of new intake at Samhain – they can't afford to slim their patrols any more than they already have.

The new influx comes with its own issues. Maisie is the most put out by it. Her predecessor, a man called Ben who must be in his seventies from the dates of his thane service, but who still has a head of floppy black hair and a distinct lack of wrinkles, leaps at the chance to come out of retirement. He enjoys making it known how *he* would have run the harkers if he was still in charge. Whenever I pass the Round Table, he seems to be there, hovering over the harkers who man it and growling complaints.

'Of course, there's probably nothing a good bit of oil couldn't have done to save these cracks . . .' he says.

'They're not *cracks*, Ben,' Maisie replies. 'I've told you again and again, they're a result of *Medraut's* power.'

'You always were full of excuses.' Ben smiles patronisingly. I catch Maisie's eye and roll my own in solidarity.

'Leave them alone, Grandad,' a familiar, strained voice says to Ben. It's Frankie, a Cambridge reeve I met last year, who made an impression as one of the most uptight people I have ever met.

'Grandad?' I ask.

'You should be up on the roof with the sentinels,' Frankie continues, guiding Ben towards the stairs.

'But they need me down here!' he protests.

'They really don't. Go on, Grandad, you're embarrassing me.'

Ben grumbles, but does as Frankie says. I stare at her as he climbs the stairs to the top of the castle.

'What?' she says. 'It's not that unusual for relatives to be recruited.'

Despite the teething problems of the different thaneships settling in together, Tintagel now buzzes with new energy. Everyone has ideas about how to tackle the rips. Asher is convinced that we should start by trying to work out how they are made.

'They're clearly something to do with Immral,' they say, looking pointedly at Ollie. For some time, my brother tries his hardest to recreate them in an unused turret room. The only thing he succeeds in doing is draining the colour from the space and giving himself an almighty nosebleed.

The archives, once dusty and quiet, now heave with reeves. Samson, Easa and I spend what time we can down there, continuing the research into how to re-start my Immral. Alongside us work Asher, Frankie and Jin, who have been tasked with looking into the Grail. Our two groups often sit amicably side by side at one of the long tables nestled at one end of the archives. Having Jin close by comes in particularly handy with my research into Immral, because she used to spend so much time studying the power, back when she thought she might have it herself.

'We should look in here next,' Easa says one night, pulling open a stack labelled *Thanes of Interest*. I stare at the rows of records, my heart sinking at the prospect of reading all of them.

'Where do we even start?' Samson says, but he is already pulling records off the shelves and flicking through them.

'You are actually loving this, aren't you?' I tease.

'Some other Immrals are in here,' Easa says, running his hands over the records. 'I just need to remember where . . .' Then, ever so casually, he asks, 'Do you think your brother might want to help us with this?'

I shake my head. 'Ollie's not in a great place right now.' I'm sure that he *would* agree to help us if I asked him, but my brother is looking so tired these days that I don't want to add more to his load.

Easa shrugs, as though he doesn't care either way. Soon

afterwards, he presents us with a thick pile of folders, each one neatly labelled with a name and a date. 'These are all the Immrals we have on record,' he tells us.

'Let's divide them up,' Samson says, taking the top third of the pile. Each folder is a different length; some hold only a handful of pages, some are as thick as a thesaurus. I scan them for any mention of Immral, trying hard not to get distracted by some of the incredible things I'm reading about. I've only got so much time before I have to wake up.

Still, none of us can help but share some of the more extraordinary people in these records.

'This is an Argentinian Immral who refused to use her power,' Easa says. 'She sounds like an amazing woman.'

'She was quite recent, wasn't she?' I ask, recollecting something Lord Allenby told me. Easa only nods in reply, his head deep in the reading.

'Did you know that some of the Fay have human children?' Samson says, holding up a folder. 'This woman was the daughter of Puck and Queen Elizabeth the First. Can you imagine?'

I show him the one I'm reading. 'This dude had Immral, and he ended up cutting off his arm and throwing it into a waterfall. I've been to that waterfall in Ithr. All the tourist stuff says it's blessed.'

'Can I see that?' Jin says, looking up from her Grail research further down the table. She takes the record from me and reads it avidly, her face clouding over.

'What? It's just a weird story,' I say.

'Yeah,' Jin replies, but there's something she's holding back. Before Samson or I can press her for more, there's a bang from the far reaches of the archives, a hushed, urgent conversation and then a reeve skids into view at the end of our stack.

'Fern, you're needed.'

I spring up. 'What's happened?'

'It's Merlin and Nimue. They want to talk to you.'

Easa pulls the rest of my folders towards him and I follow the reeve at a run up to the great hallway beneath Tintagel's central dome. It's only when I round the final staircase and push my way through the thanes gathered on the marble that I understand why we had to hurry.

Nimue and Merlin are pooled, husk-like, on the floor. Nimue is engulfed in a swathe of fabric to hide her wounds and to give her some shape, but the silk bulges and sinks in uncanny places, hinting at the lack of body beneath it. Merlin is blind; his eyes are caverns of smoke. His skin is flayed, exposing ladders of ribs. The edges of his hands and feet whisk in and out of existence. One moment they're there, the next they are trails of inspyre. A few months ago I healed him with stories. Ollie kneels next to him and Nimue now, his eyes closed, his nose bleeding. He is trying to do the same, but this time it isn't working. Who knows whether that's because he's still getting used to my part of the power, or whether Merlin and Nimue are beyond help.

'Is that her?' Merlin asks, his voice an echo.

'Yes, my lord. Fern's here now,' Lord Allenby says, ushering me closer to the Fay. I kneel next to Ollie and take the hand that Merlin is proffering. It is spongy, and smells like rotten meat. I resist the urge to pull away.

'The sword,' Merlin rasps.

'Excalibur?'

He nods. I look at Ollie: why do they want to talk to me about Excalibur? There's nothing I can do with it any time soon, if ever. Even with my Immral at its strongest, I wasn't powerful enough to wield it. Ollie's their person.

'It will find you,' Nimue says through her scarf, her voice distorted, as though she no longer has half her mouth. She tries to say more, but even as we watch, the fabric covering her face falls away. Her head has disintegrated. Her body follows, until there is nothing where Nimue once was but the memory of inspyre and a puddle of lilac silk.

Merlin takes up her words, although we can barely hear him. 'When you are ready, it will find you. Here, beneath the dome.' There is no elegant death for Merlin. He doesn't fade away like Nimue. He doesn't even burst into ash, like Andraste. He convulses, each pulse a crack of bones breaking and skin distorting. Then with one final seizure, he explodes. I look away, covering my face, and feel a rain of warm inspyre across my cheek and neck.

When you're ready, a voice seems to whisper, not in my ear but through my brain. And so passed the last of the Fay.

Chapter 12

I was never Merlin's biggest fan – he made his mistrust of me clear for several years before finally accepting that I am not evil incarnate – but his death, and Nimue's, affect me more than I expected. When Medraut killed Andraste, the shock was instant. This time, it creeps up on me in quiet moments. The strangest things set me off – the last wilting plant in the apothecaries' herb gardens, or the way the Thanes' flag flutters above Tintagel's parapets, like Nimue's silk scarf. In Ithr, I draw their final moments in all their ugliness, as though I'm trying to leach the memory through my hands.

Sometimes Charlie sits next to me in the art room as I sketch. She didn't know the Fay directly, but I tell her about them. She's a good listener, although I'm not sure how much of that is innate and how much of it is her still recovering from her father's experiments. Her gaze will sometimes turn vacant, her body stiff, until whatever shadow is passing across her mind lifts.

One day she brings me a gift: a slim box that, when opened, reveals several layers of gold leaf.

'I thought you could decorate your pictures with this,' she suggests.

My immediate reaction is to wonder who she is to tell me how to make my own drawings. But then I think about her proposal. A few dots of gold on the embers of Andraste. A wisp of it above the puddle of Nimue's scarf. Gold, instead of grey, for Merlin's eyes. Yes, there is something appealing about it.

'I guess that could work,' is all I say. 'Thank you.'

As I dip a small brush into the first sheet and wind the fragile gold around the bristles, I glance at her. 'What made you think of it?'

'Tinkerbell,' she replies.

'Obviously.'

She smiles. 'Whenever you or Lionel talk about the Fay, I always think of fairies. My nanny used to read *Peter Pan* to me when I was little. I loved the idea of Wendy flying away from her life and finding this incredible new world at the end of the horizon.'

I keep drawing, but we are both thinking why a young Charlie might want to escape the confines of her bedroom.

'The book had these amazing drawings, but my favourite was the one where Tinkerbell died. She was lying in Peter Pan's hands, and there was this tiny curl of gold coming from her mouth. It was her last breath. It was so beautiful. I remember it was the first time I understood.'

'Understood what?' I say, mesmerised.

'That life is only part of our story. Maybe it comes and goes, like with Tinkerbell – they were able to put that little curl of gold life back into her body by getting enough people to believe in fairies. But if they hadn't managed it, it wasn't really the end. That gold wouldn't have disappeared, would it? We might not have been able to see it any more, but it would be in the air around us. She'd still be there, somewhere. Everywhere.'

Charlie's words stick with me. I try to think of Andraste and Merlin and Nimue surrounding us all, urging us to keep going. I try to think of my Immral, dormant for now. Maybe that's why I do it.

'We have the beginnings of a plan,' Lord Allenby tells us one night at our regular meeting. 'We're going to need knights. A small handful of volunteers.'

'We think there's a pattern,' Easa says. 'We've been tracking the rips for a few weeks now, and there are a few that keep appearing in the same place.'

'And that gives us an opening,' Lord Allenby says. 'If those snake creatures appear near the rips, then knowing where the rips are going to be might give us a chance to catch one of the buggers.'

Fear fills me. I know what's coming. Either Samson or Ollie are going to be sent. Probably Ollie, given he's the Immral. Maybe both of them. The focus will be on who is the best fighter and the best mind. Both place Samson and Ollie right at the top of any lists. Samson takes my hand, and I force myself to listen to what Allenby and Easa are telling us.

'So far we've moved all knights away from the rips as soon as we discover them, in case they're kidnapped,' Lord Allenby continues. 'But of course that means that we haven't been able to unearth these creatures. And until we can catch one, and study it, we won't know what we're up against. So what we're proposing is . . .'

'A trap,' Ollie says. 'With us as bait.'

Lord Allenby nods, knowing that this won't be received well. It is the other lores, not the knights, who protest the loudest. 'Haven't they been through enough?' Rachel says hotly, to general agreement. Easa is looking at Ollie, mouthing, *You okay?* My brother merely nods in reply, but his cheeks are flushed.

'We're asking for volunteers. No one will be made to do this,' Lord Allenby says above the furore. 'We know it's going to be dangerous. If anyone wants to opt out, no one will judge you.'

'Speak for yourself,' Niamh mutters under her breath.

'We'll only take the most skilled knights from any volunteers,' Easa says.

I look up at Samson. 'You're going to offer, aren't you?'

'I'd be a pretty bad knight captain if I didn't at least put myself forward. There's no guarantee they'd take me.'

'Don't play humble. We both know they will,' I reply, squeezing his thigh. I try to hide my own feelings of inadequacy. Only a few months ago I would be expected to take part. As it stands now, I know that I'm not a strong enough fighter to be considered.

When you're ready.

It's as though Merlin and Nimue and Andraste are right beside me, just as Charlie had said. Formless but present. I may not be ready for Excalibur – I may never be ready for Excalibur. What I am is ready to make a difference again.

'Well, I'm in,' Natasha says.

'Me too,' Samson says.

'I'll help,' I say loudly. Lord Allenby looks at me uncertainly. The meaning is clear – I'm not skilled enough to be part of this. I feel the humiliation in front of the rest of the room keenly, but try to brush it off.

'I don't mean to actually take part,' I clarify quickly, 'I mean – let me help plan. I've been in Medraut's headquarters, remember? And I know the other knights pretty well. You're going to be busy, sir, because let's face it – you need to volunteer too. So let me run point. Let me be useful.'

My friends are staring at me but I don't want to read their expressions. Lord Allenby smiles. 'That would be incredibly helpful, Fern, thank you. I can't think of anyone better to work with Easa and Maisie on this.'

That's bullshit and we all know it, but I take it anyway. I nod stiffly, and soon afterwards we wrap up the meeting.

'You're really going into overlord mode?' Ollie says afterwards, a smile twitching the corner of his mouth.

'I'm going to be your boss lady,' I say. 'You better get used to obeying my orders.'

'Oh, we've had two years of getting used to it,' Samson says, 'I think we'll survive.'

He pulls me in for a kiss, and I let my hands roam over his chest. Sometimes, when we're alone, I slip them underneath his tunic and rake my fingernails over his skin. The sound he always makes when I do this is eminently satisfactory. But I can't do that in front of everyone, so I just press my hands over his tunic and look up at him meaningfully. The glint in his eyes tells me that he knows exactly what I'm thinking about.

'I do feel safer,' he says quietly, 'knowing you're going to be looking out for me.'

I step away, trying to hide my disappointment. I don't want to make him feel safe. I want to be by his side fighting nightmares, bow to scimitar, rescuing him. I don't want to be relegated to the sidelines. It isn't where I belong. But this isn't about me. It's about the people I love, and trying to stand beside them in whatever way I can. That desire is a stronger power than any Immral, and if it's going to help my friends survive, then I'd better step up and use it.

Chapter 13

Planning and plotting with Easa and Maisie isn't as painful as I'd anticipated. I thought I'd feel awful at not being front and centre of any attack on Medraut. So much of what has happened over the last few years is tied up in my personal grudge against him.

Easa smiles when I mention this to him. 'Grudge is a pretty small word for what Medraut's done, don't you think?'

I don't think it is, though. Grudge is a huge word. It's defined me for years. I built my personality on it. It made me strong.

We take up residence, when I'm not on patrol, in the same circular room in the veneurs' tower that was Easa and Jin's base when we were looking for Excalibur. The energy we create radiates outwards, infusing the rest of Tintagel with new purpose. Everyone wants to be seen to be helping, and as a castle we settle on a plan: small teams of knights, hidden at the areas experiencing most of the rip activity. They'll be overseen by harkers, with portals set up allowing all the teams to converge in a matter of seconds if the snake-creatures appear, trackers ready to fix to them if we can't capture one immediately.

Easa and I spend long hours poring over our small band of volunteer knights, moving them around on a map of Annwn's Cornwall. Lady Kaur lobbied for her thaneship to be our target. 'I've lost the most knights, so you stand more chance of being attacked here,' she said, brooking little opposition.

Now the map of the county is covered in ribbons that have names attached to them. The task of assigning knights to different areas is harder than any of us had anticipated.

'I think we should put Lord Allenby's team in the most likely spot,' Easa says.

'Yes, that sounds smart.' I move the pin with Lord Allenby's name on it to a place just outside Truro, where the rips have been sighted most regularly. Secretly, I'm relieved that Easa didn't suggest Samson or Ollie, and then I feel guilty because I don't want anything to happen to my commander either. Especially because I know that his life in Ithr is about as bleak as it can get.

I study the pins marking the most common places where the rips have been seen. There are five of them across Cornwall. 'We've got a problem, though,' I say.

'You figured it too, huh?' Easa looks at me. For we have four more spots to fill, and only three more teams: headed by Ollie, Samson and Niamh.

'We've got three options, really,' Easa says. 'Either we have fewer knights in each team . . .'

'Not possible,' I say. 'I know we want to keep the teams small and strong, but we need to make sure they've got backup if they're attacked. Three people is the minimum.'

'I agree. So that leaves us with trying to persuade some of

the other thaneships to help us, or recruiting more knights from our own ranks.'

Easa and I look at each other. Neither of those two options seems likely. The other thaneships have remained stubborn on donating knights to the cause, unwilling to risk their own safety when they're already stretched. And with so many serving knights on the mission already, we need everyone left to cover the London patrols that night. Nerizan is already unhappy at being left to lead Bedevere with just one Palomides knight. I can imagine her and the other knight trying to cover an entire route, just the two of them. Well, the two of them and their horses . . .

'I have an idea,' I say, and rush out of the room, bounding down the steps before Easa can stop me. Usually, the person I want to find is in the stables, but not this time. I dodge apothecaries and veneurs carrying huge straw bales as I make my way around the castle grounds. It strikes me suddenly that this place is my home, as no other place has ever been. In Ithr, I have filled my bedroom with belongings, the hallway downstairs is lined with my artwork, but I have always felt stifled there. And of course it doesn't help that for so many years I felt as though I was a one-woman army heading into daily battle against my brother and father. Here, I own every blade of grass just as much as the apothecaries who tend it or the horses who graze it. I hold my own in whatever room I enter, even now, without my Immral. This is my castle. These are my people. This is *my* world. I know it and I know them. And I will protect them, even if I'm not sure how to do that any more. Long gone are the days where I made my fortress in a corner of the knights' chamber, staking out my territory like I was under siege.

Warmth spreads from my chest, tingling through my arms and into my fingers; it feels like the warmth of hope in the face of despair.

I round the final corner of the castle's grounds and spot her. Miss D, one of the few veteran thanes who stayed on as a teacher after the events of last year, has a small herd of horses tied up by the castle well. As I approach, she pulls a full bucket from the well and pours its contents over the back of Samson's charger, who snorts with shock and pleasure, then promptly shakes the water from his back like a dog, drenching anyone in the vicinity.

'Cheeky chap!' Miss D comments, as a nearby group of apothecaries wipe their faces in disgust. I look down at my own damp uniform, hoping the reeves won't mind me asking them for a clean outfit.

'Lamb went for a wander,' Miss D says when she spots me. 'I think she's over by the lilac with that annoying dog.'

'I wasn't looking for Lamb, actually,' I say. 'I was looking for you.'

'Oh yes?' She eyes me beadily, each of her hands resting on a horse's back, as though they're the arms of a throne.

'You used to be a knight, didn't you?'

'Long time ago now.'

'We're looking for –'

'No, Fern. I'm far too old for that.'

'You don't even know what I'm going to say.'

'I have a fair idea. I hear a lot of gossip.'

I look at her in disbelief. She avoids my gaze, busying herself with scrubbing down Samson's horse.

'We really need people to help.'

That gets her to look me square in the face.

'I've paid my dues, Fern. Don't try to make me feel guilty because it won't work.' She pulls up her blouse to reveal her stomach. There, to the left of her belly button, are a series of vivid red puncture marks. I can imagine exactly what made those marks: gold claws, attached to a limb without a palm, skewering the soft flesh beneath the ribs.

'This is what Ellen Cassell did to me. She did it to me as I was running away, because she had killed the rest of my regiment.'

I can't look away from those puncture marks.

'I'm sorry,' I whisper.

'Like I said, I paid my dues. I don't owe the thanes anything. I'm not going to put myself in harm's way any more than I already am. It's just good sense.'

'We'll have to make the teams smaller,' I tell Easa later. I asked a handful of other teachers, but it became clear pretty quickly that they all felt they were going above and beyond just by showing up at Tintagel. I don't mention my failed plan to Easa, and he doesn't ask, perhaps sensing the outcome from my dejection. He rearranges some names on the whiteboard and stands back. Niamh and Natasha are now in a team of two, and Samson is on his own with Bandile, one of the newest knights, and one of the most able. 'Then that means Ollie can head up a team with Amina,' Easa explains as he writes. I nod stiffly. Neither of us like the fact that so many of our people are going in with a single backup, but it's a fine balance between strength in numbers and strength in ability, and since we simply don't have the numbers we're going to have to lean hard into ability and hope that gets them through alive.

When Ollie sees the new plans, he is less than impressed. 'I know,' I say, before he can express his displeasure, 'but we don't have a choice.'

He nods silently, but kicks the stone wall when Easa isn't looking. 'I'm sorry,' I say. 'I don't like it either. I hate it. I absolutely hate it.'

'It's not your fault,' he says shortly, but we both know it is in a way. If I hadn't let Excalibur drain me of my power, this wouldn't all be on him. If I'd focused more on improving my own fighting skill without relying on my Immral, I'd be able to boost numbers.

'We'll prepare you as much as we can,' Easa says. 'But right now, we're going to have some fun.'

Ollie snorts, as though the very concept is alien to him. Easa takes Ollie's hand and throws me the pen he's been using to plan. 'You carry on, Fern,' he tells me. 'I'm going to put a smile back on this man's face.' And with that, he pulls a protesting Ollie from the room.

Chapter 14

To my shock, Easa's plan works. Ollie returns later that night, cheeks flushed and buoyant.

'What did you do?' I ask Easa in private.

'Just reminded him what he's fighting for,' Easa says, shrugging. Ollie won't tell me what they did either, but if it works, I'm not complaining. It doesn't change his mood entirely – he's still mostly a grumpy shit – but he moves with a new determination now, in Annwn at least.

With the basics of our plan in place, and only a month to prepare the finer details, our focus turns to training. The main source of concern is Ollie. His Immral still isn't as strong as mine was, and we need it to be to give us the best possible chance against those snakes. Lord Allenby takes Ollie off patrol and makes him practise his Immral all night long, just as I did when we first discovered my power.

At first, Ollie practises with whichever reeves, apothecaries and veneurs can be spared from their duties. It does not go well.

'What happened this time?' I say, as my brother storms towards me in the gardens.

'I was trying to lift one of the veneurs, and I ended up throwing them through the window.'

I snort, then catch the eye of the veneur in question, lying in a flower bed. He is unharmed, but covered head to toe in mud.

'Sorry,' I call over, stifling another snort.

As the days go by and the time for our Cornish trap grows closer, Ollie's progress stalls.

'Why didn't they ask you to train him?' Niamh says one night. 'If anyone knows how to use their Immral surely it's the ex-Chosen One.'

I had asked myself the same question and come up with an answer: Lord Allenby doesn't want to hurt me. He's already aware that I'm resentful. Truthfully, I'm grateful, because it would have been incredibly hard to be teaching Ollie how to use the power that is rightfully mine. I tell Niamh my theory about Allenby's reasoning.

'Well, that's bollocks, isn't it?' she says. 'You're not going to put your brother in danger just because he's got something you want.'

I am wrong-footed. When she puts it like that, how dare I begrudge Ollie my help? I go to Lord Allenby that evening, and propose that I help him to train.

'If you're sure, Fern?' he says, relief etching his voice.

'Absolutely, sir. We'll get started straight away.'

And it is hard, at first. Ollie and I spend an hour or two after or before my patrol, in different empty spaces in Tintagel. Sometimes we go down to the dungeons, sometimes we requisition a spare classroom and sometimes we join the many sentinels on the dome at the top of the castle. I tell him how I used to control the power; the place in my skull that I would somehow nudge or prod to pull the Immral from me.

At first, nothing changes except he gets surlier with me, both in Annwn and Ithr. When Saturday comes round and it's time to visit our friends' graves, Ollie's still in a foul mood. He crunches his toast as though it has personally insulted him.

'Shall I go on my own?' I ask.

'No, no. I'll come.'

'Well, don't act like you'd be gracing me with your presence or anything.'

Ollie sighs. 'I'm sorry. I just spent so long being jealous of you getting the cool part of the power, and now I've got it and I'm shit at it.'

I had always known in an abstract sort of way that Ollie was jealous of my half of the Immral, but this is the first time he's admitted it. It feels pointless to gloat – I'm in exactly the position he used to be in. I try to be gracious instead.

'You're no worse than I was at the start. You just need practice,' I say.

He grunts. 'What do you think I'm doing all night?'

The lock goes in the front door, and before we can react Clemmie has breezed in. She pauses when she sees us. 'Oh, I thought you two would be out somewhere.'

'We do live here,' I point out.

'Yes, but – well, I thought you'd be with your little group.'

'You mean Shout Louder?' Ollie says, his voice deliberately calm.

'Don't get snappy with me.'

I grab Ollie's arm. We both know there's no point getting into an argument with Clemmie.

'We're not being snappy,' I say to her. 'Do you want to come for a walk with us?'

Ollie looks at me sharply, but I ignore him. I have to try – maybe there's still a chance to turn her back into the old Clemmie, who cared for us, protected us, loved us. But Clemmie just shakes her head, doesn't even deem us worthy of a reply. I pull Ollie to his feet as Clemmie turns her back to us and makes herself a tea.

'Come on. Let's get some fresh air,' I tell my brother.

'Off you go to your protests, while you can,' Clemmie sing-songs behind us.

I slam the door shut in reply.

'What do you think she meant, *while we can*?' Ollie asks as we traipse down the street.

I shrug. I haven't been back to Shout Louder since the single meeting that made me feel so uncomfortable. Ollie is a regular, though, as is Kieran. I resist the urge to ask him whether his obvious attraction to Easa is making things awkward with Kieran now – I'm trying to put him in a good mood, not start another argument.

We pass a group of kids playing in their front garden a few doors down. The oldest, a sweet boy with freckles and a lanky gait, runs out of the gate to retrieve their football, which has been thrown into the road. Ollie kicks it back to him.

'Alright?' the boy says, watching Ollie with the kind of

admiration someone his age would usually reserve for Spider-Man or Captain America. The door to the house opens and the kids' mum peers out.

'Don't ever go into the road, David, okay?'

'I didn't, Mum, Ollie got it for us.'

Ollie lifts a hand. 'You okay, Miss Moore?'

'They're not bothering you, are they?' she says, signalling to her children. The youngest two, a boy and girl, take the ball from David and carry on throwing it to each other as Ollie and Crystal Moore chat. I lurk awkwardly, wanting to get on our way even though it's quite amusing watching David try to surreptitiously impress Ollie.

'Well, you better be off then,' Crystal says. 'Take care as you go.'

'Bye, Ollie!' David shouts, right before he takes a football to the cheek and topples out of sight.

The flowers we laid at Ramesh and Sachi's graves are gently wilting in the November chill. They have been joined by a handful of other bouquets. I check their parents aren't here this time, as I have every week since we spotted them. There was something about the way Mrs Hellier stared that unsettled me. I remove our old flowers and rearrange the newer ones to cover the space. That's when I spot it – a card in a plastic sandwich bag, beneath the flowers we left last week.

'Rubbish?' Ollie asks.

I look at the envelope. It is addressed to *The Girl with the Scarred Face*. That must be me. My first instinct is to try to conceal it from Ollie, in case it mentions the letter I slipped through the Helliers' door so many months ago. But I'm too late.

'Oh God, what does it say?' Ollie asks, peering over my shoulder. I'm left with no choice but to slide the envelope out of the bag and pull out the card inside. The writing is neat and clear.

Was it you who sent the letter?

We believe you.

Is this you too?

There's a web address underneath it – long and complex and entirely forgettable.

'I've never heard of this website, have you?' I show it to Ollie.

He shakes his head. 'What do they mean, *We believe you*?'

I think about denying all knowledge, but only briefly. It's time for truths to be told. So as we walk on, I confess to my brother. I tell him about the letter I sent to the Helliers, but I don't tell him that there was a second letter – one I gave to my brother under the guise of being from our mother.

'That was bloody risky, Fern,' he says when I've finished.

'I know.'

'They could've reported you to the police for harassment.'

'I didn't sign my name. They wouldn't have known who it was from.'

'Still.'

I look at him, needing approval. 'Do you think it was the right thing to do?'

'Oh, definitely.'

His confidence throws me. I had expected judgement and perhaps a rueful, 'Well, you're lucky it didn't turn out worse.' Not full-on support. But then Ollie laughs. 'You really have changed,' he says, nudging me. 'Look at you, wanting to help strangers. Thinking the best of them while the rest of us avoid doing the right thing because we're thinking the worst of them. A few years ago you wouldn't have given a second thought to the Helliers.'

He's right, although I hadn't thought about it like that before. All I knew, at the time, was that I could imagine how much pain they were in. I could imagine them questioning, in the long nights when irrationality sets in, whether it was karma for a forgotten sin. I know that's what I would wonder, if I had been them. They have a younger child too, and it seemed important to reassure them that she is too young to be called to the thanes for some time. But back when I first joined the knights? It wouldn't have even occurred to me that Ramesh and Sachi's parents might need to ascribe some meaning to their children's deaths.

'Well, you know what we always say,' I joke.

'Yeah, yeah. I got the looks,' Ollie replies, but he's grinning for the first time in weeks. 'Give me that then.'

He takes the Helliers' card from me and taps the website into his phone. A page loads, mostly full of text, except for six symbols that sit in a row along the top. They look as though they've been drawn by hand and then photographed, but the shapes are unmistakeable: they are the five symbols of the lores, and the five-pointed star of the thanes.

Ollie and I read someone else's version of the truth about Annwn. It's not exactly like the letter I wrote to the Helliers, but the sentiment is the same: all of these deaths had meaning. The sleeping were murdered, and the prime minister is responsible.

'Who did this?' I ask.

Ollie points to two typed signatures at the bottom: *Irish and Penn*.

We look at each other, working it out, then both speak at the same time. 'Niamh!'

'But who's *Penn*?' I say.

'Natasha,' Ollie replies. 'She's from the USA, right? Pennsylvania?'

I dance with glee. 'They did it too!' I don't know why I'm so giddy, until Ollie articulates it.

'God, it's nice to not feel so alone in Ithr, isn't it?'

That's it. It's a connection to our friends, who we've never met in real life. Who, if we stick to the thanes' rules, we never will truly meet. But there they are, on the page – proof that they exist in Ithr and that they're thinking along the same lines as me. Ollie laughs too as he puts his phone in his pocket, 'Alright, sis, let's smash it tonight.'

We attack Ollie's training with renewed energy, and for the first time he starts to make progress. He's not as good as I was – and I allow myself a small amount of satisfaction at that – but there's definite improvement.

'Well done, Fern,' Lord Allenby says one evening, after Ollie has demonstrated his new skills by taking out a whole tranche of trickster nightmares, then reassembling them as dreams. That last part wasn't strictly necessary, but one of the things I learned about Andraste and the Fay last year was that they valued me not using my Immral to simply destroy inspyre, nightmare or not. It felt like a way to honour Andraste and her faith in me – to pass on those values to my brother.

As I watch Ollie grow in power and confidence, something strange happens. My own confidence grows. *I did that*, I realise. *That's my victory too*. Only a few years ago, my happiness and Ollie's would be in direct contradiction to each other. But now, seeing Ollie look at me with a renewed sense of purpose through eyes that are slowly turning from blue to violet, and seeing the pride Samson and my friends take in the way I am teaching my brother, I start to find some peace.

And, because I have always gone to extremes, it becomes something of a drug.

Chapter 15

'Maisie?' I collar the harker captain one night before patrol. She looks at me, frazzled. I probably shouldn't have approached her right after Frankie's grandfather, Ben, had been on one of his *I know best* rants. 'I wanted to ask about Rachel.'

'What about her?' Maisie starts walking towards the Round Table, where the cracks that began the night I crossed over into Ithr are growing by the day.

'She's good, right?'

'Very.'

'Can I ask why she isn't a sentinel then? Only I noticed that one of the other harkers from our year was promoted the other week, and I think Rachel's just as good as them.'

Maisie looks at me oddly. 'Hasn't she told you?'

'Told me what?'

Maisie sighs, then pulls me into a side cloister. 'I offered Rachel a promotion months ago. She turned it down.'

'But why?' I know that Rachel's dearest ambition is to work her way up to being one of the harkers who mans the Round Table. She needs to become a sentinel first. Why on earth would she refuse?

'You tell me.' Maisie shrugs. 'No, seriously, please tell me. I'd give her that job in a heartbeat if I knew what was stopping her.' She is about to say more when she looks over at the Round Table and spots Ben fiddling with one of the buttons. 'What are you doing? Don't touch that!'

Ben grins at her. 'This one's new since my time. What's it do?'

Maisie storms over and pulls him away. 'It's a self-destruct button, Ben. You almost destroyed Tintagel.'

I keep thinking about Rachel, wondering why she would turn down the sentinel job. I know she won't give me a straight answer if I ask her directly. It's only a few days later, when Bedevere is passing her on our way back from patrol and Samson says, 'Good work, Rachel. We'd be lost without you,' that I understand. Loyalty. A few months ago she was suicidal over not being able to do more to save the knights. Of course she'd martyr herself now for the sake of her friends.

Well, I'm not having any of that. I bring it up with the rest of the knights later.

'You've got a good one there,' Natasha comments, when I describe my dilemma. 'I wouldn't be too quick to get her that promotion if I were you.'

'Natasha's right,' Amina says. 'We got a new harker after Tom left last year, and I swear she doesn't understand the concept of passing on sentinel knowledge straight away. Twice this evening we walked into packs of Medraut's dreamers a full five minutes before she thought fit to tell us they were there.'

Samson turns to me. 'Are you sure she does still want that promotion, Fern? She might have changed her mind, you know. She might genuinely want to stay with us.'

I shake my head. 'I know I'm not exactly great at understanding people's feelings, but I know that deep down she wants to be a sentinel. I even asked her about it a few weeks ago and I thought she looked a bit odd. She's staying out of loyalty to us.'

'Fern's right,' Ollie says, then catching the others' eyes hurriedly adds, 'I haven't read her mind or anything, don't worry. But I know Rachel pretty well. She wants that promotion.'

'I could talk to her, I suppose,' Samson says.

'No,' I say, suddenly realising something. 'Leave it with me.'

Niamh grins. 'She's the woman with the ideas and she's on a mission.'

'It's important to get people to see the truth, isn't it?' I say, then add more quietly, so only Niamh and Natasha can hear, 'Irish and Penn?' It's the first time either Ollie or I have let slip that we know about their website. The shock on their faces almost makes me laugh. A moment later, though, Niamh winks at me and puts a finger to her lips. Our little secret.

I have a feeling that getting Rachel to accept that promotion will be a lot easier if it's done by stealth. I need to show her that she can be just as useful to the knights if she becomes a sentinel. And as it happens, I'm in charge of a mission that could use some good harkers.

‘I have a favour to ask,’ I tell Rachel the next night.

‘Anything,’ she says, as I knew she would.

I bring her up to the room where Easa and I are plotting and explain what we need her to do.

Doubt clouds her features. ‘I don’t know, Fern. This is a big responsibility. I’m sure there are other harkers . . .’

‘No, we need you for this,’ I say. ‘Besides, Maisie can’t spare any of the sentinels. They’re short-staffed, aren’t they?’

Rachel blushes. ‘Well, if you’re sure, and if there really isn’t anyone better who’s free.’

Easa smiles. ‘Who would be better for this than the person who worked out how to alter the Round Tables last year? You do realise you’re a legend in the reeves for that research, don’t you?’

‘Hardly.’ Rachel shrugs, but I think she’s pleased by the compliment.

The night before the mission, Easa and I gather our team. I look around the room at the faces I have come to love. And I know – we all know – that I am putting them in great danger. I’ve tried to mitigate it as much as possible, and luckily Lady Kaur has volunteered herself and a couple of her remaining knights to bolster our teams, but there’s only so much I can do. If I’d been riding alongside them, perhaps it wouldn’t feel so bad. But now, looking at Lord Allenby in the front row, for once taking orders from *me*, I understand how difficult his job is. Sending people you love and respect into the line of fire night after night, every wound must feel like a blow to your conscience.

‘No heroics,’ I tell them, giving every one of them my best

don't mess with me glare. 'Obviously we want to catch one of those snakes. But if I tell you to get out of there, I want you through your portal and back in the Cornish castle without a second's thought, okay?'

Niamh mock-salutes as the others nod.

'Come see me to get your portals redirected before you head back to Ithr,' Easa says. Whispers, sober and serious, break out across the room. Lord Allenby rests a hand on my shoulder, but doesn't say anything. I find my way to Samson – it will be the last chance I have to speak to him before we're in the thick of it tomorrow night. He snakes his arms around my waist and touches his forehead to mine.

'How are you feeling?' he asks me.

'Really hoping I'm not sending you into a trap.'

'Even if you are, it won't be your fault.'

We walk through the castle and out into the grounds, finding our spot – the place beneath a willow tree where Samson first admitted he liked me as more than a friend and colleague. It's where we always go to have important conversations, and I don't know whether it's an effect of our feelings or just coincidence, but the willow itself seems to understand our need for privacy, draping its brown and curling leaves down to the ground to make a veil.

I push Samson up against the trunk and press my lips to his. I have become bold – less worried about imposing on him. But there's something else niggling at me, even though I know that now's not the time to have this conversation.

'What's bothering you?' he says. Is my poker face really that bad?

'It can wait.'

Samson runs one hand up my arm and into the crook of my neck. 'Can it? If something happens tomorrow –'

'Nothing's going to happen tomorrow.' But my words are hollow.

'Come on, Fern. Don't play games.'

'I'm not.' I wrestle with how to make my point. It's so tied up with secrets that I can't share with Samson yet: Natasha and Niamh's website, the letter to the Helliers, Ollie's relationship with Kieran . . . But the can's been opened now. I can't close it again.

'In all the stories, people talk about love like it's a dream,' I say. 'That's how I feel with you, all the time. But it's different, because we *are* in a dream, aren't we?'

'Don't tell me that what we have isn't real,' Samson says.

'But it isn't. Not properly. I never thought I'd say this, because Annwn is the only place I've ever really been happy, but I don't want to always be in a dream. Dreams don't work without reality, just like reality doesn't work without dreams. I want real, Samson.'

'You want us to meet in Ithr.' He looks away, conflicted. Is it because he's worried about what I'd see, or find out? Or is it because he knows it's against the rules for us to have a relationship in the real world? One I can stomach, the other I can't.

'Yes. That's what I want. Not now. Not even this week. But if we're going to be together, I need us to be together properly.'

Samson nods and kisses me again. As we step onto the

platform that will take us back to our respective homes, halfway across London from each other, I can't help but worry that this uncertainty between us will have been the last conversation we'll ever have.

Chapter 16

I wake up with a nausea that only grows throughout the day. The journey to school may be uneventful, but as soon as I reach Bosco things get significantly worse. Charlie's old friends are on the warpath, especially when they see her sitting with me at break times.

'Get a room,' they spit at her. Then they look at the make-up I now use to cover my burn scar and jeer.

'Fake,' Victoria Von Gellert says. 'As if we don't know what it looks like.'

But insults like that don't phase me. I am far more worried about Charlie's safety.

I half wonder if this is being engineered by Medraut directly. Has he decided that she's no use to him in Ithr as well as Annwn? The thought of a father abandoning his own child like that is horrific, but then some of the things Medraut has done to his daughter are beyond that. He has experimented on her in the cruellest of ways. He killed her dog years ago. I know that this can only build to something worse, but Charlie doesn't seem to care.

At lunchtime we go to the art room, where we can be alone

and where I can continue my sketches of the Fay. Charlie watches me impassively, then says, 'Lionel told me he might not see me for a few days.'

I pause, taken aback. I knew Lord Allenby spent a lot of time with Charlie, that he was protective of her. I knew he'd arranged for her to get her own portal, so she's now an aventure instead of a dreamer, but this makes it sound like . . . like they're family.

'Yeah. He's helping out with a mission,' I say carefully, unsure how much I should tell her.

'Is it to do with those rip things?' she asks.

I nod.

'Couldn't you try to recreate them instead of doing this mission?'

'We tried. My brother – we thought his power might help but it didn't work.'

Charlie considers this. 'Maybe he just needed an extra burst of energy.'

I stare at her. 'Since when did you turn all scientific?'

Charlie smiles wistfully. 'I used to love science. Dad didn't like that.'

Yet another thing that Medraut took from his daughter. I grip Charlie's hand briefly before going back to my drawing. I know that if I try to get her to talk about it more she'll clam up. Anything she tells me about her dad has to come from her alone. But my mind is also racing – *an extra burst of energy.* Could that be the secret? We don't have time to test it now – the mission is scheduled for tonight and we can't risk any more delays. But if it doesn't work, then perhaps we can get Charlie to help us with a plan B.

'I tried to get into my dad's office last night,' Charlie says, breaking into my thoughts.

I drop my brush. 'You did what?'

'I wanted to see if I could find anything useful.'

'Lord Allenby put you up to this?'

She shakes her head. 'He told me to stop worrying about helping and focus on getting better, but you're all risking your lives every night to try to stop my father. I want to help.'

I have never told Charlie about the time I tortured her for information in Annwn. Selfishly, I don't want her to hate me. But perhaps I should – maybe it would cure her of the idea that she owes us anything.

'I couldn't get into his desk drawers,' Charlie continues. 'And I don't know the password to his computer. I'll keep trying, though.'

Another ugly thought pops up – it *would* be useful to have someone on the inside. We are under siege – literally in Annwn, metaphorically in Ithr. Maybe it's time that we used Charlie to attack her father. I balk. This is the kind of person I am now, is it? The kind of person who's considering using a traumatised girl to spy on her abuser?

'Don't do that, Fern,' she says, watching me shrewdly.

'Do what?'

'Treat me like a damsel in distress. I'm not any more, thanks to you. Let me decide what to risk.'

'Alright,' I say, but I don't really mean it.

'Just stay safe tonight. And Lionel. Please don't let my dad hurt him.'

I just smile at that, in what I hope is a reassuring way, but

I cannot bring myself to promise anything. I know only too well that promises like that shouldn't be made in a world like this.

My worries about Charlie become just one layer of many anxieties. When I get home from school, Clemmie is already in the kitchen. I smell her cloying perfume as soon as I set foot in the house. I watch her quietly from the doorway, wondering whether there is anything I can now do to bring her back. She starts when she realises I'm here.

'Oh, it's you Fern,' she says primly. 'Angus told me he'd be back early today so I thought I'd make him dinner.'

'Right.' I note the way she makes it clear that I'm not invited to this dinner. That rejection stings. There was once a time when she'd have done practically anything to gain my acceptance.

'Are you licking your wounds?' she asks as I head for the stairs.

'My wounds?'

'The announcement. Didn't you see? Our prime minister's banned all protests.' Clemmie is back to using her sing-song sweet voice, and it makes me want to punch her.

I run up to my room to look up the news. I don't have to search hard, the headlines are everywhere and they all have the same angle.

PRIME MINISTER CALLS FOR UNITY.

PEACE IN OUR LAND.

And one tabloid's take: *SHUT UP AND SIT DOWN.*

The articles all note how Medraut has banned protests and protest groups 'in a move to bring the country together as one'.

Shout Louder is pinpointed everywhere as the main target of the new law, but it takes me a while to find a comment from them. Their new leader, a woman with cropped, grey hair and a sharp voice, talks about free speech but it's clear that the paper quoting her sees her as a troublemaker. I wonder what Constantine Hale, the founder of the group, would make of this if he were still alive.

Sitting back in my chair, I probe my feelings. Nothing Medraut does surprises me any more. Clemmie had even hinted at this happening, and it makes sense given Medraut's aim of silencing every voice except his own. I had never been convinced that Shout Louder was particularly effective. Perhaps it was more useful than I'd given it credit for, if Medraut sees it as a threat.

I'm pulled out of my reverie by a pair of familiar voices outside. Peering out of my window, I see Ollie and Kieran at the front door.

Clemmie's here. This can't end well, given the mood she's in.

I tap on the window, hoping to get Ollie's attention, but he and Kieran are deep in conversation. Before I can text him, Ollie has opened the door and they're inside the house.

By the time I get downstairs, there's a stand-off in the hallway. Clemmie has barred the way into the kitchen and she's staring at my brother with disgust. Kieran is trying to moderate.

'Nothing we do affects you, Clemmie.'

'If my work found out, I'd be a laughing stock,' she spits.

'How terrible for you,' Ollie says. His voice is cold but he's shaking.

I'm about to stick my oar in when Dad ambles in. It takes

him a few seconds to notice the tension in the house, and the four people blocking his route to the kitchen. If it weren't all so tragic, I'd laugh.

'What's going on?' he says, although from the way his eyes dart from person to person, I'm sure he realises.

'I have to insist that Ollie's *friend* leaves the house,' Clemmie says. She speaks confidently, knowing that Dad will back her up.

'If Kieran leaves, so do I,' Ollie says.

'And me,' I pipe up. My brother looks up at me, only just noticing I'm here. 'As long as you don't mind me being a third wheel.'

'Why would I make Kieran leave?' my father says mildly.

Clemmie splutters, 'Isn't it obvious? How can you allow them to live their lifestyle under this roof?'

'What lifestyle would that be?'

Ollie, Kieran and I stand back. Clemmie hasn't noticed what we have: the undertone of danger beneath Dad's gentle voice. It's an undertone I've never heard before.

'Don't be ridiculous, Angus. It can't be allowed to continue. Ollie needs help. He needs an intervention. I've stayed quiet until now because I love you, and I love Ollie and Fern, but you've been letting them get some very dangerous ideas in their heads. Unnatural ideas. It wouldn't be tolerated in my household, and it won't be tolerated in my country soon. So I'm saying this for your own good: that boy needs to leave, and we need to take Ollie somewhere that'll straighten him out.'

'Pun not intended,' Kieran says.

There's a long silence. Something in the house shifts. The

atmosphere thickens, until it is almost claustrophobic. Dad is the one who breaks it. 'You should leave.'

Clemmie smiles triumphantly.

'Clemmie,' Dad clarifies, 'I'd like you to leave.'

Something releases in my chest. I have known for months that Dad was more accepting of Ollie than I'd thought he would be, but he's never stood up to Clemmie's increasing bigotry. He's not the kind of person to stand up to anyone, or so I'd thought.

'I beg your pardon?' Clemmie says, inflating with indignation.

'I've tolerated your intolerance of my boy for far longer than I should have. I'd hoped you'd come round, but clearly that's not happening.'

'If I leave now, I won't be coming back,' Clemmie says, as though she's wielding a trump card.

'I think that'd be for the best,' Dad says. 'I won't have my child made to feel unwelcome in his own home.'

I bite my lip to stop from cheering. Clemmie splutters some more, then storms out, giving Ollie and Kieran as wide a berth as she can in the narrow hallway. She pauses when she's halfway out of the door, and looks up at Dad. Her eyes are brimming with tears, but resolute. 'I've kept this house safe for a while now, Angus, I hope you know that. You won't have my protection any more. Not as long as those unnatural children of yours are under this roof.'

And she walks off down the street, her heels tapping on the pavement. Dad closes the door smartly behind her, and a part of me that I didn't know existed – the part of me that quietly loved her against my will – breaks at the abandonment.

'What did she mean,' I ask, 'about protecting us?'

'It's bluster,' Dad says wearily. He looks at Ollie. 'I'm sorry it came to that, Ols. I know I should've thrown her out months ago. I was just hoping she'd find herself again.'

Ollie hugs Dad, Dad pulls Kieran in to join them, and once again I feel left out of their little tribe. Dad's the one Ollie turns to. Dad stands up for him when he didn't stand up for me. I try not to think about Dad's lack of action over Jenny. I don't want to let the bitterness creep inside me again. So I close my eyes, and I let the disparity wash over me.

Even though the rest of the evening is a relatively pleasant affair, full of forced jollity to make sure that Dad's okay with the sudden breakdown of his relationship, I can't help but feel as though Clemmie's behaviour is an omen of what's to come tonight. As I watch Ollie looking over at Kieran, something clouding his face, that feeling grows. We just lost one member of my 'family'. I don't think my poor, scarred heart could bear it if we lost any more.

Chapter 17

My fears are not allayed when I land in the thanes' Cornish castle. I have been here once before, last year, when I was sent to alter the Round Tables across the country. It gave me the creeps back then and it does so even more now. For the Cornish castle isn't a castle in the traditional sense of the word: it is an underground lair, a network of caves that spin out from a ring-like portal that sits directly beneath an ancient stone circle. There are no towers, no windows, and the air is close. Inspyre flickers down the fortified earth walls like lightning, offering the only decoration in the main chamber.

We arrive in the open air, inside the stone circle that covers the castle. Ollie is already there when I materialise, and soon after the other members of the team – Lord Allenby, Samson, Natasha, Niamh, Amina, Bandile, Rachel and Easa – arrive too, each one with a little *pop*.

'You made it alright then?' Lady Kaur says from just outside the circle, and we stride over to her. Lord Allenby shakes her hand warmly and we follow them into a cave that leads beneath the earth. This is where Rachel, Easa and I will be stationed for the operation.

'Your veneurs sent your horses on earlier. They're being taken care of in our stables.'

'Thank you, my lady,' Lord Allenby says. 'Let's see if we can work out what's going on here, eh?'

'Indeed.'

Rachel, Easa and I are shown into a small, circular room where the Cornish harkers have their Round Table. The space was once a well. Far above us, a distant light streams down the vertical tunnel. Rachel is given a sentinel's helmet and shown to a seat where a periscope leads up to the outer air.

'It stretches up far higher than the ground,' one of the harkers explains, 'so you can instantly see anything that our sentinels might spot, and match it to the Round Table's map.'

As Rachel settles into her seat, I sneak a quick peek through the periscope. The view flits between dozens of different places in Cornish Annwn, in line with what the sentinels are seeing from their different positions. Easa and I duck out of the chamber and find our way back to the rest of the knights, who are waiting in the underground stables with their horses.

They turn to us, faces tense. Apart from Lord Allenby, they've all been standing in a circle, arms around each other. Samson and Natasha open their arms for me to join them, and even though I do, I feel like a fraud. I may be a knight, but this time I am not putting myself in danger. I am thrusting them – my friends, my lover, my brother, my commander – into the line of fire, and if I mess up, their lives are at stake. I, meanwhile, will be waiting behind, watching and listening but unable to step in front of them to save them.

'You're all going to be fine,' I tell them out loud as I pair them off in their teams and Easa hands each of them a tracker. Lord Allenby is with one of the last remaining Cornish knights. The knight is apparently older than Niamh, but he looks very young in the dim light of the stables. Samson and Bandile comprise the next group. I want nothing more than to hold Samson close, but we both know that wouldn't be professional. As Samson mounts his horse, I mouth *Love you* at him. He doesn't smile in return, just holds my gaze. It's the first time I've said those words to him, and they feel like a desperate goodbye rather than a romantic declaration.

'It'll be okay,' he says softly.

Lady Kaur is next, leading a team with one of her knights. Niamh and Natasha follow them. As Natasha mounts her horse, Niamh digs in her pockets and produces a treat for Domino. Seeing this, Amina's horse nuzzles her. Niamh bats him away. 'Back off, these are for my favourite lad.'

Ollie and Amina make up the final group. The horses frisk and stamp, picking up on their riders' nerves. Amina rubs her horse's neck, making soothing noises. 'Come on, old girl,' I hear her whisper, 'we've been through worse.'

Easa looks up at my brother. 'We'll go to that place again when you're back, if you'd like?' he tells Ollie.

Ollie nods tightly. He puts a hand lightly on Easa's arm. The change in Easa's expression is immediate: a kind of contented focus on my brother. I look away, feeling as though I've witnessed something intimate.

The first sun sets, drawing its blistered fingers behind the horizon. That's our signal. 'It's time,' I say.

They lead their horses out of the stables and into the dim

light of the cave entrance. I stroke Balius's muzzle with a whispered, 'Take care of him,' and then hold up a hand by way of farewell as they ride out of the cave.

Lord Allenby growls, 'Stay safe, everyone.'

Five portals glint in between the megaliths of the stone circle, each one set up to transport our knights to a different part of the county. Ollie smiles back at me, and Samson salutes, and then they're urging their horses forward. They leap through the portals and vanish, as though swallowed up by the air itself.

Heart heavy, I make my way back to the Round Table chamber where Rachel is already seated. Easa places a hand on my shoulder.

'You okay?' he says.

'It's not me I'm worried about,' I say. 'I don't know how you guys do this every day.' Rachel grimaces at me in solidarity.

Easa says, 'Well, historically I just haven't let myself get close to any knights. That got shot to pieces last year, though, didn't it?'

We sit at the table and Easa pulls out our plan. I don my own harker helmet. 'Can you hear me?' I say into my helmet.

'Loud and clear,' Samson says, and the other team leaders respond too.

'Nothing sighted yet,' Rachel says, her eyes glued to the periscope.

'Remember, any sign of a rip, even if it turns out to be a false alarm, you alert us,' I say into my helmet. I try to keep my voice even and calm. If I'm going to lead this mission, I'd better do it with the appearance of confidence.

We sit like that for what feels like hours. Every few minutes I do a roll call, just in case something's meddled with the periscope. After a while, it starts to feel as though this was all a big anti-climax. Maybe there won't be a rip tonight, even though there has been every night for the last few weeks. I try not to think about what that means for us – does it suggest that we've got a spy in our ranks who is relaying our plans to Medraut?

'I bloody hate waiting,' Niamh says into her helmet, and the others mutter their agreements.

'Here, snakey-snakey,' Bandile sings, trying to lighten the mood.

'Quiet,' Lord Allenby says. 'Keep the channels for real news, please. This isn't a social engagement.'

While Lord Allenby's right, I can't stand the silence that falls over the group. It emphasises the distance between us and makes the minutes stretch. Every time Rachel takes a breath or shifts in her seat, I startle, thinking, *This is it*. But then she settles and the waiting goes on and on.

'Come on, come on,' Easa mutters.

'What are you up to, Medraut?' Lady Kaur hisses over the helmet.

Time for another check-in.

'Is everyone still there?' I say into my helmet

'Yes,' the Cornish contingent say.

'Yup,' Niamh says.

'Yes,' Lord Allenby says.

'Here,' Samson replies.

There's a pause.

'Ollie?' I say. 'Amina?'

There's another long pause. 'Ollie? Are you there?' I say again.

Rachel mutters directions into her helmet then peers into the periscope. When she pulls away, her face is paler than usual. 'They're not there,' she whispers.

'What do you mean, not there? They must be,' Easa says.

'They've disappeared,' Rachel says, looking to me. 'Fern . . .' She peters out, because what can she say? What can anyone say to the girl who's just lost her brother in a scheme of her own creation?

Chapter 18

'Do you want to divert knights, Fern?' Lord Allenby says.

I close my eyes, trying to clear the fog of panic. My instinct is to jump on a horse, any horse, and ride as fast as I can to find my brother. But what use would that be? If Medraut has managed to abduct two knights, one of them with Immral, without anyone seeing, then what good could I possibly do? We have to be smart; we have to think through all the possibilities. But that's easier said than done when every particle of my body is screaming, *You've lost your brother*.

'Help me,' I whisper. I don't even know who I'm talking to – perhaps Rachel and Easa; perhaps the knights who are listening for my orders; perhaps Annwn itself. My hands tingle, as though they've got pins and needles.

'Stay on plan for now. But keep talking to us,' Easa says into his own helmet. Rachel tells the sentinels to focus on the place where Ollie and Amina were just stationed, and to look back through footage to see if they can spot the moment they were taken. Their voices calm me: cracking but determined. They may not be hurting as much as I am, but Ollie and Amina are their friends too. I have to hold myself together as well. If I fracture, then what am I except a burden? My devastation isn't going to save Ollie. There will be time for tears later.

'The sentinels can't find anything on the footage,' Rachel says. My fingers tingle again, and for an instant I feel sure that there is inspyre gathering there, as it might have done when I had Immral. *Could* Annwn have heard my plea?

'Let me look,' I say.

Rachel swaps places with me and I peer into the periscope as a reeve instructs me how to use it; bending the view backwards and forwards with willpower. I watch my brother and Amina sitting, tense and upright, on their horses. They are neatly camouflaged by a low-hanging tree. You would need to know they were there to see them. Ollie glances over at Amina. Balius flicks his tail at a fly. And then . . . they're gone. Balius and Amina's horse stamp their feet, suddenly riderless. Then they take off, spooked. I rewind the scene again and again, and every time I watch it I feel the snap of my heart as my brother blinks out of existence.

'There must be something else,' I mutter.

'We checked – it hasn't been tampered with,' the reeve says.

My fingers tingle again, and it's as if I hear a voice, distant but familiar. *Look*.

I deliberately calm myself. Going on instinct, I welcome the tingle into my body. It floods up my fingers and into my chest and for a brief moment I have a flash of knowledge, as though my body is no longer present but is everywhere. I can see everything; I am losing myself and am the most powerful I've ever been. And in that moment, I see what the voice wants me to see. Ollie and Amina did not vanish – something reached through the fabric of Annwn and snatched them. The rope of thorns. It grabs my brother and friend, and before they can react they have been pulled beyond this world.

But the knowledge, whatever it is, doesn't stop there. It tells me things I shouldn't know. It tells me that Ollie is still alive. It tells me that the original plan was good. That I should forge forward, no matter what.

Then I come back to myself, and once again all I can see is Ollie and Amina simply vanishing. The certainty and peace that I briefly felt as the inspyre flowed through me disintegrates. I have to trust that voice, whatever it was. I know the voice of Immral – I'm sure it's wasn't Medraut, manipulating me. It was someone, something, else.

'It was a rip,' I tell the others. 'The snakes are definitely coming from them.'

'There's no sign of a rip there now,' Rachel tells me.

I talk into my helmet. 'I want everyone to join Lord Allenby. Now. But stay at a distance.'

Easa looks at me but doesn't question my command.

'They're hunting us. Let's see how they tackle trying to take eight knights instead of two.'

'You think they'll try to take Lord Allenby next?' Easa asks.

'Him or Lady Kaur. I don't think it's a coincidence that they took the Immral first.'

Within minutes, the remaining teams have assembled in a cave not far from the ruined castle, where Lord Allenby and the Cornish knight wait.

'All eyes on team one,' I murmur. Rachel relays my order

to the sentinels above without taking her eyes from the periscope.

All I can hear is my heart thrumming. Ollie's disappearance is the only thing that matters to me, but I force it into background noise. I cannot wonder where he is, or what is happening to him, or I'll fall apart.

'I think I see something,' Rachel says at last.

'Where?' I hear the distant voice of the sentinels say. 'We can't see anything.'

'Oh, maybe I'm wrong . . .' Rachel says.

'You're not.' I scoot over to her. 'Trust yourself. What do you see?'

'A shimmer, I think. Very faint.'

'It's a rip. Sir, you're bait. Everyone else, forward, as fast as you can.'

Rachel looks at me with wide eyes. 'Fern, it might not be – don't compromise the mission on my hunch.'

Then there's shouting from above and through Rachel's helmet. 'We see it! It's forming!' the sentinels say.

'See. You were right.' I grip Rachel's arm. Her sight might have just given us the warning we needed to get ahead of those snake creatures.

There's shouting from the knights at the rip. 'Have you got it?' I say into my helmet. 'Can you get the snake?'

More shouting, incoherent and panicked. Then Lady Kaur's voice comes through clearly. 'We need backup. All knights here, here now!'

With another tingle of my fingers, I know that I need to be there. 'Can I borrow a horse?' I ask the nearest reeve.

'Come,' she says, and we run towards the stables.

I shout instructions into my helmet as we go. 'Backup is on its way. Remember the plan! Capture one if you can!'

The reeve throws open a stall for me. 'One of the missing knights used to ride this one.'

I vault onto the mare's back, silently asking Lamb to forgive me. A handful of knights, freshly back from their patrols, run in behind me and climb onto their steeds. Together we canter out of the stables. 'Follow me,' I shout, racing towards the shimmering portal that will take us to my friends and whatever fight they're battling.

We emerge on a cliff edge, with a violent sea dashing against the rocks below us. The waves reach higher here than they would in Ithr, salt spray coating my face and making it hard to see. The wind is sharp, but there's an uncommon power behind it. Something of the tornado. I can glimpse some of my friends battling their way through the wind ahead of us. Beyond them, violet rips across the landscape. I have seen photos and videos of the northern lights, and it reminds me of that, except that this isn't peaceful. It's a violent cascade punching across the sky and the earth, like a glitch in the fabric of Annwn.

Beneath it, the rip expands. In texture, it is akin to the one that divided Annwn and Ithr that we found in Richmond Park a few weeks ago. The borders are like the edges of a geode. In places, I spot the moonlit peace of Ithr, but beyond that sight is a deeper rip that reveals a different place entirely.

It is an endless grey. A purgatory that knows no time or space. I am reminded of a place I went to two years ago. An underground warren, created by Medraut to house the treitres he was training, and the puzzle box that held his ambition. Instead of a series of tunnels, though, this is an entire world, mapped out in the space between – or maybe beyond – Annwn and Ithr.

As I gallop closer, I spot the knights doing battle at the rip's edge. Snakelike tendrils, longer and more numerous than any we've seen before, reach out from the grey. Samson and Natasha are clinging to one, dragging it away from the rip, trying to pin it down. I crest the final hill and the question that has been plaguing me for so long – what's at the end of those snakes? – is answered in the most horrific way.

A human, wearing the blue tunic of the knights, emerges from the grey world inside the rip. Their face is a mass of thorns. Snake-like tendrils wind around their body, sprouting from their back, from every limb. I cannot tell who the knight once was.

The thorns controlling the knight's body snap this way and that, extending far beyond human reach. More shapes appear behind it, their movements jerky, like puppets controlled by an inexpert master. And then another, beyond them, appears. A shape that I do recognise, despite the fact that it is wound round by thorns that pierce every part of its body. A shape I know well.

It is not my brother, as I had feared.

It is Ellen Cassell.

Chapter 19

The last time I saw Ellen, she was being feasted upon by morrigans. She shouldn't be able to exist in Annwn – the morrigans removed her ability to dream. But then, as the thorns that control her weave out through the rip, I realise that she alone of the figures does not step through to this world. She remains hidden, a shadowy figure beyond the veil, but the snakes emanating from her body are longer than any of the others. They reach through the rip and snap at us, tearing great scars in our horses, who don't have the same protection that we do. Lord Allenby vaults off his charger's back and sends him away from the danger.

'Niamh – now!' I say, hoping she'll hear me through our helmets. Niamh doesn't have a horse; she flips her wheelchair high into the air. In one swift stroke, she detaches one of her wheels and brings it down on the snake that Natasha and Samson are fighting. The wheel severs the creature from its knight, and the snake disintegrates into a spark of Immral. We cannot cut them from their hosts.

'We're going to have to bring one in whole,' Easa says over the helmets.

The thought of capturing one of these creatures, now that

we understand what they are, is an abomination. But Easa's right – if we want to work out how to defeat them and, perhaps, save the knight inside, then we have to try.

As if they have heard our plans, the snake-knights retreat back into the grey. The spots of Ithr grow larger, and the rip begins to shimmer at its edges.

'I think it's going to close,' Rachel says.

'No, we have to get one!' I shout. I look at Lord Allenby. This may have been mine and Easa's mission, but we are so far off plan now that I need my commander's permission for what I want to do next. He nods reluctantly. I leap off my horse and run to the edge of the rip. Something tells me that if I still possessed Immral, I would be feeling sick at the lack of inspyre. I wonder if Ollie is in there somewhere, and what he must be feeling.

'No one goes too far inside,' I say, as Samson, Niamh and Natasha join me. 'Quickly in, grab one, out before the rip closes.'

Bandile approaches. 'How many of us do you want?'

'You and the commanders stay here. Do what you can to keep the rip open for as long as possible.'

'We need to go quickly,' Samson says. 'They're getting away.'

Together we move inside the rip. An empty sensation settles in my chest. My skin drains of colour – still white, but somehow muted. Lifeless. Lethargy spreads across my bones.

'Be careful, everyone,' Samson says.

Something is blanketing my brain, telling me that nothing matters. Telling me to give up and give in, although I'm not sure what I'm supposed to be giving in to exactly. *What am I doing here?*

Lord Allenby calls from the rip's edge, 'Move quickly. Remember, keep an eye out for Ollie and Amina.'

I peer through the grey, but there's nothing here. It's hard to tell whether I'm seeing a blank landscape or whether my view is being blocked by mist or something else. 'Hurry,' I say, and we lope forward. The grey clings to us like treacle. The snake-knights are receding.

'Ollie!' I call. 'Amina!' My voice doesn't stretch as far as it should. In fact, it barely comes out at all. There's some dampening magic in this new world-between-worlds that prevents loud noises. That shouldn't be surprising, I suppose, if Medraut is the one who made this. But I'm not sure he did. This place is the world Medraut would have created for himself, but there's something about it that feels older than him. As though it has always been here, waiting to be discovered.

I wrestle my mind back into focus – capture one of the mutant knights, and rescue Amina and my brother. If only I had my Immral I could search for them that way. I call to the tingle in my fingers that I'm sure was inspyre, but I cannot summon it again. I suppose that we are not in Annwn any more. This is a place where no inspyre can live.

'We've lost them,' Samson says. 'We have to turn back.'

'No, keep going. We didn't go through all this for nothing,' Niamh says.

The mutant knights are finally swallowed by grey mist. I look back. The rip is further away than I thought, and it is closing.

'Samson's right. We have to get back or we're going to get stuck in here,' Natasha says.

'You all go back,' I tell them. 'I'll look for a bit longer.'

Samson grips my hand. 'Fern, you're not going to find Ollie and Amina right now. Not on your own. I know it's hard, but we have to get back to Annwn.'

I know he's right, and I hate him for it. Ollie wouldn't have given up on me. But I have to think about more than Ollie. Every moment I delay here is another moment that everyone else is in danger. Despising myself, I nod. We turn and race as fast as the lethargy allows us towards the closing rip.

'To your right!' Lady Kaur calls.

A dozen shapes rear out of the mist. It's the mutant knights, Ellen amongst them, somehow transported to a totally different place. They are going to cut us off. Samson fits an arrow to his bow, but it is snatched from his hand by one of the snakes. One of the Cornish knights who accompanied us slashes his sword at one of the creatures, but it tears it from him, not just taking the blade but the knight's entire hand.

Ellen is moving towards me, the snakes snapping this way and that to clear her path. The rip slivers together like a zip from either end. We're on the wrong side of it.

'Go!' I shout to the others, pushing them ahead of me. Niamh pauses only to throw one of her wheels at a nearby mutant. Her aim is true: it cuts through a swathe of snakes, but more leap to take their place, sparking with violet Immral. It's enough of a distraction for the rest of the knights to slide past the mutants and throw themselves through the rip. I dart after them, except that the body that was once Ellen Cassell intercepts me.

I parry the snakes that stretch from her with my scimitar,

and slide beneath them, racing towards the closing gap. Even so, I'm not sure I'm going to make it in time. Other snake-knights are here now, and they're all heading for me.

I spar once, twice, and then a third time before one of the ropes lashes against my calf.

'Hurry, Fern!' Natasha shouts.

I limp onwards, trying to ignore the pain in my leg. The rip is nearly closed now. I'm not going to make it out. I'll be turned into one of those thorny creatures, my mind filled with spikes, and together Ollie and I will help Medraut achieve his grand purpose.

There's a scream of rage and desperation from just beyond the rip, and the next thing I know, Samson appears. He squeezes himself through. The rip tries to consume him, but he holds fast, one arm reaching for me, the other pushing at the edges of the gap, stopping it from closing with superhuman willpower.

'I've got you,' he says, his eyes locking with mine. 'Come on, Fern, I've got you.'

There's another lash from the thornlike snakes, this time against my waist. It tries to pull me away, but I keep my eyes on Samson. The rip is fighting him, fighting to close, and his arm strains against the pressure. I reach for him. I'm going to make it.

Then a force stronger than any other I've experienced curls around my waist and arms, drawing me back into the grey. Samson shouts my name, but his voice is too distant. I cannot reach him. I cannot hear him. And then the rip overcomes him, and he's gone.

The grey suffocates me. More snakes, their necks covered in

thorns, twist around my body, turning me this way and that in an agony of punctures. A tortuous cradle. Ellen Cassell, thorns protruding from her arms, her hair a Medusa of them, her eyes a mass of writhing ropes, is carrying me into the depths of this new in-between.

'Ellen,' I whisper, through bouts of pain, 'Ellen, I'm Fern. Una's daughter.'

There's no reaction, although what kind of reaction could I really expect? There can't be any Ellen left inside that body now, not if Medraut has been working on her since she was expelled from Annwn.

In no time and forever, we come to a new grey space. I can tell that something's changed not by the landscape, but by a shift in the air and the way the snake-knights move. The ropes constrict, as though they are being forced into a tunnel. The air, such as it is, becomes closer.

Ellen stops, and pins me down upon an unforgiving, invisible surface. I writhe against the ropes that bind me, but all that does is force the thorns deeper into my body. I wonder why I'm struggling then. Is there any need for it? I'm just being dramatic.

Mmmm. Someone nearby is making a muffled noise, as though they're having a bad dream. The sound is familiar. I force myself, through a fog of indifference, to look for its source.

Across the space, pinned down by another thorned figure, are two people. One is Amina. The other is Ollie. And he has snakes sprouting from his back.

'No,' I whisper, 'not them.' I look up at Ellen, praying that there is still something of my mother's friend in that husk of a body. 'Please,' I say, 'not him. Just not him.'

Ellen doesn't flinch. Instead, she raises one of her arms and, before I can say anything further, brings it down hard on my head. All goes black.

Chapter 20

I wake up in my bed, my head foggy and my sheets sweaty. There is a mirror in my hand, although I can't think why. Oh well, it doesn't really matter. I have to get ready for school. I put my make-up on, making sure to cover every inch of my burn scar. It's important to look nice. To look like a decent person, who's going to fit in and be a useful part of society.

Downstairs, Ollie silently hands me a cup of tea, his eyes pleasingly unfocused. Dad is bustling around the kitchen far too quickly. There's no need for his urgency. It's unnecessary.

'Is Kieran coming over tonight?' he asks Ollie.

Ollie frowns. 'No, why would he?'

Dad smiles at him oddly. 'You two have a fight or something?'

Ollie shrugs and turns away. I feel as though maybe this is wrong, but something worms through my brain, telling me that it is right. This is as it should be. Ollie isn't bothered. Kieran was just a phase. My brother will find someone far more suitable now. I try to ignore a deep unease. I don't like it. I don't want to feel uncomfortable. That's why I covered up my burn scar. The scar that only came about because I was too stubborn to make friends. I should have played nice with Jenny. She must have been right all along if she was so popular.

My journey to school goes by without incident. I've put more effort into looking normal. Why didn't I do this before? Stubbornness, again. A stupid desire to stand out. To make a difference. As if one insignificant girl could have any power.

But you did. You do. Fight, Fern.

I shake my head. Unsettling memories of horses and a London that is both familiar and strange rise to the surface of my deliciously treacly brain. There is a face, too. One that stirs complicated feelings in me – I have an impression of a strong mind. Eyes like deep, warm springs. No, no, that must be wrong. I don't remember his name.

'Fern!' he shouts, reaching for me through a rip in the world that must close.

Stop it, Fern.

The train grinds to a halt at Westminster, and I get off, melding with the other commuters. Left, right, our feet go, and the bliss of fitting in helps me to forget the thoughts that shouldn't be there. Left, right, left, right. I fall in behind another young woman, her brunette locks swaying neatly with our matching pace. I almost feel sad when I have to take a different route to get to Bosco College, except that sadness is a useless emotion. In fact, all emotions are useless. They are not productive. And productivity is key. Onwards, upwards, with my fellow human beings. A common purpose. A single voice. It's so peaceful.

I sit neatly in my seat all morning, writing down my teacher's lecture, word for word. There is a spare notebook in my bag – one labelled *Knightbook*. I vaguely remember that it was something to do with dreams or sleep. I have no use for it any more. I drop it in the bin as I leave for lunch break.

At some point, I find myself sitting on my usual bench. A girl called Lottie joins me. I smile at her, but do not offer my hand as I once did. That would be *wrong*, although I can't quite place the reason why it would be wrong.

'Lionel says you have to fight,' Lottie whispers.

She must be confusing me with someone else. I don't know any Lionel.

'They're working on a way to get you and Ollie out, but you have to fight, Fern.'

'Ollie and I are fine,' I tell her, smiling reassuringly.

'Samson wants you to know that he's never going to give up on you. He's going to find you in Ithr.'

'Where's Ithr?' I say. 'I live in Stratford.'

I push away the creeping sensation that tells me that I *do* know a Samson, I *do* know a Lionel. Those sensations are wrong. *Wrong wrong wrong*. But even as I think it, I wonder whose voice it is repeating that word. Lottie seizes both of my hands in hers now, so that some of the delicious fog clears.

'You saved me once, Fern. I'm going to save you now.'

She pulls me to my feet, ignoring my protests, and drags me to a place I know I should not go. The art room. Pain prickles across my back, punishing me for being here. Lottie pulls a sheaf of paper from a drawer in the corner of the classroom, and lays each piece out across the desks. I close my eyes, desperate not to look at my transgressions, but Lottie forces me. So many people are drawn. Some of them are human – a girl with red hair and a kind face. Two siblings, their deep eyes and weak chins identical. A boyish man, a creature perched on his shoulder, part crow, part bat. Looking at them all makes something in my chest ache, and the pain along my back increases unbearably. I am not supposed to care about these people, yet I do, even though I can't remember their names. There are more drawings of older beings, who do not look entirely human. One – a warrior woman with bird's-nest hair and a face covered in scars – makes me feel something else. Sad, yes. Indescribably so. But also powerful, and desperate for revenge, although I don't understand why.

'I am ordering you: *fight my dad,*' she says. 'Whatever he's doing to you, *fight him*. Remember what he did to these people you've drawn. Or I . . .' She casts around for a suitable threat. 'Or Loco's going to die. And Lamb.'

'Lamb?'

'You remember Lamb, don't you? Lionel took me to meet her.'

I don't know Lamb. I don't know what she's talking about. But I do know that I don't want Lamb or Loco, whoever they are, to die. Something deep inside me screams against the very idea of it. But she said I had to fight her father, and I don't want to do that either. I wouldn't know how to even if I did. Sebastien Medraut is stronger and cleverer than me. He is perfect. I wouldn't stand a chance against him. But apparently I need to, if Lamb and Loco are to survive.

'How do I fight?' I say.

'Use your imagination,' she replies. 'Samson says, *remember the bird*.'

I carry this advice with me into my afternoon lessons,

although it doesn't make any sense. *Remember the bird*. I find myself doodling birds on my lesson notes, even though I know I shouldn't. Doodles are useless. Art is useless. Why do I need to remember a bird?

After school, I leave the building and spot the same man from my muted memories. Something stirs inside me – more than recognition. There are feelings there, emotions that are dangerous. I duck my head and join the throng of students leaving Bosco. There is safety in numbers, that's what they say, isn't it? It has never been true for me in the past, but it is true today. And they accept me, these students, now that I am making an effort to fit in. That's all it took – a small effort. The little matter of removing who I am and becoming who they want me to be.

'Fern,' the man says, pushing through the crowds. Some of them hiss at him, at the intrusion into our safe pack by this stranger who doesn't conform. One or two of them cast me dark looks, suspicious of him wanting to talk to me.

'Leave me alone,' I say, my voice flat.

His eyes linger on the make-up concealing my burn scar. Something seems to break inside him – is he disappointed in me? Why does that matter to me the way it does?

'Let's talk quietly,' he says eventually, 'just for a few minutes. Then I'll go, I promise.'

The people around me move on, although some of them push and shove the man. 'Stop that,' I say, surprising myself. 'Leave him alone.'

'You *are* one of them,' someone hisses as she passes, and there's a sharp pain in the back of my head, as though my brain is rebuking me for stepping out of line.

I follow the man down the steps of Bosco and towards a quiet garden, one of the tiny courtyard spaces that punctuate this part of London; a shared haven for the houses crammed into these streets. A bird sings, lonely, from one of the trees. *A bird. A bird in a grey space, long ago.*

'Samson,' I say, finally naming the man. How did I know that his name was Samson?

'You remember.' He smiles, and it makes him look even more handsome.

'No,' I say, the sharp pain in my head returning. 'No, I don't. It's fuzzy. Who are you?'

Samson leads me to a wooden bench in a secluded corner of the garden. 'Listen carefully, Fern,' he says. 'Medraut has you trapped somewhere. We're working on a way to free you and Ollie and Amina, but we need a rip to open up again. We've got every thaneship working on it, okay? But we need your help. Can you remember anything about what happened before you woke up? Anything at all?'

I shake my head. He's asking about dreams, but I don't dream, not any more. Dreams are pointless. That's what I'm supposed to think.

But, unbidden, a fleeting memory comes to me. A woman covered in snakes, marching me through a bleak landscape. A terrain so different from the richly flowered garden we sit in now, that I cannot help but feel the difference in my gut. I tell Samson what I remember, and describe the woman, and how she made me feel.

'Ellen. I think it's Ellen who has you.'

He pulls me to my feet, looking something up on his phone.

The pain at the back of my head is spreading now, into my shoulders and down my spine. It reprimands me, telling me to leave Samson, to accept, to surrender.

'I've got it,' Samson says, and my hand automatically finds his. I know I shouldn't be with him. With him I am vulnerable. With him I am not part of the pack. We are Different. But he also makes me feel as though I am his, and he is mine, and that feeling is worth any pain.

Chapter 21

Samson brings me to an imposing building set back from the street, talking all the way. His voice clears some of the fog in my head. He tells me what Ellen did for me as Helena Corday, and the terrible crimes she committed in a place called Annwn, and every word makes the prickles along my back ache and burn. A bushy hedge obscures all view of the house from the road, as though trying to pretend it's not there. The gates are locked shut, but Samson blags his way in on the intercom. He speaks differently, erasing all trace of his south London accent. He glances at me. 'Don't want to give them any more excuses not to let us in.'

As the pain in my body grows, flashes of memories return. Lamb, I now realise, is a horse. A horse that I ride, although I can't work out where I would ride a horse in London. We can't afford riding lessons. Samson keeps looking at me. I think he's worried.

'I'm fine,' I tell him, but he just shakes his head.

'Fern would never let me pull her along like this. She'd be the one leading the way,' he tells me.

'*I'm* Fern,' I snap at him. 'I know what I'm like.'

He smiles. 'That's more like it.'

I pull my hand from his, even though the loss of his warmth makes me feel bereft. The pain lessens, like a reward. But I keep following Samson, instead of running away like I'm supposed to. The receptionist studies Samson suspiciously, as he explains that we are old friends of Helena Corday's.

'Visiting hours are nearly over,' he tells us.

'We'll be quick, sir,' Samson says. He is still using his posher accent, but it's not going to be enough. I'm not sure why Ellen is so important to him but apparently we simply have to speak to her. I step forward, and parrot some of what Samson told me on the way here. 'I'm a student at Bosco College. She got me my scholarship there, and I'd just really like to update her on how it's all going. To thank her. If you don't mind.'

The man settles back in his chair, regarding me more warmly than he did Samson. 'She won't really understand you,' he warns us, then, when we don't move, he sighs. 'Fine. Go on through. Room eleven.'

'Brilliant,' Samson mutters as we pace up the stairs.

The room is sparse, but a decent size for a bedroom. There's a large window looking out over grounds where other residents are gardening. Two chairs sit on either side of the window. The bed, which is the only other significant piece of furniture in the room, is neatly made.

Ellen, sitting in one of the chairs, doesn't respond when we enter the room, or when Samson says her name. In appearance, she hasn't changed much from the politician who visited me after the fire three years ago, and promised to help get me into Bosco. But as Samson directs me to the spare chair and I see

Ellen's face properly, I realise that there's a looseness to her features and a stiffness to her limbs. I reach a hand up to my own face. Something tells me that this is how I look right now too. I certainly feel the solidity in my bones, keeping me more upright than I would otherwise be.

'Talk to her, Fern.' Samson says.

'What should I say?'

He huffs.

'Miss Corday?' I say, viscerally aware of Samson's growing irritation. Ellen pulls her gaze away from the window with great effort, and I know exactly how she feels. For me to say even a word is a feat of great strength, requiring far too much energy to be worthwhile. Better to stay silent. Then her eyes settle on me. They are blank for the longest time, not a hint of recognition. Then she tilts her head, ever so slightly. She mouths something, although no sound comes out.

'Yes,' I say, 'I'm Una's daughter.'

It begins to come back to me. Ellen and my mother are connected. Ellen . . . killed my mother.

'Ask her about the rip,' Samson prompts me. I jerk my head at him, my eyes still on Ellen, as if to ask her if she heard him. She is frowning now. Then she winces and clutches the back of her head, curls over as though something is raking down her spine.

'Do you hurt there too?' I ask her.

She nods through silent pain. She's muttering something. I lower myself to the floor and place my ear close to her face.

'It grows,' she's saying. 'It grows, it grows, and you cannot cut it off.'

Samson's next to me now as well.

'Do you mean the snakes?' he says, but the urgency in his voice silences Ellen. She cringes away from him.

'If you can't cut it off, how do you stop it growing?' I ask her, only understanding that this is important to Samson.

'The root,' she says. 'You must destroy the root.'

'Can you help Fern?' Samson says. 'Can you help Una's daughter, Ellen?'

She starts to shake. A quiet tremble that vibrates her whole body. It takes me a while to realise that she's laughing.

'I already did,' she says, looking up at last, her smile a pained grimace. 'I planted it in the wrong place.' She emits a single, loud peal of laughter that's cut short by a painful gasp. She is being punished for being loud, for being disobedient.

'Thank you,' Samson says. Silently, I offer Ellen my hand. She stares at it incomprehensibly, until gradually her fingers crawl their way into mine, like a baby looking for reassurance in a parent's embrace.

'Can I help you?' I ask her.

She meets my gaze properly for the first time. 'Kill the root,' is all she says.

Samson leads me out of the room, out of the building, and we are far away from there before we speak again. 'Okay, this is our plan, Fern. I need you to try to remember this, no matter what they do to you, okay?'

I may not fully understand what is going on, but I trust Samson, and enough memories are coming back to me now that I know that something is happening to me. Something to make me not myself. I am learning that the pain is a sign that

I am fighting whatever it is. If I embrace the agony, maybe I can find a way back to myself.

As Samson finishes talking me through his scheme, I do something that is going to make the pain in my head shoot right across my shoulders and back. I pull him towards me and kiss him, pressing my body against his. I am right; the pain is almost unbearable. But in a flash, I am more myself than I have been all day. This is where I am meant to be. I remember everything: Annwn, Ithr, Tintagel, the rip and the snake of thorns encasing the kidnapped knights, encasing me.

I release Samson and step back, fog already threatening to cloud my memories and my reasoning once more. Samson looks at me hungrily. 'Hello, my love,' he says. 'It's good to finally meet you.'

I move away from him, stiff and aching, and walk towards my home. 'I'll see you tonight, girl,' he calls after me. I lift a hand in response. Saying anything back will only make the pain ricocheting around my body greater. I have said what I wanted to say to him in that kiss.

At home, Ollie sits on the sofa, staring straight ahead, upright and unfocused, at the news on the TV. I feel as fuzzy as he looks, but now I am beginning to understand that this is not natural.

'Something's happening to us,' I tell Ollie.

'Yes,' he says, 'I'm getting better.'

'What do you mean?'

Just then, the doorbell rings. Kieran stands outside, looking pinched.

'Is Ollie in?' he says.

'Umm.' I get the feeling that my brother doesn't want to

see Kieran. And even though I know that what I am thinking is wrong, a throb in the back of my head is telling me not to let Kieran in. I stand aside to allow Kieran through. I follow him into the sitting room where he stands over Ollie. 'Why haven't you been replying to my messages?' he asks my brother.

Ollie just shrugs in reply.

'Is this your way of breaking up with me?' Kieran says. 'God, you're such a coward, Ollie. You've been off with me for weeks but you couldn't just come out and say it, could you? Trying to make me the bad guy. Well, congratulations, you've got your wish. We're done.'

Ollie doesn't look at Kieran, doesn't even move, and I can feel the anger and hurt radiating from Kieran in waves, crashing against Ollie's immobile form like water against rock. Kieran stands there for a moment longer, waiting for some kind of reaction, but when he doesn't get it he shakily steps back and pushes past me.

'Wait –' I say to his back.

He pauses at the door. 'Something's wrong with you both,' he says, and I get the feeling he doesn't just mean what's happening to us the last day or so. 'Take care of yourself, Fern. And take care of him.' Then he's gone, pulling the door shut behind him in a not-quite-slam.

'That was too loud,' Ollie says monotonously from his position on the sofa.

Kieran's right. There is something wrong with us, and tonight I'm going to try to set it right.

Chapter 22

Samson explained the mirror's purpose to me earlier today, but I'm still shocked when light pours out as I open it. So this is why I'd been clutching it when I woke up. I tried to explain to Ollie that he had something like this too, but he wasn't interested. I hope that won't affect Samson's plan.

I find myself in dark waters that hold me close, like being inside a womb. I can't find it in me to swim up, so I let myself fall instead. Eventually, I come to a barrier at the bottom of the pool, and find myself sinking into something resembling light. Everything is grey. I am inside a body that is and isn't mine. The body is strapped to a surface that I cannot see. I look to either side of me and realise that I am just one of a row of people. I recognise some of them – my brother and a girl with braided hair. We are all wearing the same clothing – a blue tunic. Around us move a mass of creatures, half human, half snake. They work upon our bodies, inserting ropes of thorns into our heads and attaching them to our backs. Their movements would be robotic, if it weren't for the way the snakes attached to them twist and weave – like thunder, a slow roll followed by a clap of sudden movement.

The creature working on me is familiar. I met a version of her earlier today: Ellen Cassell. She is more snake than human, though. The snakes operate every limb, pushing them here and there to make the body move.

It's hard to remember the plan, but I hold on to Samson's earnest expression, the passionate way he talked to me, the way he pleaded with me to remember. That is my anchor. That, and something deep inside me that curdles at the ropes already working their way through my body. It revolts against them, creating a storm inside me. Sometimes pain can be useful, just like fear and anger, when you know how to direct it.

I try to reach Ollie, but he's too far away. I'm not going to be able to do this unnoticed. I look up at Ellen. Meeting her earlier today told me that there was still some part of her in there, rebelling against the snakes. But can I speak to that part now, in this place?

'Help me,' I whisper to her. I cannot hold her gaze, for she has no eyes. I grasp her hand, ignoring the pricks of the snakes as they flick against my wrist and fingers, trying to pull me away. 'It's Una's daughter,' I say. Violet sparks bolt across Ellen's skin. A low groan from the depths of her throat tells me that she is in pain. Awful though it is, that means there's hope. She is being punished for an emotion. I grip her hand tighter.

'I need to get to Ollie,' I say, but I don't know if she can hear me properly, not with those things winding their way through her mutilated ears. I direct her hand towards my brother, hoping that she will understand. Slowly, she looks towards Ollie's bed. The snake-like ropes reach out towards my brother, digging into his body with sharp little pincers, as though they're taunting both me and what's left of Ellen. Ellen's hand twitches. The ropes attack my brother with increased fury, but they do not seem to notice that Ellen's hand is moving closer to me, closer and closer until it has found its way to the invisible ropes that bind me to this surface. The pressure on my chest and legs lifts.

Slowly, trying not to alert the snakes, I inch my way across to Ollie, who is still lying prone on the table. He now has snakes protruding from his back, and with a lurch I realise that I alone of all the people in this space, have been left untouched. Was this all Ellen's doing? She had said that she planted them in the wrong place, but I don't have any on me now.

On the other side of the space, the woman who I now remember is called Amina, gives a great cry. It is like a final exhale. She is covered in the thorned snakes. They rise from hundreds of punctures in her body, but as she cries out, a ripple of blue light runs across her skin. The snakes, as one, fall from the perforations and writhe on the floor before they are collected by the other snake-knights. Amina opens her eyes, bloodshot but whole, and looks around blearily. She spots me.

'Fern?' she says.

But the snake-knights have seen her. They understand that she is not a good host for them, and they descend upon her, hissing and stabbing. Amina screams. I reach towards her but something stops me. Ellen is holding me back. She makes the same noise in her throat, and I only hear it above Amina's screams because it seems to reverberate through her arm and into mine. I understand what she is saying: *You cannot help her*.

One of her snakes becomes aware of what she's doing. It snaps its way towards me. I freeze as it arches over me, hoping it will not have noticed how much I've moved. Then the snake shifts, nudging me onto my side. There's a deep pinch on my spine, as though something is being attached to me. The pain in my head tightens, like a wrench on a nut. My stomach somersaults. Something sinks inside me – the same feeling I had when I realised Ollie's betrayal three years ago. I know what this means. The snakes have attached themselves to me again. Maybe I'll still have time to get to Ollie before their effect takes hold . . .

Unbidden, an image of a bird comes to mind. A little bird, fluttering in mid-air, looking at me with meaning. There's a twinge in my head. Something blue and beautiful crackles across my skin. There's another pinch in my back, and whatever was inserted there falls to the floor. It is a sliver of a snake, searching for me, and finally disintegrating into nothingness. It's the same thing that happened with Amina. That means I only have a matter of seconds before the snakes realise that I am not a good host either.

I move quickly towards Ollie. A snake-person is hovering over him, holding his eyes open. One of the snakes comes closer, and with a lurch I realise that it is about to replace his eyes with snakes. I whisper, 'Ollie, it's Fern. Remember – Samson and Lord Allenby. Remember Ramesh.'

Ollie's fingers twitch in mine, but he doesn't show any other sign of having heard me. The snake moves closer to his eyes, and I take a risk – I reach out and grab the creature. It rears backwards, the thorns that line its body digging into my palm, soaking us all in my blood. An image of Brandon, who was killed by thorn-like creatures earlier this year, comes to my mind, and I think of the power that allowed me to transform those larvae into something harmless and delicate. My skin crackles with blue light once more, and the snake makes an awful sound, like nails on a chalkboard.

The blue light that repelled the snakes ripples across my arms and into my brother. He twitches again, and the snakes already buried inside him writhe and hiss. *Destroy the root,* Ellen had said. I turn Ollie over and pull at the snakes embedded in his back. They snap at me. They were planted deep, but their purchase isn't as strong as it should be. I can feel them giving way, slowly sliding from the sheath of Ollie's spine.

One of the snakes hisses in a strange way – a series of snaps. As one, the other mutant knights turn towards us. It has raised the alarm. I am out of time.

'Remember them, Ollie, please,' I say. A flicker of insight plays across my memory and I find myself saying, 'Remember Easa.'

With another crackle of blue light that emanates from inside Ollie's body, the snakes slide out by the root, and I throw them as far away from us as I can.

'Fern?' he croaks.

'Now, Samson,' I mutter.

As if he has heard me from across the worlds' divide, the space around us shimmers. I pull Ollie away from the advancing mutants. 'I need you to use your Immral, Ollie,' I tell him.

'What? I can't –'

'You have to. The others are trying to make a rip, but we need you to activate it.'

I press my brother's hands against the shimmer. 'Now, Ollie, or we die.'

The way my brother looks at me, in total confusion, tells me that this isn't going to work. He has forgotten who he is and what he can do. But I keep his hands pressed there, as the air makes mother-of-pearl lights, unwilling to give up until the very end.

The snakes advance.

Fern, we're coming. Hold on.

It's Samson. Samson and . . . Charlie? I look back at the shimmer. Ollie's hands are sparking with violet light, and the shimmer is expanding.

'You're doing it!' I grin at him.

Like an earthquake, the grey is pulled apart, Ithr just visible in the jagged seams between this place and Annwn. Hands reach for me, but I push Ollie through first. Samson's face appears. 'Come on,' he says, grabbing me, 'I've got you this time.' Other knights appear, some I recognise and some I don't, all wielding guns, bows and arrows and other devices that hold the mutants at a distance. I clamber through the rip and into Samson's arms. Easa is carrying Ollie in his arms towards the hospital wing, muttering words of comfort.

'Close it,' Lord Allenby says.

'Sir, we need to get those snakes,' Samson says.

'It's too risky,' Lord Allenby replies.

But there's another *Uuurrrggghhh* from Ellen's body. With a superhuman effort she is moving towards us, despite the cuts and wounds inflicted upon her by the knights' weapons. Then I realise something: the snakes are trying to pull her back, away from the rip. It is Ellen who is trying to get through, not Medraut's creatures.

Kill the root.

'She can't survive in Annwn,' I whisper, realisation dawning. *She* is the root. The snakes couldn't survive when they were *cut* from a body, but maybe if the body disappeared . . .

Despite everything she's done, I want to help her. There is no way to save her if she crosses into Annwn. Briefly, I wonder if we can hasten the rip closing and lock her in that grey-between. But then I remember the way she looked at me earlier today in Ithr. She had told me how I could help her: *Kill the root*. This is what she wants. It's what I would want, too, if I had become one of those creatures. It's not murder. It's mercy.

'Let her come through,' I tell the others.

'What? Fern, are you mad?' Samson says.

'Trust me.'

The knights aim their weapons at the other mutants, and Ellen comes on, slowly because the snakes are using all their might to try to stop her. But she is determined to die. First one hand, then the other, stretches through the rip to Annwn. The grey skin, puckered with tiny snakes, withers before our eyes. But before it does, it grows pink again, and whole. For a brief moment, she is human once more.

As her skin withers and vanishes, the snakes fall from it, onto the marble of Tintagel. This is her final gift to us.

The apothecaries scoop the snakes into jars as Ellen tries to pull the rest of herself through. She seems to look at me through the rip, even though she no longer has eyes, and I understand.

'Help her,' I say.

More arms reach to pull her through, but then one voice

says, 'I'll do it, old friend.' Lord Allenby pushes me to one side and lifts Ellen's body, with greatest tenderness, through into the light of Annwn. As her flesh falls away, and the snakes are released, she gives one final sigh, and then she is gone.

Chapter 23

'He couldn't let her go, could he?' Lord Allenby says softly. 'He had to find another use for her.'

As the reeves and knights hovering at the edges descend upon the rip to close it, I sink back into Samson's arms. I have no energy left – surviving in that grey place drained me.

Niamh and Natasha push through to check on me. 'Amina?' Niamh says. I shake my head. Natasha turns away.

'Hospital wing first, explanations later,' Samson says, and for once I don't argue. He pulls a curtain around the closest available bed and helps me to peel the tunic and soft leather leggings from my aching body. Beneath my clothes, my skin is a mess of bruises and cuts. 'Oh baby, what did they do to you?' he says.

Jin pokes her head around the curtain. 'I need to check the patient.'

She rubs a cooling gel into the bruises, then probes the cuts with greater care. 'These are deep,' she comments, shining a light into them. 'Clean, though.'

'How's Ollie?' I ask, wincing as she stuffs the wounds with goldenrod and yarrow.

'Much the same as you.' She's frowning.

'But?'

'His cuts are in different places, and they were even deeper than yours.'

I piece the truth together. 'It was Ellen,' I tell Jin and Samson. 'She told us that she planted the snakes in the wrong place. I think it bought me more time. They must have put them in the right places with Ollie and Amina.'

'Well, you'll heal nicely, I think,' Jin says brusquely. She lets me leave my bed under Samson's supervision. 'You could let me carry you, you know,' Samson says. 'No one would think worse of you and I'd get to look like a romantic hero.'

As it happens, I can't face the knights' chamber and the questions and crying from Amina's other friends. Plus, there's someone I have to check on. I peer round the curtain that is protecting Ollie from the curious gaze of the other thanes. Easa sits by his side, my brother's hand clasped in both of his, his head bowed to it.

'He'll be okay. He just needs rest,' Easa says when I join him. My brother's face is covered in bruises and cuts. His ears look as though they've been passed through a grinder. But his breathing is steady.

We stay like that for a while, until Samson leans down and whispers that Lord Allenby has asked to talk.

'See you when we wake up,' I tell Ollie, squeezing his hand and Easa's shoulder.

When we reach Lord Allenby's office, Samson insists on putting extra cushions on my chair to soften the impact on the worst cuts. There I tell Lord Allenby, Maisie and Samson everything that happened when I went through my mirror tonight, right up until they created the rip. Then it's their turn to tell me what they'd been doing.

'It was Charlie who had the idea,' Lord Allenby tells me, and I suddenly remember the conversation she had with me, the day before the mission. 'She thought that we might be able to use the power of the Round Table and Tintagel's portal to boost Ollie's Immral and create a rip in the right place. Luckily, Ollie and Amina still had the trackers on them, so we could use their signals to direct our work.'

'Those creatures have a name now, by the way,' Samson tells me. 'We're calling them *sluaghs*.' He draws the word into two syllables, the first a long *sloo*, the second a staccato *ah*. I remember reading something about these creatures in the archives. It was thought that they were a type of vampire nightmare, although in Ithr they're believed to be the deadly ghosts of unforgiven souls. I think of Ellen, and shiver.

'Poor Amina,' Lord Allenby is saying. 'At least she didn't die as one of them. I wonder what it was about her and you that didn't agree with the sluaghs. If we can work that out, it might help us defeat them next time. Because believe you me, there'll be a next time.'

But I'm too tired to think about that right now. All I want to do is rest, and to allow myself to weather whatever emotions are coming. I've lost enough loved ones now to know that Amina and Ellen's deaths are going to hit me, and soon.

It happens after I wake up. The marks on my body are fainter than they are in Annwn, but I can pick out the rash-like pattern on my wrist where Ellen's snakes tried to stop me from holding her hand. My grief for Amina is pure, but around Ellen it is far more complicated. Part of me feels guilty for being sad about her death. After all, she killed my mother and Ramesh and so many more. She deserved her death, as much as anyone can deserve it. But she tried to redeem herself too. She played a big part in Ollie and I getting out of that grey world alive. And she gave us the snakes. For all our planning, she was the reason our mission to capture one of those things succeeded.

I find myself digging out Mum's old diaries. It's been ages since I've pored over them, but now I find comfort in reading her cryptic clues. There were a handful, written over the course of a decade or so, that she wrote in a code that I cracked a few months after joining the thanes. They tell of her secret life in Annwn, and talk about her friendship with Ellen.

It's late in the morning and I'm just up to the part where Mum has written in code *I have met the man I'm going to marry*, when I hear shouts on the street outside. I peel back my curtain. A gang, mostly white, mostly men, strut along the road, leering at anyone who dares to look at them. I draw back. They come to a halt in front of Crystal Moore's house, pointing and jeering. Unease stabs at me. I consider calling the police, but something tells me they wouldn't do much about it at the moment. After all, Clemmie's a police sergeant, and her behaviour hasn't exactly been sympathetic towards the victims of these kind of attacks. But then the gang moves on and passes out of sight. Trouble averted, for now.

As I'm settling back to reading Mum's diaries, Ollie knocks on my door. His face still bears the scars of the sluaghs, although in Ithr they could be explained away as the imprints from pillow creases. It's his eyes that worry me the most. They are bloodshot and haunted.

'How much do you remember?' I ask him as he sinks into my desk chair.

'Not very much of that grey place. I remember everything I did yesterday, though.'

'Ah.' I think of poor Kieran, hurt and lost, as Ollie didn't even give him the courtesy of a proper goodbye. Miserably, Ollie picks up Mum's open diary. A look of confusion and then shock passes over his face. He peers at the cover.

'Everything alright?' I ask.

Ollie throws the diary down and mashes his face in his hands. 'I'm an awful person, Fern.'

'You're not. You were being controlled by those things. I didn't behave very well yesterday either. You should've seen me when Samson found me. I was horrible to him.'

Ollie stares at me blankly, and for the first time in a while, there's a distance between us. I don't know whether it's my admission that Samson and I have now met in both worlds, or whether there's something he's not telling me. Either way, I know what he needs to do to make it better.

I had thought that once I gave him a plan of action and cajoled him out of the house, Ollie would cheer up, but he remains sullen and withdrawn all the way to Kieran's house. It's a large Victorian semi, with patterned tiles and neatly trimmed flower beds leading up to the front porch.

It takes three knocks for the door to be answered. Someone who I imagine is Kieran's mother looks none too pleased to see him, but shortly afterwards Kieran himself comes to the door. I watch them exchange quiet words from the end of the path.

'You can't just pick me up like this because you've worked through your issues,' Kieran is saying.

'That's not why I'm here,' Ollie says.

Kieran pauses, then steps out of the door and closes it behind him. I turn away, wanting to make it clear that I'm not there to eavesdrop, even though that's exactly what I'm doing.

'I shouldn't have ghosted you,' Ollie says. 'I was going through some stuff, but it doesn't . . . I wanted to do it right. Give you some closure.'

Kieran scoffs. 'Get over yourself, Ollie. I got all the closure I needed yesterday.'

'I'm sorry.'

'I've moved on already,' Kieran says, quickly and loudly enough for me to suspect he's bluffing. 'I don't need your apologies, or whatever it is you came here for.'

'Okay,' Ollie says, 'that's good. I never wanted to hurt you. I wish I hadn't behaved the way I did. I can't take it back, but I wanted you to know – that I know you deserved better. It's just that I don't have the energy for the fight any more. Not like you do. It's too much. I'm sorry.'

Ollie leaves. Kieran stands as upright as he can, but no one can mistake the way his gaze lingers on Ollie's retreating form. I raise a hand – my own apology and farewell – and follow my brother as we walk away from his first love.

Chapter 24

With Kieran out of the picture, I expected Ollie to spend more time with Easa. But instead of returning Easa's embrace when he steps off the platform in Tintagel's grounds that first night, Ollie skirts him with a high five and an excuse that he needs to get ready for patrol. I follow him in awkwardly, past Easa's hurt confusion. But my brother isn't getting ready for patrol, he's busy chatting to Rachel.

'What was that about?' I ask him, annoyed. He clearly wanted to dump Kieran for Easa, and now he's messing Easa around too. Why did he moan about being a bad person if he's going to repeat the same behaviour?

'I was talking to Rachel about her brilliant sentineling,' Ollie tells me breezily.

'Oh, it wasn't really anything special,' Rachel says.

'Nothing special?' I say. 'You probably saved Lord Allenby from being snatched before we could get to him.'

Rachel just shakes her head.

'Come on, Rachel, why are you being like this?' I ask her gently. 'I know Maisie offered you the sentinel position. You want to take it. You've earned it –'

'No, I haven't,' Rachel cuts me off.

I pull over a spare chair and face her over her desk, feeling like a headmistress. 'Why do you think you haven't earned it?'

Rachel chews her lip and doodles on her paper. 'I just don't think I deserve a promotion when I helped Medraut gain power, that's all. I'm lucky I've even been allowed to stay.'

I gape at her. Before the battle at Trafalgar Square, Medraut had revealed that he had brainwashed several thanes, Rachel amongst them, into retrieving the puzzle box that helped catapult him to power. None of them had a clue that they had been used by him until the revelation. I had thought that Rachel was refusing the promotion out of loyalty, but it's far worse. She's refusing it out of guilt.

'You're kidding, right?' I say. 'Lord Allenby helped Medraut too – do you want him to resign?'

'No, of course not.'

'You weren't in control of yourself. It wasn't your fault.'

'But there must have been a reason he chose me. It must be some weakness that made me an easy target. And if that's true then there's no way I should be given more responsibility.'

'Has it ever occurred to you that Medraut chose you because you're mine and Ollie's friend, and he wanted to taunt us?' I ask.

Rachel thinks this over. 'Do you really think that could be it?'

'I've no idea, but it's way more likely than him thinking you're weak. He probably singled you out because he thought you were a threat. It's like some twisted way of showing respect.'

My words are clearly having some effect on Rachel, but I know better than to push it. Feeling pressured would be sure to make me dig in my heels, if I were her.

'Think about it,' is all I say.

She evidently does, because a few days later Maisie pulls me to one side.

'I don't know what you said, but I've got a new sentinel starting in the New Year. Thank you.'

While Bedevere is thrilled for Rachel, her imminent departure does inspire some mixed feelings. With no new squires this year at Samhain, we're going to be assigned one of the retired harkers. To be precise, we're assigned Ben.

'Nooooooo!' Nerizan groans when we get the news. Ben has made a name for himself as a fussy know-it-all who doesn't listen. His granddaughter, Frankie, is intensely embarrassed by him. She collars us shortly after we're told the news.

'I'll try to keep him in line for you. He really did used to be the best back in his day, you know.'

None of us are reassured.

'Maybe I should request a transfer to the harkers,' Easa jokes one night. 'Reckon I could do a better job for you than Ben.'

But Ollie only smiles quietly and turns away. Easa's clearly as confused about my brother's behaviour as I am, but whenever I raise it with Ollie he has a tendency to snap my head off. Torn between my twin and my friend, I take the coward's way out and choose to spend most of my time in Annwn with Samson instead. That's not hard, given that when we're not on patrol we spend every moment either in each other's arms or searching for the key that might help to kick-start my Immral.

We've moved on from Tintagel's archives and have free access to Oxford's now as well, working alongside the team assigned to research the Grail. Almost every night, we knock on

Lord Allenby's door and select the doorknob that will lead us directly from the back of his office into the gardens of Oxford's headquarters. There Asher escorts us as we pore through the castle's vast underground resources, which stretch for miles beneath the city. Asher turns out to have a memory almost as encyclopaedic as the records they help to maintain. All we have to do is mention a sentence in a book, and they'll run off to find something that might be related.

That's how we find it.

I'm flicking through an ancient manuscript that supposedly details a reeve's experiments on several Immrals. All I can tell from the archaic language so far is that the reeve in question was extremely easy to manipulate and probably shouldn't have been a scientist. When I get to a page covered in obscure mathematical equations, I throw the manuscript into our 'useless' pile and continue playing footsie with Samson as I pull the next book towards me.

Samson's eyes land on the equations. He frowns. 'What's this?'

I explain what it's supposed to contain. 'But it's crap,' I tell him.

'I don't think so, Fern.' Samson skates over the figures. Jin puts her book down – I glimpse a series of illustrations of knights performing increasingly difficult tasks, culminating in one who seems to be stabbing himself in the stomach. I look away from the gruesome image, my hands prickling strangely. Jin and I wait for Samson's verdict. 'Shit,' he says quietly. 'Shiiiit.'

'Please feel free to keep us in suspense for as long as you like,' Jin remarks.

'Sorry.' Samson looks up at us. 'These equations – they're saying that Immral can be *passed* from person to person.'

'No way,' Jin says. 'You're born with it or not.'

'You might be born with it, but that doesn't mean you have to die with it,' Samson says, his finger tracing the sums. 'If I'm right, an Immral can *give* their power to someone else.'

Jin calls Asher over and we relay this new information to the reeve. They nod. 'That reeve did some later experiments if I recall correctly. Let me see if I can find them.'

I don't think I've ever felt time stretch as long as the mere minutes it takes for Asher to return with another slim volume written in the same hand. All four of us eagerly lean over it. My heart is pounding with so much anxiety I can barely read the writing.

'Get this,' Samson says, pointing to more diagrams. 'These sums say that when an Immral drains another Immral, the receiving Immral becomes disproportionately powerful.'

'What do you mean *disproportionately*?' I ask.

Samson pulls two glasses of lotus juice towards us, and fills both of them a third full. 'These are our two Immrals, okay?' he explains. He pours one glass into another, so the second glass is now two-thirds full and the first is empty. 'When this Immral gives their power to the other, how much Immral do you think the one getting the power should have now?'

'Twice what they had before,' Asher says, 'or however much the giving Immral has.'

'Wrong,' Samson says. He pours juice from the jug until the second glass is totally full. 'This is what happens. It's like it sparks some kind of growth.'

'Well, this is very interesting, but it doesn't help us, does it?' Jin says. 'Medraut's the only Immral we can steal from, and we all know how that attempt will go.'

I bang the table. 'There is someone else. Jin, do you remember the record you found back in Tintagel? The woman from Argentina?'

She grins. 'Yes. Sophia Parriego. The one who refused to use her power.'

'She might not want it,' I say, 'but I definitely do.'

Chapter 25

My fevered excitement over what we've discovered lasts until Christmas. No one can find out what happened to Sophia after she refused to use her Immral. Lord Allenby contacts the Argentinian equivalent of the thanes, but they can't help us either. Apparently, she disappeared shortly after resigning from the thanes back in the 1960s, when she was still a teenager.

'We'll keep looking,' Samson tells me, but I try not to get my hopes up. For a few, blissful weeks, my Immral felt within reach. I try to focus on Christmas instead. It will be the first time in a few years that Dad, Ollie and I have spent it just the three of us. I feel oddly protective of Dad, who hasn't mentioned Clemmie since she left. He now roams the house looking lonelier than ever.

In Bosco, I spend more time in the art room than ever before, usually with Charlie by my side.

'Lionel wants me to join the Christmas celebrations,' she tells me as I put the final touches to my presents for Dad and Ollie. Charlie hasn't been permitted to leave her tower room in Tintagel because of fears about what she might unwittingly tell her father. If Lord Allenby thinks it's safe for her to come down, though, then who am I to say otherwise?

'Do you want to?' I ask her.

'What will it be like? Will there be a lot of people?'

'Yes. But everyone's nice, mostly. And this is me saying that. I don't think many people are nice.'

Charlie smiles. 'It will be the first time I've gone to a party as Charlie, not Lottie. Do you think everyone will judge me for being his daughter?'

I put down my sculpting tool. 'Honestly, yes, some people will. It doesn't mean they're bad, or that they won't come round.'

Charlie nods, pensive.

'Plus –' I grin – 'you can stick with me. I'll show you the ropes. Introduce you to the cool kids.'

'Well, that decides it then,' Charlie says. 'But I'd better give you your present now.'

'Present?' I say, alarmed. I haven't got Charlie anything, and hadn't planned to. I hadn't realised we were good enough friends – more like allies weathering a tempest together. But then Charlie produces a shabby envelope.

'Relax. It's not really a present. Just returning something I thought you might have missed.'

Inside the envelope is my knightbook – the one I threw away when I was under the influence of the sluaghs. I had already mourned its loss. Impulsively, I throw my arms around Charlie.

'Thank you,' I whisper into her hair.

'It's the least I could do,' she replies.

I pull away, guilt squirming. She still doesn't know that just over a year ago, I tortured her for information. I don't deserve her kindness.

'Charlie, listen . . .'

'I know, Fern.'

She looks brittle, fragile but brave. 'Lionel told me what you and Ollie did to me. I'm not going to pretend it's okay. But *we're* okay. You have my permission to let it go.'

Tears bubble their way up my throat as I cling to her hand. 'We're going to make sure you have the best time at the Christmas party.'

And so Charlie agrees to make her grand entrance into the heart of the thanes. Ollie uses his Immral to help decorate the central hall, so that glittering snow falls gently from the inner dome and settles in attractive waves on the marble. On Christmas Eve, we all gather after patrol beside the snow drifts. Maisie is already tipsy, and floats around the room holding mistletoe over people she deems 'a good match'.

I had assumed that I would be the one to bring Charlie down from her tower, but just as I'm thinking about asking Lord Allenby if it's time for her to join us, he appears in the doorway of the turret. He stands to one side, Loco darting past him. Charlie follows, wearing a tailored trouser suit of deep red velvet and a sprig of holly in her hair. Lord Allenby points me out in the crowd, and she squeezes past thanes to reach me. Lord Allenby is smiling with pride, and jealousy flicks through me like a blade. I push it aside, introducing Charlie to the friends she doesn't already know. Rachel bounces up to us with all the enthusiasm of Loco, and I listen for a while as Rachel tells Charlie about the joys of being a sentinel.

'I'll take you up there if you like. Sometimes I feel as though I could see to the other side of the world if I wanted to.'

'She probably could, you know,' I tell Charlie. 'Her eyesight's incredible.'

I leave them to it, and wander past little groups of friends. The castle almost feels normal, like it did two years ago when I first joined. I find a bench in the cover of a cloister, and people-watch. I spot Niamh and Natasha, deep in conversation, and wonder whether they're talking about their alter-egos, Irish and Penn. Then my eyes are drawn to Ollie and Easa, who are standing back to back, talking to different people. Maisie drifts past them and pauses, holding her mistletoe between the two.

'Kiss!' she shouts drunkenly.

Ollie and Easa look at each other, smiling awkwardly. But Maisie hasn't picked up on the tension, and stands there stubbornly until they peck each other on the cheek. I can't work out what's going on between those two. I had thought that Ollie had lost interest in Easa, but from the way Ollie glances back at him, I can see that he hasn't. Why on earth did he push him away?

'Do I need mistletoe to get a kiss?' Samson says, approaching with two mince pies. I take one from him and lean into his embrace. We sit there for the rest of the evening, mostly in silence, because words aren't needed for how contented we feel.

As the party draws to a close, and people begin to drift back to Ithr, I pull Samson into the knights' chamber and draw something from my locker above the mantelpiece.

'Happy Christmas,' I say, nervous. I hand Samson a canvas wrapped in muslin. He flips back the fabric and lets out an exclamation of recognition. The image is of a dragon, grey and fearsome, rearing over two figures. One a girl with blonde hair and a scimitar; one a boy with dark curls and a bow and arrow. From them both emanates a blue light that forces the dragon back.

'It's a shameless rip-off of yours,' I admit. A few years ago he painted this on a wall near my house as a way to convince me to re-join the thanes. In his version, there's only one figure facing down the dragon. Samson pulls me in for a kiss. 'The two of us together, always,' he whispers into my hair.

Later, as he walks me back to the portal, he says, 'I got you a Christmas present too, you know.'

'Oh?'

'Look underneath that flowerpot next to your front door.'

I gape at him. 'You got me something in Ithr?'

'Something real. That's what you wanted, right?'

The first thing I do when I wake is skid down the stairs and unlock the door. The flowerpot is perched on top of a tiny package wrapped in blue paper. I carry it back to my room and tear it open. Inside the box is a delicate silver bracelet. Hanging from the chain is a series of crescent moons and stars set with tiny crystals. A note inside the wrapping reads, *To go with your necklace. S.* Beneath it, he has written his phone number.

I am giddy. Far more so than a serious knight with a serious mission to bring down the prime minister has any right to be. This is the first gift I have ever received from my first ever boyfriend. I clasp it around my wrist and jiggle it, watching the star crystals cast dancing lights on my bedroom walls. Then I retrieve the necklace, a gift from Ollie long ago, from my desk drawer and put that on too. They look like a matching set, although the necklace is battered. And, of course, the necklace forms the basis of my weapons in Annwn: the crescent moon pendant a scimitar, and the three stars set around it now two fire-destroying marbles. I take a selfie wearing the bracelet and send it to Samson. Samson, my boyfriend in Ithr now, as well as Annwn. Real and dreamlike.

Nothing can quite beat the high of this moment, but the day tries its best. I present Dad with a set of clay coasters and placemats inscribed with his family's old Scottish crest, while Ollie gets a pair of earrings I made from polymer clay, designed to resemble a pair I saw him eyeing in a magazine recently. We sing carols and watch *Home Alone* and Dad lets us have mulled wine rich with cinnamon and oranges.

I am just about to go up to bed, groggy with happiness, when the credits of the film we were watching stop abruptly and a newsreader's face appears. *Breaking News* scrolls in bold letters across the screen. Dad stops washing up, and Ollie pokes his head out of his bedroom.

'In what is being called an unfortunate tragedy, today in a small town in Northumberland, a community has been devastated . . .'

A photo of a hospital pops up onscreen. Dad, Ollie and I gather, sickness building in my stomach. CCTV footage plays, blurry and grey, under the newsreader's bland voice. A mob of people, so similar to the mob I spotted on our street just days ago, is advancing through the building. A doctor tries to stop them, and that's when it happens: one of the mob raises his hand, and I see that he's clutching a crowbar. The footage cuts just as he brings the bar down on the doctor's head.

Ollie lets out a strangled cry.

'Oh my good God,' Dad whispers in horror. 'What is wrong with us?'

I cannot say anything, do anything, except look at the screen in horror. The newsreader describes how the mob systematically murdered every patient, nurse and doctor they came across.

'They think that because people inside are ill, that they're useless,' Ollie says. 'And the doctors and nurses were just collateral. That's what they're thinking.'

The same image – of that crowbar being swung with such force, such certainty, upon the doctor's skull – plays over and over in my head. But there's something else I see – something not visible on the grainy footage. I can see the threads, violet and sparking, that power the blow. I can see how those threads are controlled by Medraut, with his ideology of usefulness and practicality, like a puppet-master. And I can see where those threads lead. It won't stop here.

Chapter 26

Fury prevails in Tintagel after the attack. I can't look at the dreamers I patrol past without wondering whether one of them was involved. I have, up until now, thought that most dreamers wouldn't actually hurt anyone in Ithr, even if they're violent in Annwn. The hospital massacre has proved me wrong.

I'm not the only person who feels that way. Niamh goes round the knights' chamber telling us about a series of countrywide protests that are being organised. 'We've got to make sure that the killers get a proper sentence,' she says. 'You're in, right?'

The police issue a warning, reminding the public that protests have been outlawed. But for those of us whose very existence is under threat, the possibility of jail no longer holds so much fear. Our collective anger splinters us along different priorities. Samson disappears for long tranches of time outside of patrols, and when I ask him what he's doing he only says, 'Something to finish this.'

Most of us retreat to the archives, throwing ourselves more fervently into researching the Grail. We're joined by Charlie and even, occasionally, Lord Allenby. But we have nearly exhausted the vast resources of the thanes' archives.

'There's got to be *something* here,' Jin says, pushing away her book. She takes it personally when libraries let her down. The book flaps open at the inside cover, where the names of those who've read it scroll across the page in glittering ink. My heart catches.

'Mum?' I pull the book towards me and stare down at the name – *Una Gorlois* – as it slides across the paper.

'Your mum read this book?' Easa asks curiously, but he doesn't understand the importance of this. Ollie, though, does.

'Give it here,' he says, and I pass it over immediately. Ollie's face tenses in concentration as the table falls silent. He flicks through each page, his eyes closed, and then pauses part way through the book.

'This one,' he says.

Everyone leans in. It's a page I noticed before when I looked over Jin's shoulder – full of gory illustrations of knights performing violent tasks.

'I don't understand,' Easa says.

Ollie and I stare at the drawings, trying to figure it out. 'We know that Mum spent a lot of time researching ways to bring down Medraut,' I say into the silence.

'Excalibur,' Jin says, but Ollie shakes his head.

'That's what we could never work out – why would she say she was trying to kill Medraut and then go looking for the one thing that would make him stronger?'

'Because she knew that Fern –'

'No,' I say. 'She was looking before Ollie and I were born. She wasn't looking for Excalibur. She must have been looking for the Grail.'

Asher lets out a low whistle as Ollie smiles bitterly. 'Always one step ahead of us, Mum.'

'Do you think she found it?' Charlie asks.

I consider the possibility, then shake my head. 'She'd have left a message for Ollie and me if she had.'

Ollie tenses, but doesn't contradict me. Mum would only have left *me* such a message, but hopefully my fake letter to Ollie last year has persuaded him that she'd send it to both of us.

'So,' Jin says, bringing us back to the matter at hand. 'She was looking for the Grail, and found something interesting on this page. But what? It's just a load of pictures. The words don't mention the Grail at all.'

I flick to the text accompanying the illustrations so we can all read it.

Our dreams make no sense on a realistic level: they are chaotic and muddled. However, often there is a moral logic that runs through them. Have you ever dreamed that you committed a crime, and must decide whether to confess? Have you ever betrayed a loved one and then woken, riven with guilt? Have you ever been forced to choose between saving two people you love in a dream? These are moral quandaries, and they are an essential part of the fabric of Annwn and the power of inspyre, for what is imagination if not the ability to strive for self-betterment?

The ancient storytellers understood this, and so did the founding knights and their compatriots on different continents. The notion of worthiness is woven through the dreamworld. Throughout our history, we have been asked to prove that we are worthy in order to attain our goals – treasure, enlightenment, ascension . . .

The text goes on, but Jin and I pull away at the same time, realisation hitting us.

'You have to prove you're worthy of the Grail,' I say.

'And that's how your mum came up with the Excalibur tasks,' Jin adds. 'All these pictures are of knights trying to prove they're worthy.'

'This is good. This is progress,' Easa says, but I can't agree with him. To me, it feels as though we've just been set an impossible mountain to climb, when we're already fighting on empty.

The others carry on looking for more clues as to what tasks are needed for the Grail quest, but I bow out. Another set of tasks, and what at the end of it? A treasure that we don't even know exists, that might be another poisoned chalice, like Excalibur. There are more practical uses for my energy, like the protests scheduled for the first week of the New Year.

Kieran turns up on our doorstep on the morning of the protest. 'Are you coming?' he asks Ollie. 'We could go together, if you're up for the fight again.'

'You're not mad at me any more?' Ollie asks him.

'I'm still pissed at you,' Kieran admits. 'But if you want, we could try to be friends.'

Ollie nods, and together he and I pull on our coats and scarves. Dad blocks the door. 'No, absolutely not. It's illegal. I don't want you putting yourself in danger.'

'Dad,' I say, pushing past him, 'look at me. Look at Ollie. We're in danger already. We're just fed up of pretending that we're not.'

The three of us lock arms, like we used to do when Ollie and

Kieran were a couple, and stride down the street, ignoring Dad's shouts for us to come back. We pass Crystal Moore ushering her children inside. 'Be careful, you lot,' she calls, nodding towards the houses around us. I become aware of dozens of faces watching us from behind their windows, radiating judgement through the double glazing.

The crowds have begun to gather already. A huddle of protesters hold cardboard signs with photos of the hospital. Others have cut out Medraut's face and scrawled *Murderer* across it in red marker pen.

On the other side of the road, a larger crowd gathers silently. I start to wish that I'd listened to Dad's warnings. I have no scimitar here, no ability to fly out of trouble's reach.

'Do you think . . .' Ollie says, faltering.

Then the police arrive. Their vans block the street, a barrier between Medraut's followers and the protesters.

'Thank you,' Kieran says softly, but as they leap from their vans and don riot gear, I am not convinced that they're here to protect us at all.

'We're not doing any harm!' someone shouts from our side of the street.

Someone from the One Voice side throws a glass bottle. It hits a boy at the front of our crowd and he goes down like a skittle. Instead of looking for the bottle thrower, the police march forward, riot shields clasped in front of them. Kieran, Ollie and I run forward to help pull the boy out of the fray, as all around us the protesters use anything they can find to throw back. Their missiles bounce off the shields and skitter across the street. The police keep coming.

Kieran gets up to help the protesters push back. Ollie and I look at each other over the body of the unconscious boy. We are kneeling, penned in by a forest of legs and noise. 'This was a bad idea,' I say. We're not going to win anything here.

'Let's go,' Ollie says, and together we push our way through the crowd, always moving sideways, back the way we came. But the protesters' numbers have swelled, and they keep carrying us forward, closer to the police. 'Nearly there!' I shout, leading the way. At last, I come to the end of the crowd and burst out of the scrum.

Ollie is no longer behind me. I crane my neck to catch sight of him, and at last spot him stuck in the worst of the fight, leaping and shouting at me. 'Get Dad!' he calls over the crowd. 'Get help!'

We're too far away from home for me to get Dad quickly, though. Anything could happen to my brother in the time it would take to get there and back. Medraut's followers set up a low hum: *One Voice, One Voice.* They march forward, their feet machine-like on the tarmac. The police let them through.

'Ollie!' I call. I have no idea what to do.

As Medraut's acolytes go in with fists and feet on the protesters, the police stand by, impassive. One protester tries to escape, and the police close ranks, pushing their riot shields into the man's body, throwing him back into the crowd. I catch a glimpse of my brother, side by side with Kieran. A dozen men and women, silent disgust etched on their faces, bring their fists down upon him. Ollie raises his arms, trying to defend himself, but then one of the attackers swings at his stomach and my brother disappears beneath the mob.

Chapter 27

'No!' I scream, trying to reach Ollie, but there's no way in any more. I run back along the street, behind the line of impassive police. They can't all have been turned by Medraut. One of them must still have a conscience. But every face is stony, the helmets turning them into robots.

Then I see a familiar body. 'Clemmie!' I shout. 'Oh my God, Clemmie!'

Clemmie fidgets, dwarfed by her riot gear.

'Clemmie,' I plead, 'please, Ollie's in there.'

'Move away, girl,' one of Clemmie's colleagues says.

'He's my brother!'

'Then you should have stopped him from being so stupid,' one of the other officers sniggers.

I turn my attention back to Clemmie. 'He's hurt, Clemmie, please.'

'I can't help you,' she says, refusing to look at me.

I paw at her arm. There's no dignity left in me, not when Ollie is in danger. 'Clemmie, you used to love us. You know Ollie. You know he doesn't deserve this. Please.' I break down, sobbing right there in the street.

Clemmie wavers, I can feel it. The shift in her weight, the lowering of her riot shield. Her colleagues sense it too.

'Hold the line, officer. If the girl's brother gets hurt, it's his own fault.'

'Please, Clemmie. I thought you were safe.' I clutch her arm pitifully. 'I loved you.'

'Hold the line, officer,' the man next to us repeats. To emphasise his point, he raises his arm high and smacks me across my burn scar. Pain glances through my jaw. I am sprawled on the street, my hands covered in grime. I cough up blood and think dimly, through the ringing in my ears, that it's been a while since that happened.

There's chaos all around me. Clemmie has bashed the officer who struck me with her riot shield and he is nursing his arm and shouting obscenities. She pushes the crowds aside, using her shield as a ram, and is swallowed up by people.

Strong hands are upon me, but they're not the police.

'Fern,' Dad says as he lifts me up. 'I've got you, darling.'

'Ollie's still in there,' I say, twisting and thrashing in his arms.

'Clemmie will find him. She'll find him.' Dad carries me to a quieter part of the street where we both wait, watching the pulse of the crowd where it swallowed Clemmie, where I last saw Ollie. The officer she hit is saying something to his colleagues, but I can't hear over the roar of the protest and the steady chant of *One Voice*. It seems to me that the fray becomes a single beast, heaving and hauling and stretching this way and that, until finally it convulses and spits out three figures.

Clemmie and Kieran are supporting Ollie, bloodied but alive. Dad and I rush forward as Clemmie shoves my brother through the line of riot shields. We grab him and drag him away from the police. I turn back for Clemmie. 'Come with us,' I say. She sways, tempted, but then the officer she hurt makes a movement with his hand. A signal.

Down the riot shields come on Clemmie's back. The officers crowd in, intent on punishing one of their own. Clemmie looks up at me from between their legs. They've ripped her helmet off, and beneath it she looks so young and so small.

'Stay safe,' she mouths at me, then another shield cracks across her head, and she crumples.

'We can't leave her,' I tell Dad. Kieran is frozen, unable to tear his gaze away from what is happening to the woman who might have been my stepmother.

'I've got to get you both back home,' Dad says, refusing to look back at the mass of officers surrounding Clemmie's form. 'That's my job. To keep you both safe.'

He drags me and Ollie onwards, away from the fray, his expression etched with guilt. Kieran follows us like a stray dog for a few streets, then trails away without a word. I don't have the capacity to do more than send a wish into the ether that he makes it home. At our house, we tend to Ollie's bruises in the silence that comes from knowing we have sacrificed someone for our own survival. I could have fought Dad. I could have run back to help Clemmie, but I didn't. She was only attacked because she was helping us. How could we have left her there? Dad hands me an ice pack for my stinging jaw, his hand shaking.

The protests are all over the news. They have flared across the country, but the reports are all the same: a small group of dissenters sparked violence, necessitating police intervention.

It's all lies – the protest here wasn't violent until Medraut's crowds got involved and the police refused to do anything. I'd be willing to bet anything that it's the same elsewhere. Then –

'In east London tonight one police officer is in hospital in critical condition after being violently attacked by protesters.'

Dad and I rush to turn the volume up. It's Clemmie, I know it is. It says something about the state of my life recently that I'm more relieved she's alive than worried about her being in hospital.

'Go,' Ollie croaks from his place on the sofa. 'Go and check on her.'

Dad and I rush to the car. He nearly crashes several times on the way to the nearest hospital, where we're counting on her having been taken.

'Family?' the receptionist asks suspiciously.

'Yes,' I reply.

Clemmie is hooked up to a mass of machines and monitors. Her face is swollen and red, and one of her arms and legs are in plaster casts.

'Will she wake up?' I ask the nurse as he checks her vitals.

'It's hard to tell. The head's a funny thing. But you want my honest opinion? Don't get your hopes up. Absolute animals, the people who did this,' the nurse says.

'Animals,' Dad echoes, staring down at the woman who gave so much of herself to him and his family, and who rarely received anything in return.

We enter the New Year with a mixture of anger and guilt, which feels like an appropriate set of emotions to greet a year that will, one way or another, decide our fates. Ollie's physical wounds heal relatively quickly, but the emotional scars take much longer. Quick movements make him flinch, so Dad and I float through the house like monks. Kieran, bearing his own bruises, visits when he can. His shame about leading Ollie and me into the fray has swept away any residual awkwardness about the break-up with my brother.

Ollie and I try to find Clemmie in Annwn, thinking that he might be able to ease her suffering with his Immral, but not even Rachel's sharp eyesight can find where Clemmie's battered imagination is hiding.

During the protests, I had a vague sense of victory, even as I was worried sick about Ollie and Clemmie. *Medraut can't hide who he is any more,* I thought. *Everyone will see what's really happening*. How naive of me. Just as they did with the attack on Clemmie, the TV reports and newspapers fed people stories of maniacal protesters looking for a fight, and heroic police and passers-by wading in to try to calm the situation. Medraut shook his head patronisingly, and talked about how the troublemakers were a minority, and must be sent a message that such unrest wasn't patriotic.

Samson rages at the injustice. 'He may as well have patted the police on the back and given them a cookie.'

I've never seen him loudly furious before. I run my hands up and down his arms, but he pulls away. 'It's not you,' he says, his voice tight with emotion, 'I've just – I've got to go.' And he marches out of the knights' chamber and disappears, as he has every night for weeks.

Niamh watches him go. 'If he'd stayed a little longer I could have given him some good news,' she says.

‘There’s such a thing as good news?’ I say.

‘Too right. That website Natasha and I set up to tell everyone about the thanes and Annwn? Well, it’s gone viral.’

I lean forward. ‘You’re kidding.’

‘Nope. There *are* people out there who see what’s happening, Fern. And they’ve found us. It was all over the internet a few hours ago.’

‘Not any more,’ Natasha says, slumping down in her chair. ‘I checked before coming to Annwn and all of them have been wiped. Our original website too.’

Niamh swears, but hope lights my chest. ‘That means it worked,’ I tell them. ‘Medraut wouldn’t have had them taken down if he didn’t think they were a threat to him.’

‘That’s all well and good, but what are the people who know the truth going to do now?’ Niamh grumbles.

‘We’ll figure something out,’ Natasha says. ‘We always do.’

But between visiting Clemmie’s motionless body in hospital whenever I can, surviving school and surviving patrols, there is precious little time to think about doing anything else. If a permanent state of crisis can become a routine, then that is what my life’s routine becomes. In Ithr, now that Medraut has successfully stifled all meaningful protest, his new laws come thick and fast. Rumours swirl through the halls of the thanes’ castles: rumours of new buildings and fences being erected around the country in secret, rural locations. Places where, in Annwn, the landscape is barren and rotting, and no inspyre dares to tread.

The apothecaries, reeves and veneurs team up to investigate the thorned snakes we took from Ellen Cassell, occasionally recruiting Ollie and I to help, either with his Immral or my uncanny ability to repel the creatures. They hiss and rear away from me whenever I approach. They soon outgrow the jars they were scooped into, and are moved to the most secure of the dungeons, where they snap at anyone who comes near them. 'I wish we had Brandon,' one of the veneurs admits. 'He'd know how to talk to them.'

'Well, we don't,' Ollie snaps, 'so we'll have to make do.'

'Easy,' I say. More and more these days I am forced into a peacemaker role. It's not a natural fit for me, but someone needs to rein Ollie in when his temper frays. In fact, I'm the only one he can talk to like a normal human being.

'You really are turning into me,' I comment in the stables after a particularly rocky night that culminated in Ollie blowing up at old Ben for giving us the wrong directions.

'Shut up.'

'I'm serious. Carry on like this and I'll be the popular one and you'll be the one sulking in the corner. It's a miracle Balius and I still put up with you.'

Balius snorts in agreement.

'We shouldn't even have been leading patrol tonight anyway,' Ollie complains. 'Where's Samson gone off to?'

I shrug, concentrating on brushing a particularly tricky knot out of Lamb's mane.

'Isn't he your boyfriend? Aren't you supposed to be keeping an eye on him?' Ollie sneers.

I point Lamb's comb at him. 'Stop it, Ollie. Whatever's eating you up, either talk to someone properly or deal with it yourself, but do not keep talking to us like this.'

I give Lamb a last cuddle then stalk out of the stables, straight into Easa.

'There you are,' he says, glancing towards Ollie's back. 'I've been sent to get you. Both of you.'

Ollie follows Easa and I through the castle, ignoring the shouts of alarm as another crack forms across the Round Table. Easa throws open the door to Lord Allenby's office. A group of people wait there for us. I know all but one of them.

'Fern?' Samson says. He and Jin are standing with a woman, wrinkled and stooped, her wispy hair scraped back into a bun. 'Fern, there's someone here we'd like you to meet.'

Natasha is shown in behind us, looking just as confused as I am.

'You speak Spanish, right?' Samson asks her. When she nods, he explains, 'Can you be our translator?'

He turns back to me. 'Fern, may I introduce Sophia Parriego? *Señora, esto es* Fern King.'

Sophia Parriego – the Immral who turned away from her power many years ago. The one we've been trying to find for weeks. Sophia bows her head, and sinks into a chair.

'You found her?' I say, looking at Sophia in wonder.

'No, she found us,' Samson admits ruefully. 'I asked Natasha and Niamh to add a message to her on their website before it was taken down. She saw it when it went viral.'

I glance at Lord Allenby, gauging his reaction to the news that our knights have been broadcasting the truth about Annwn to Ithr, but he only looks resigned and a little amused.

'She made herself known to Argentina's equivalent of the thanes and, well, here we are.'

'Brilliant.' I grin, hope building.

'Why am I here then?' Sophia says, Natasha translating.

'We have a favour to ask you,' Jin says, modifying her voice to be more charming than she usually is. She explains our predicament – that we really need my Immral to return.

'We understand that there is a process whereby Immral can be transferred . . .' Jin peters out, evidently unsure of how to baldly ask Sophia to hand over her power like it's the last chocolate in a bag.

'Ah,' Sophia says, 'so you were hoping to persuade me to give my unused power to you, is that right?'

She is eyeing Ollie and I with interest, her gaze roving over our eyes and skin. That's when I notice – her eyes aren't violet. My stomach sinks. She doesn't have Immral. How could that be? Does Immral fade with disuse? Does it fade with age?

'That's what we were hoping, I must admit,' Lord Allenby says, 'but it seems we're too late.' He has made the same connection as me.

'You are indeed,' Sophia says, smiling. 'I'm afraid you are seventeen years too late.'

'What do you mean?' Ollie says.

'I mean,' Sophia talks in halting English now, 'that I already gave up my Immral. I gave it to you. That's my power you're wielding, boy.'

Chapter 28

2005

It had taken some doing, finding a portal between London and Argentina in Annwn. There were portals that led all over the world, of course, dotted around the city, but mapping them was an impossible job for the reeves, as the portals switched so quickly. Una couldn't let the thanes discover her plan, so she had to explore them entirely by herself. No matter, she had done it before. The thrill of finding a new place in Annwn hadn't worn off. After all, last time she had gone rogue, she had found the love of her life. It stood to reason that it would work out well for her again. Besides, she had a new purpose growing inside her. Two new purposes. She and Angus had found out a few weeks ago. The news had inspired her idea – a determination to make the world safe, once and for all, from people like Medraut and whatever was killing her friends.

But it turned out that finding a portal to Argentina was the easy part. Finding the woman was impossible. Una had reached out to her contacts in the South American arms of the thanes, but they were no help. Sophia still had her portal, though, which gave Una hope that she was in Annwn somewhere, perhaps as an aventure. It had taken all of her investigative skills to track her down. When she found her, Sophia was not in Argentina at all.

She was in Antarctica, next to an ice cave that glittered like crystal. Una first caught sight of her squatting beside a deep well, fishing patiently. She didn't look up as Una approached, but Una could feel her presence from a distance, like a magnetic pull. That was how she knew she had the right person – it was the same feeling she had in Medraut's company. That feeling of not being in control of herself. It was a sensation she had never enjoyed.

She bowed, and Sophia laughed. 'It's exactly that kind of behaviour that I wanted to get away from.'

Una's Spanish was rusty, so it took her a moment to parse what Sophia was saying. She smiled and sat opposite the woman, peering into the ice well. Very suddenly, a white shape, with black bulbous eyes and a humanoid expression, emerged from the water, snapped at the humans, and then submerged once more. Una threw herself backwards, shocked.

'Don't mind the ningen,' Sophia said. 'He likes to check up on me every now and then. Make sure I'm safe.'

'You probably know why I'm here,' Una said, in broken Spanish.

'I do indeed, and you're not the first to come to me with such a request. You lot are all so obsessed with this idea that Immral is the only thing that will make the world safe. You have no clue, any of you, even when you know how destructive the power can be.'

Una leaned forward. 'Look into my soul. You'll see that I *do* understand how dangerous it is. I've risked my life to bring down the only other Immral in this world. I saw it when hardly anyone else did. I did something about it.'

Sophia leaned forward too, insolent laughter dancing in her violet eyes. 'I looked into your soul the moment you sat down, young woman. You think you can hide your true self from me the way you hid it from Sebastien Medraut? That young man's power has nothing on mine, believe you me. I see you, Una Gorlois. I see you.'

Una couldn't take her eyes away from Sophia's, even though she wanted to run. She couldn't stop herself from hearing everything that Sophia was saying, and feeling its truth in her gut.

'I see your selfishness, and the way you wrap up that selfishness in a cloak of helpfulness. I see how your quest for knowledge is not *true* curiosity. It is always for your own gain. So when you tell me that you want my Immral to rid the world of Sebastien Medraut and all like him, I tell you this: you *are* like him. You are exactly like him, and if you had my Immral you would be no different. And you know this, Una. You know this, and you hate it about yourself and you are proud of it too. I see you, and I will not give my power to someone like you.'

Sophia sat back on her haunches. 'You can go now, young lady.'

It was a command, to be obeyed with every fibre of her being. Una fled, all the way back to Ithr, where she lay awake from the early hours of the morning, thinking about all that Sophia had accused her of and knowing that it was the truth.

She went back there, though. Whenever she could be spared from patrol, and sometimes even when she couldn't, she found herself winding her way back through whatever portals she could, to a dreamscape Antarctica. Every time she came, she would sit, sometimes beside the ice well, sometimes inside Sophia's cave. Sometimes she would ask questions, sometimes she would stay silent. And every time, the conversation would end with Sophia telling her something truthful about herself. It was never pretty. Una's faults were laid bare in a way they had never been before. It was masochism. But it was important. Someone was finally putting her on trial for her crimes. Someone was finally reminding her of her limits. And finally someone was showing her a way back.

Gradually, Una came to relinquish the idea of making Sophia's Immral her own. At first the loss was painful. She held out hope that she would be able to change Sophia's mind if she swayed this way or that; showed so much contrition. A redemptive arc. That would be the satisfying way to get it. The mercenary turned entirely altruistic. Deserving of absolute power at the point where she no longer yearned for it. But Una knew – and Sophia knew – that it was never a path open to Una. There would always be something of the grifter about her.

Then came the night when the treitre attacked, and Una barely escaped with her life. As soon as the apothecaries had sewn her arm together again, she found herself going not to Ithr, but to Antarctica, stumbling blindly through a snowstorm – she didn't know if it was conjured from the tumult in her mind, or Sophia's way of telling her to turn back, or simply a part of Annwn. She somehow found her way to that ice cave and sat, alone and shivering, beside the well. She waited there for what felt like days, although really it could only have been minutes in Ithr. She waited until the wound at her shoulder began to bleed freely, so that the snow at her feet turned scarlet.

At some point, she looked up and realised that Sophia had joined her. Was, in fact, sitting next to her rather than opposite. Silently, Sophia opened her arms, and Una toppled into them and cried. She sobbed as she hadn't sobbed since the news of her father's death all those years ago, the night she met Angus. She sobbed for Ellen and Clement and the rest of her fallen friends. She sobbed for the life that she had almost lost, and the unborn lives she had put in jeopardy. She sobbed because she knew that it was time to stop being a knight. It was time to give it all up, and she hated herself for resenting that.

Eventually, Sophia dried her cheeks on the rough fur of her coat, and Una got up, and walked back to Ithr. The two women had not said a word to each other. Yet something had shifted between them. Una didn't return for several days. Long enough to hand in her notice to Lord Richards and to tell Lionel that she was getting out ('Thank God,' was all he had said). When she did return, she intended to say goodbye, and that was all. She had meant to merely thank Sophia for what she had done – for her comfort, but mostly for her insight.

But when she arrived and saw Sophia waiting – standing outside her cave, as though she knew it would be the last time, she couldn't help but ask. Before she had opened her mouth, Sophia said, 'No, young lady, I will not give you my power.'

Una laughed bitterly. 'Even when I'm going to leave it all behind, I had to have one last try.'

Sophia caught her up in a hug. 'You should not be ashamed of this part of you. But you are also not meant to have Immral.'

Una nodded through her regret.

'I am ready to give it up, though,' Sophia added. She pressed Una's stomach, and looked into her eyes. 'But I will give it to one of your children. How would you like that?'

Una felt Sophia's hand pressed against her belly. She seemed to feel the twins, for the first time, beneath Sophia's grip, as though she was bringing them to life, as though they were eager for the power she was willing to give them. Una probed her feelings. She knew what it would mean: watching one of her children grow more powerful, more charismatic, than she was. Was she equal to that? Was she truly the kind of parent she would need to be, to steer that child through the responsibility of being an Immral? She thought of it, and she knew she was.

'The girl,' she breathed, 'give it to my daughter.'

In her head, in her heart, the girl was already hers and the boy was already Angus's. She knew that was wrong, but that's the way it was. And somehow it felt right, the power passing to another woman. Three generations of females, to bring down Medraut. *Yes, this is how it is meant to be*. She was at peace.

They performed the ritual then and there, the purple light of Sophia's Immral glowing brightly beneath her hands as they clasped Una's stomach. Una felt nothing but a residual warmth, but she knew it had worked by the way Sophia's eyes turned brown.

It was a few months later, when the midwife laid the twins into Una's arms and she peered at them through tired eyes, that she saw what must have happened. One pair of eyes red; the other bright blue. *Was it intentional?* she had wondered.

Surely not. But when she had recovered, she had gone back to Antarctica to ask Sophia. She could find the ice cave nowhere, nor Sophia. That disappearance was all the confirmation she had needed that Sophia had tricked her, and divided the power between the children, instead of giving it wholly to Fern. She couldn't have felt more betrayed than if Sophia had been her own mother.

Chapter 29

I am reeling with what Sophia has told us. The way my mother courted her, groomed her, tried to grift her Immral for herself. It's so . . . distasteful. I look across at Ollie and see only resignation there. I know how much it will hurt Ollie that Mum wanted just me to have the power. Will this revelation undo my attempts to make him feel better with the letter I forged in Mum's name?

I can't help but be angry at Sophia as well – her trick may have been a final lesson for Mum, but it destroyed the relationship between Ollie and I for years, because of my red irises. And what has it done to our worlds? It's meant that neither one of us is strong enough to bring down Medraut.

'Well, that's a blow,' Lord Allenby is saying. 'But at least now we know what we're working with.'

Jin makes a strangled noise in the back of her throat, and I think I understand why. It's another door closed to us. Another avenue to victory shut off. We can't find the Grail, or even work out what tests we might need to pass to prove ourselves worthy of it, and now we can't return my Immral. That leaves all of our hopes resting on a depleted collection of exhausted and besieged thanes, and my brother, whose power still isn't as strong as mine was, when I had it.

'There must be another Immral somewhere on the planet,' Easa says, but I am watching Ollie. His gaze is fixed on Sophia with an intensity that I can't translate.

'So it *can* be transferred? The power?' he asks Sophia.

'Yes, it can be done,' she says. 'But I have none left to give.'

Ollie turns to Samson. 'And that equation you found – it definitely means that if someone gives their power to another Immral, it boosts that Immral's power even more?'

Samson nods slowly. 'I'm pretty sure that's what it was saying.'

Ollie pauses, not meeting anyone's eyes, weighing something in his mind. Then he turns back to Sophia.

'Will you show me how to give mine to Fern?'

Everyone looks at my brother, collectively stunned. I am hot and loved and unworthy. 'What?' I whisper.

He looks at me. 'It's simple. I want to give what's left of our Immral to you.'

I gape at him. Lord Allenby says something, and everyone leaves the room apart from Sophia, who sits back in her chair, giving us some space.

I want it. There's no denying that I want it. But it's not mine, it never was. I was never the Chosen One, as Niamh put it. Nor was Ollie, for that matter. We weren't chosen by fate – we were chosen by our mother, in her quest for power, influence, victory. Ollie would do better to give the Immral to someone else – to Lord Allenby, or Jin or Rachel. Any one of them would be a more humble and generous recipient. I am scared that I have too much of our mother inside me. I was proud of that fact once, but not any more.

Ollie follows me to a corner of the room.

'You should keep it,' I tell him. 'You're getting better at using it, and I don't really need it.'

'You don't get it, Fern.' He smiles. 'I. Don't. Want. It.'

I want to believe him so badly. To believe that he won't feel the same resentment for me as I have felt for him at times over these last few months.

'Stop thinking that,' he says. 'I can read your mind, remember? I won't resent you, I promise.'

'Why though? I wouldn't give you mine, if it was the other way around.' No matter how much I want this, I owe Ollie the truth – that I don't have the generosity of spirit to do what he would.

'I know,' he says easily, 'but that doesn't really matter, does it?'

It does matter. It matters to me. Seeing my hesitation, he sighs. 'You want a reason? Here's three, Fern. One: I've made a lot of mistakes with this power, and if I carry on having it I'll make even more. I've hurt people who I don't want to hurt.'

'But *I've* hurt people with it too,' I protest.

'Then that's between you and your conscience,' Ollie says, 'Once I give this to you, it's yours, and you can do what you want with it. Personally, I trust you to do the right thing, even if you haven't always. I've had years to see how evil this power can be and that still hasn't stopped me from doing wrong with it.

'Two,' he continues, before I can ask him what he means.

'When all this is over, one way or another, I'm leaving the thanes.' I can't help but gasp. Leave all of this? This wonderful group of friends we've found? This place where we belong? He smiles wryly at my expression. 'I know. You can't understand it, can you? But what happened to me in that in-between place isn't something I want to go through ever again. I might carry on teaching so I stay in touch with everyone, but as for actual fighting? I'm done.'

He pauses, and drops his voice. 'Three. This makes us even. For everything I've done to you. The fire. The betrayals. The bullying. For being a total dick to you. It would make things square between us, right?'

I nod, then with a burst of emotion throw my arms around his neck. He holds me tightly, both of us trying to express what we mean to each other without saying the words – the words we've never said.

'Anyway,' Ollie says, pulling away, his voice hoarse with unshed tears, 'it's the least I could do for the sister who forged a letter from our darling mum to try to make me feel loved.'

I gape again. 'You know about that? Of course – you read my mind. I hate that I keep forgetting you can do that.'

He laughs. 'I didn't read your mind, actually. I knew the moment you gave me the letter in Ithr what you'd done. You've got a terrible poker face, Fern.'

'Why didn't you say anything?'

He shrugs. 'I didn't need to. It did exactly what you wanted it to do. Exactly what I needed it to do.'

'Made you realise Mum loved you too?' I ask.

'No. Made me realise I didn't need Mum's love when . . .'

He trails off, awkward. The end of the sentence sits between us, warm and full.

'This is very sweet,' Sophia says, her eyes glittering, 'but I believe you have many people standing outside this room, wanting to find out what you've decided.'

We open the door to let Lord Allenby back into his own office, and behind him trails Samson, Natasha, Jin and Easa last. Something passes between Easa and Ollie – a promise, on my brother's part. How strange, that Ollie thinks Easa would prefer him to be without his Immral, while Samson has searched continents to give mine back to me.

'We're going to do it.' Ollie grins to the room. 'Fern can have it. She was always better at the fancy stuff anyway.'

The room erupts in applause and cheers, but through it all I lock eyes with my brother. It is the settling of our final accounts with each other. Now, perhaps, we have a chance at being the siblings we always should have been.

Chapter 30

With the Immral transfer ceremony set for the next night, I wake up in Ithr coated in sweat. The possibility of getting my power back has shaken me more than I thought. Not just getting it back: having the *whole* power. For if those old reeve's experiments are right, then Ollie giving me his entire power will complete mine. All of the things I said to Ollie about not feeling worthy are true. And the news that Mum chose Immral for me – it makes me even more certain that I should never have had Immral in the first place. And yet . . . I'm still going through with the ceremony. Of course I am. I had carved a place for myself in the thanes over the last few months as a peacemaker and planner, but I was missing part of myself. Now I discover that that part of me – the part of me I've relied on for years, the part of me that caused so much suffering – was never supposed to be me at all.

I used to wonder what I would have been like, how my life would have been mapped out, if Mum had lived. Now my thoughts take me in a very different direction – what would my life have been like if Mum hadn't found Sophia, or if she hadn't even been a knight?

Dad fell from the podium of parenting a long time ago. But Mum – she's been on a pedestal as high as the one I fought Medraut on in Trafalgar Square last year. I've kept her up there for so long. Sometimes it looked as though she would topple and I put all of my strength into keeping her upright; a fierce, uncompromising mother to be proud of, and if she didn't get things right with Ollie then that was a shame but it didn't diminish her, not really. After all, fierce people sometimes have to do fierce, unlikeable things.

It fills me with shame that it has taken this long to admit that she was so deeply flawed. It shouldn't have taken something that affected me to make me realise it. It should have taken the same reason it took for Dad to fall – the mismatch in how she treated her children. The more I understand people, the more I realise that how someone behaves towards their children is the mark of who they truly are as a person. Lord Allenby left his to keep them safe, even though it broke him. Medraut mentally tortured his daughter but uses her in Ithr to bolster his reputation as a family man. If Mum chose greatness for me to the detriment of Ollie, then that says a lot about her choices as well, doesn't it?

The bittersweetness of the moment leaves me feeling more alone than ever. Mum's faith in me is no longer a support. It is a condemnation. An alliance I don't want any more. And yet I now have to bear this power by myself. I have to be equal to it, not for her, but for my brother who is sacrificing so much, and for the other thanes, both living and dead.

I haven't earned it yet, but I have to. I have to live up to it, to live up to their belief.

It takes me a long time to go downstairs. It's a weekend, so there's a lot of time to fill, and I don't want to be stuck in the house with Ollie and Dad. Luckily, Ollie has a plan for that.

'Come out with me today?' he offers over toast and Marmite.

'Where are you going?'

'Irish and Penn left something for us. They told me about it last night.'

Niamh and Natasha? I'm intrigued enough to set aside everything else and follow Ollie out into a bright chill that speaks of spring. The blossom is just starting to emerge on some of the trees, pure and timid. We mostly walk in silence. Words aren't needed between us any more. The knowledge of what Ollie is going to do tonight has filled the gap that once gaped like an open wound whenever we were around each other. We are healed. The plaster has been peeled away, and the skin is mended; fresh but no longer tender.

We make our way to the outskirts of Epping Forest, where it is easy to get lost in the many pathways that criss-cross this stretch of land on the edge of London.

'There.' Ollie points to a symbol drawn on the earth with flour – a five-pointed star, its longest point indicating a direction. That leads us to a set of twigs shaped into an arrow – a treasure trail for those still curious enough to follow. After a while we come to an opening of the path that leads down to a lake.

A few dog walkers and some children, wrapped up in layers, amble by the path. My own hood and scarf disguise my burn scar well enough that I don't get too many suspicious looks. A red ribbon flies from one of the reeds sitting at the edge of the lake.

We must look strange, craning our necks to see if there's anything hidden in the reeds, trying not to fall into the water.

'Here,' I say, pulling at a little box attached to one of the stems. It snaps off in my hand, and Ollie joins me as I open it to see what's inside. A tiny booklet, its cover emblazoned with the sigil of the thanes, sits inside a little plastic bag to keep it safe from the water. Someone has written in the front page, *Keep remembering. Write the names of your loved and lost here, and we'll remember them for you*. Underneath, in a different handwriting I recognise from patrol notes as Natasha's, are the words, *Never forget*.

The pages that follow are filled with names. More than I could have thought possible from a tiny, hidden memorial in a little-known part of east London. The first few I recognise as the names of dead knights and thanes – Brandon, Rafe, Phoebe, Ramesh and Sachi, Emory – placed there by Natasha and Niamh. But the names that come after are all in different handwriting, a list of the dead every bit as powerful as the scrolling memorial in Tintagel. A few pages in and some people have added explanations and doodles. One has drawn their pet cat, with the note, *Midge was hit by a car last week, and I found this on the day we got her back from the crematorium. I hope you won't mind.*

Niamh has replied beneath: *If anyone minds, they can answer to me. This is for remembering anyone who was precious to us. I'll add a name – Gavin. He was my imaginary friend when I was a kid and didn't have any real ones. I'd like you all to remember him too, please. Maybe he can give Midge a treat.*

Beneath Niamh's words people have written *RIP Gavin and*

Midge; Gavin & Midge 4ever! and someone else has doodled a boy, who I assume is Gavin, with a cat twined over his shoulders. The conversation continues through the notebook, little snippets of merriment amidst the names of the lost. A sense of camaraderie grows and builds, until the notebook takes on a life of its own as people dredge loved ones, real and imaginary, from the depths of their hearts. When we get to the end, I fish a pen from my pocket and with Ollie's blessing, add: *Una Gorlois – she was our mum, and we never really knew her. She's part real, part imaginary to us; part heroine, part villain. And that's okay. I'm writing her name here not to remember her, but to let her go.*

Ollie squeezes my shoulder. Writing feels like an exorcism. A way to establish me, with the power that will be mine, separate from my mother and the life she wanted for me. As I close the notebook and replace it in its plastic bag and then the box, I can feel the weight of Mum's expectations fall away from my shoulders. The path I will tread now is mine alone.

Chapter 31

When I land in Annwn, there's a strange feeling in the air. A sense of expectation that comes not just from my fellow thanes, whose eyes linger on me in hope and excitement, but from the air itself. As though the little inspyre left powering Tintagel, holding together its decaying rocks, is waiting for me to receive my inheritance. Alternatively, it could just be nerves.

The knights' chamber is deserted when I arrive. I'm a little bit early so perhaps I shouldn't be surprised. I move into the centre of the room, drawn to the fire crackling under the mantelpiece. Just over there, in the corner, is the chair I once haunted, on the periphery of the group. Later, it was occupied by Sachi, before she too yielded to the friendship offered by her regiment. This room isn't empty after all: it is full of ghosts. Sachi there. Ramesh in front of the fire, in the middle of the chat. Phoebe beside him, perched on the arm of the sofa, laughing, her eyes inviting me to join them. Over there, by the lieutenants' tables, is Rafe, his head deep in patrol notes. And now all around me are my old Bedevere regiment: Vien, Linnea, Milosz – the scars of a hard year's battle in their rough laughter. Brandon, head peeking around the door, his hooded morrigan perched on his shoulder. They are all here with me in this moment. I have felt the weight of their losses for years, but right now I feel the weight of their presence. It's as though they're reminding me what matters, lashing me to humanity before I gain inhuman powers.

I was sure that the day patrols would be coming back by now. Worry crawls over me – what if Medraut has heard about our plans and has done something awful to stop us? What if he's attacked enough knights that even with full Immral I don't stand a chance of beating him?

Just as I'm starting to spiral, a pair of hands covers my eyes.

'Feeling ready?' Samson whispers in my ear. I pull his hands away and spin to face him. Behind him, the others are beginning to trickle through the door.

'I thought you might want a bit of space, so I asked everyone to stay outside,' he says.

I nod, my heart full. How does this man, who's only known me a few years, somehow understand what I need better than I do?

My fellow knights are quiet, but not subdued. As they pass, they squeeze my arm reassuringly, or smile tearfully. But one person is missing. 'Where's Ollie?' I say.

'He's gone ahead already,' Natasha explains.

'Think he wanted some space too,' Niamh adds.

Sophia told us that the ceremony would be easier and more effective if we hold it at a place of significance in Annwn. There was one place that we all agreed would work. I don't relish the thought of returning there – it's always been a place of promise and danger, a place where one's soul is laid bare and tested in unexpected ways.

Stonehenge.

This time, there is no huge gathering of squires and thanes and Fay. There is only my brother and I, Lord Allenby, Jin, Natasha and Sophia. We climb through the portal from Tintagel into oppressive sunlight. But something is different about this place now: the grass is dying, and so, I think, is the henge. There are gaps in the elaborate pattern of bones in each slab, as though the skulls and fibulas that were once glued there have disintegrated. The remaining bones creak eerily.

My brother is sitting on a slab of stone near the centre of the circle; the slab that squires must bleed onto to activate the tournament.

'Give us a moment?' I say to the others, and they hold back as I move across the grass. I sit quietly beside Ollie, my hand palm up on my knee – an offering. He rests his hand on mine, lightly, non-committal.

'I won't be upset if you've changed your mind,' I lie.

'I haven't. I'm just saying goodbye, that's all.'

'It's not like you're dying,' I joke lamely. 'You're just going to be an ordinary, good-looking, popular guy who fights in a secret army.'

He smiles faintly, like he's humouring me. I get it. He's giving me this willingly, but that doesn't mean it's easy. And for anyone to suggest that he could back out or that he can't want to do it if he's upset about it cheapens the sacrifice he's making. So I lean into him, resting my head on his shoulder, and he rests his head on mine. As he says his farewells to the person he was, I offer a silent thanks to him for doing so.

Eventually, he squeezes my hand properly. 'Okay,' he says, 'I'm ready.'

As if she's heard us from so far away, Sophia steps forward.

'Take each other's hands,' she says, as Natasha translates. 'It will be a little different from when I did it with your mother, because I was using her as a conduit. But I remember the principles.'

Ollie and I clasp hands across the slab. I can't tell if it's him or me who's shaking. I focus on his hands and plant my feet, feeling the soft earth beneath them.

'Now, Ollie,' Sophia says, 'you remember what you need to do?'

'Yeah.'

'It will hurt,' Sophia warns. 'Draw your Immral into your hands. All of it. Now. Go.'

Ollie's jaw is set, his face determined. His eyes fix onto mine, but they are focused on an inner struggle. It's the strangest feeling, to be so intimately connected to someone – his hands clasping mine, his eyes on mine – and yet so distant, for there is a war raging in my brother's body. Sophia had told us that it was like drawing your own blood – all of it – into a syringe and injecting it into someone else. She hadn't sugar-coated how painful it would be, and I can tell from the blood now seeping from my brother's nose and ears that this is costing him immensely.

'Stop, Ollie,' I say quietly.

His violet irises bore into my hazel ones, until the whites turn red as something pops there.

'Stop,' I say more urgently.

Blood trickles from his eyes.

'You have to push through the pain,' Sophia says.

'No,' I say, trying to pull away, 'it's going to kill him.'

I know what happens when an Immral's eyes start bleeding. He's going to pass out. The doctors have warned us that if it happens too often we risk brain damage.

'I'm okay,' he mouths at me, even though I know he's lying. He won't let go of my hands, and he won't stop.

Then something strange happens. Our hands, which were simply holding each other, become magnetised. His skin grows warm, as though it is on fire from the inside. It is so hot that I can feel my own hands blistering beneath his. It's as though a flood of boiling water is waiting there, with power immeasurable, only held back by the dam of his skin.

'Is it ready?' Sophia says.

Ollie nods.

'You know what you need to do?'

At last, Ollie closes his eyes. He breathes deeply in . . . and out. And with that outward breath, he releases whatever was holding back his power, whatever was keeping it inside him. Now the pain is mine to bear, mine to accept. I try to clear my head, to welcome it in, but my body revolts. There is no space inside my veins for the raw Immral mingling with my blood. It is as though a million needles are injecting the power into me through my palms, and it is at once familiar and strange. I remember what this feels like – the sense of being able to stretch out a hand and command the air.

But there's something new too. A prickle at the back of my head sparks, and then ignites. A dormant creature – the

Chapter 32

Ollie teeters, and I reprimand myself for getting so caught up in my new power that I had forgotten the person who gave it to me. I catch him before he falls. He glances at me through bloodshot eyes. They are no longer the blue they were when we were younger, or the violet they had become over the last few months. They're hazel, like mine are . . . were . . . I resist the urge to conjure up a mirror to check whether my eyes are now violet. I catch glimpses of Ollie's memories, fleeting as a butterfly, through my hand on his arm. Running through London with a grinning Easa; Easa pulling faces, cartwheeling, doing anything in his power to make my brother forget the weight that was crushing him. The weight of his Immral. It's the first time I have been able to use what used to be Ollie's half of the power. Now it's *mine*, all of it. The joy and longing that swirled through Ollie at that memory swirl through me as well, so that I'm not sure where my brother ends and I begin.

'Are you okay?' Ollie asks me, and I laugh nervously.

I'm more than okay, I want to say, *I'm invincible*. I feel the tiredness in his body. The ache. The memory of his ordeal permeates my brain, showing me just how much he has given up. I taste his loss like iron, but there's a richer taste on top of it – the bergamot smell of having made peace with himself and his past sins.

Easa comes to his other side. 'Let's get you cleaned up,' he says, and reaches across to wipe the blood from my brother's face with his bare hands. I *see* the heady tension between them so keenly that I pull away, letting them have their moment.

'You look incredible,' Samson says, keeping his distance. I can feel his uncertainty, but also his pride, both in me and in the fact that he put his own insecurities aside to make this happen. I close the space between us, pressing my lips to his. 'Thank you,' I say. The old Fern would have wanted him to know that I mean it; would have stared at him a little too intensely to try to get her point across. The Fern I am now doesn't need to. I can feel the Immral sparking in my throat, imbuing my words with sincerity.

He steps back, and covers the move with a smile. But I can feel how disconcerted he is. I understand it: after all, I've been in Medraut's presence when he's turned the full force of his Immral on a crowd. I know how odd it is to feel someone else's wants and feelings imprinted upon you; to not have full control of yourself. It's a kind of desire, but not the one he and I have shared these last few months. For a second, the urge to reach out and soothe his concern with a little Immral takes over me.

'Shall we go back to Tintagel?' Lord Allenby says. 'I believe Jin was going to run some tests, Fern, as we agreed?'

'Alright,' I say. Her experiments are going to be psychological, when all I want is to test the limits – or lack of limits – to my renewed power. I want to show Lamb what she and I can do together now I'm even stronger than I was. I link arms with Ollie as we walk back towards the portal.

Samson and Lord Allenby stride ahead, talking in low voices, and I resist the temptation to reach out with my power to listen to their thoughts.

'Wait, please,' Sophia says in broken English. It's more of a command than a request – perhaps having Immral is a hard habit to break. She hobbles up to us and I fall back to allow her to take my arm.

'Go, go,' she says, gesturing Natasha forward. Natasha glances back at us curiously as she joins Ollie and Easa. I wonder briefly how Sophia is intending to communicate, given my Spanish is minimal at best, until she says, with mischief in her voice, '*You* do not need translation any more, do you?'

Then the strangest thing happens. A wave of emotion flows into me through the papery skin of Sophia's hand. It's akin to the tastes I get when I use my Immral on other people and objects, but now it's more defined, more nuanced. I see a series of memories through Sophia's eyes, layered on top of one another like a disjointed flip book: flashes of my mother visiting her all those years ago; of Sophia's thaneship when she was a young woman, and the look of disappointment and hunger on the faces of her fellow thanes as she told them she didn't want to use her Immral. Through them all I decipher a single, connecting question: *What are you going to do with your great power now?*

Up until this point, I had only been thinking about the Immral as a means to defeat Medraut. That has, after all, been the overwhelming purpose of my life for the last two years.

Victory always seemed so impossible that nothing beyond that concept existed. But now, for the first time, I understand that if we succeed, then there will be a future after Medraut. A time when my Immral isn't needed for war. What happens to me when I no longer have a purpose? What happens to any great power when it can no longer be directed towards some notion of 'good'?

'Why did you give the power up, when you could have used it to help against people like Medraut?' I ask Sophia. I say it out loud, but I push some of my Immral into the words, flowing them back through her arm, so that she will understand me.

The reply comes back almost immediately, in a flurry of memories and rough emotions. *Power never interested me. I wanted to live lightly. Saving the world sounds fun, but not when you must really do it.*

I don't agree, I think, then add, *Do you ever regret giving it up?*

'No,' Sophia says softly, 'I do not.'

Do you think I'm the right person to have Immral? I ask her.

I cannot tell you that, she replies, in thought. *The answer will shift from moment to moment, depending on what you do. If you want to prove that you deserve it, then you will have to consider everything you do, from all angles, interrogate whether you do it for you or for others.*

Sophia imagines a long road that winds through desert and jungle and ice, climbing and falling until I can no longer see the place where the thought started. I understand what she's trying to say: everything I do from here on out will need to be measured against who I am now and the values that brought me here. I will need to work out whether I'm staying true to those values, or whether it is right that those values have shifted. The truth of what lies ahead of me, whether we win or lose against Medraut, presses down on me.

'You're scared,' she says.

I nod.

'Good.'

She gestures to the small band waiting for us at the entrance to the portal back to Tintagel, and sends me one last thought. *Use them. Always use them. Let them become your guiding angels.*

As though conjured by her advice, something materialises on my wrist: the moon and stars bracelet that Samson gave me in Ithr. Not a guiding angel – a guiding star.

'Everything okay?' Samson asks as we approach.

'Yes,' I say, and I turn around to cast one final look back at Stonehenge. I still see the roots that spread from its foundations, like a spider's web stretching across Annwn, linking everything together in this world through threads of shared imagination. I let Samson help me into the portal and land in the centre of Tintagel to a mass of waiting thanes. They take one look at the violet light that crackles around my form and burst into applause. I spot Rachel and Niamh, eyes shining, at the edge. Charlie is there too, an odd smile playing over her face. She alone of all those waiting walks away.

Before the eyes of Tintagel, I walk towards one of the crumbling walls. Grey nothingness – the in-between world Medraut created, peeks through the cracks in the stone and mortar. I glance back at Sophia. 'You asked me what I would do with my power now.'

I place a hand on the stone and feel the weary inspyre inside it stir at my presence.

'This is what I'm going to do.'

I close my eyes, gathering my power and the inspyre that always seems to rest inside my bones, and send it out through my fingertips. It answers my call, rushing outwards, into the stone, mending the cracks then leaping up, up, up to fix the broken dome. I call to the memories of St Paul's Cathedral, and the worship that happens here in Ithr, and angels burst from the parapets, naked and powerful like the stone they came from. I cast my inspyre across the grounds, and ivy and honeysuckle once more spring from the earth and wind their way up the outside of the castle, dusky flowers sprouting. The bare willow tree in the centre of the gardens pops with buds and uncurls fresh leaves, tender as the sun.

Spent, I open my eyes at last and pull away from the stone. All around me, people are peering out of the windows and exclaiming in wonder and joy at the transformation. My palm is blistered and raw, and when I look closely I see that the skin hasn't burned away – it has disintegrated, as though I have given part of my actual body to Annwn.

Sophia takes my hand, peering at the wound. 'That was not your Immral, child,' she says, looking at me warmly for the first time. 'That was your soul.'

Chapter 33

The second thing I attempt with my Immral is to restore the Fay. I recall the stories we told over Merlin's failing body last year, injecting the full force of my Immral into the inspyre in my hands, but nothing except a faint, human outline appears. Bringing a god back from the dead remains beyond me.

The next thing I attempt is to find Excalibur. Merlin and Nimue had told me that it would appear when I was ready. Everyone assumed that reviving my Immral would be that moment. They can't see inside my heart. They don't know I'm still terrified that I won't be strong enough to wield it, and in doing so that I'll be drained of my power once more. Secretly, I'm relieved that the Fay understood this, and had mercy on me.

Sophia stays in Tintagel for a few weeks, to help me master my new Immral. Some of the power is familiar, but it's like driving a supercar when you've only ever driven Dad's Fiat before.

'No, you need to be subtler,' she tells me, Natasha translating. We are in the airless dungeon room where the snakes are being held. The reeves and veneurs have been running tests on them ever since Ellen's death, trying to work out a way to use them to our advantage, or render them harmless, but their efforts so far have been fruitless. I'm trying to mould them into something new, to turn the Immral that binds them together into something that we might be able to use. But just as Ollie had found when he had my power, the Immral is twisted so tightly and so complexly that all I am doing is angering them.

In frustration, I throw my Immral at one. The violet light from my hands hits it like a plate shattering against a wall. The snake doesn't reel back, injured – it absorbs my power as though it were cream.

'Did it just . . . grow?' Natasha whispers.

The snake does seem to become longer, its grey skin shimmering purple.

'You just fed it,' Sophia says. 'Foolish girl.'

'Well, *you* try it then,' I snap. 'Oh no, wait, you can't, because you gave your Immral away.'

Sophia casts me a look of deepest disappointment, then limps from the room. Natasha pats me awkwardly on the shoulder as, in the corner, the snake writhes and hisses at us. What Natasha doesn't know – can never know – is how much I wanted to use my Immral to make Sophia like me. If my friends knew how often I wish I could do that at the moment, they'd never come near me again.

The truth is, that even having only had the power for a few days, I feel more sympathy for Sebastien Medraut than ever before. I used to puzzle over how he was so disconnected from other people, so determined to force his will on them. But if he's always wielded this power then he probably never made the true friendships that I did. He was never given that chance. My friends' and colleagues' trust in me, sown gradually and naturally over the last few years, is my only anchor. I can't let them down. But it's hard, and every day it gets harder.

'Come on, come and get some air,' Natasha says, leading me from the room. We pass through the cloisters, where harkers listen through their helmets to whatever is happening across the London thaneship. I miss seeing Rachel at her desk, even though I'm pleased that she's finally advancing as she deserves. Now Ben sits in her place, frowning over his notes and muttering, 'I can't hear you, sentinel, speak properly for goodness' sake.' I send up a silent prayer that Ben isn't mishearing crucial information that's going to keep Samson, Ollie and Nerizan safe out on patrol.

We wander into the gardens. The only people here are a handful of veneurs and apothecaries. I briefly think about visiting Lamb, perhaps taking her out for a gallop across the city, when I hear laughter. It's such a rare sound, either in Annwn or Ithr nowadays, that I'm drawn to it like the sea to the moon.

The laughter comes from two people, Charlie and Lord Allenby, as they throw sticks for Loco across the lawn. I've never seen either of them look so free. Lord Allenby says something, wry smile on his face, and Charlie looks up at him in a way that makes my stomach jolt. It's the way she used to look at her father, except that this time there's genuine trust there.

'Fancy joining them?' Natasha says.

I shake my head. There's no place for me there. But as we move away, Charlie spots me and waves us over.

'How's it going, Miss King?' Lord Allenby says. His formality is another blow; I'm just another thane to him. Charlie is Charlie.

'Not brilliantly,' I reply honestly.

'She'll be fine. She just needs to settle into her new body,' Natasha says, casting me a reassuring smile.

'Is it those snake things? The ones my dad made?' Charlie asks anxiously.

'It feels like the best thing I could do with my Immral is to fix them, doesn't it?' I say. 'But all I can do is make them stronger. I'm just no match for him, even when I've got the full power.'

Charlie turns away from us, and Lord Allenby puts a steadying hand on her shoulder. He murmurs words to her, and I use my power to hear what he's saying. 'You're not him, Charlie. You're not responsible for anything he does.'

'I know,' she whispers, 'I know that.' But she doesn't sound as though she totally believes it. There's another urge, driven by my sympathy for her – it would be so easy to *make* her believe that. She would feel better, it would be helping her, wouldn't it? And that's something I *can* do. My hand twitches towards her. Just a tiny nudge of the mind . . .

'Maybe,' Natasha says, folding my hand between both of hers, 'we shouldn't look at it from an Immral point of view.'

That gets both Lord Allenby's and Charlie's attention. I've lost my chance. I study Natasha's expression as Lord Allenby asks her what she means. Then I quietly look inside her mind, to see whether she knew what I was about to do – whether she was stopping me on purpose or whether it was a coincidence. But all I find there is a deep contentment as long as she is in Annwn, although I get the sense that she is far from content when she is in Ithr. She cannot be who she truly is when she's in the real world; her body is divided from her mind. In Annwn, though, they are one. I pull away, suddenly aware that I only meant to find out whether she knew what I wanted to do – I never meant to look deeper.

'You make a good point,' Lord Allenby is saying. 'All the research that Jin and Easa have done suggests that Inspyre is the opposite of Immral. Do we think that we've been using the wrong weapon?'

'You could do an experiment,' Charlie says, her eyes lighting up as they always do when someone mentions science.

'That might not be a bad idea,' Natasha says. 'I mean, there were some knights who didn't become sluaghs, weren't there? Amina didn't, and Ollie eventually. They couldn't get the snakes to stick to Fern at all . . .'

'I always guessed that was because of my Immral, even if it wasn't working then,' I say.

'But the snakes were starting to work with Ollie, weren't they?' Lord Allenby says, 'and he had more Immral than you back then.'

I think it through. 'You think it was my imagination?'

By the time the rest of the knights have come back from patrol, Lord Allenby, Charlie, Natasha and I have a plan. We also have every thane in Tintagel gathered in the central hall, beneath the portal dome. Loco is ecstatic – he's never seen this many people in one place before. He rolls from hand to hand, encouraging belly rubs.

'What's going on?' Samson says, pecking me on the cheek as he takes in the gathering.

‘Science.’ I grin. For the first time since rebuilding Tintagel, I feel on solid ground about what I’m doing – that I’m definitely in the right. ‘Pop over there with the other guinea pigs, please.’

Samson smiles bemusedly, but wanders over to chat to Rachel, who is glowing from a night spent up on the castle balconies in the blustering wind of Annwn.

‘Can I not at least get the sweat and horse smell off me first?’ Ollie complains.

‘No time, sozzles. Go on, off you go.’

When all the knights have mingled with the rest of the thanes, Lord Allenby raises a hand for silence. I am struck by the fact that only two years ago, this circular space was barely big enough to fit one set of squires. Now there is easily room for every thane from Tintagel as well as those on loan from the other thaneships.

‘We’re looking for volunteers to test a theory that might help us to combat the sluaghs,’ Lord Allenby says. A handful of thanes raise their hands eagerly.

‘Not so fast.’ Lord Allenby smiles. ‘I’m afraid we’re looking for a very particular quality. Fern?’

I close my eyes, calling to the part of my Immral that allows me to see the inspyre that makes up every object in Annwn. It has another purpose – one I only realised recently. For I can see the inspyre inside dreamers and aventures. I saw it once in Samson, before I went on my tour of Annwn’s Round Tables. When I open my eyes, everything is bathed in blue light. It pulses across the spots where I recently mended Tintagel’s crumbling walls and tapestries and paintings. But it isn’t the decor I’m focusing on this time, it’s the people.

I can't pick out individual faces easily, because I'm only seeing inspyre, but I recognise some shapes. Samson and Ollie, Natasha and Niamh are as well known to me as my own figure. They pulse brightly with inspyre. I touch them lightly on their arms, and Lord Allenby directs them to stand in one cloister. I move amongst the group, picking out everyone who shines more brightly with inspyre than others. By the time I'm finished, I've chosen twenty or so thanes from those assembled, and the corner where they now stand is so bright that I can barely look at it.

'Are you done, Fern?' Lord Allenby says, his figure outlined in blue.

'Nearly,' I say. 'There's two more.'

I walk over to the one figure who stands on the periphery of the group, outside the dome. I touch her on the arm.

'Me?' Charlie says, bewildered. 'I'm not a thane.'

'That doesn't matter,' I say. 'We're looking for imagination, and yours is brighter than almost anyone else's here.'

I can't see Charlie's expression, but I can feel it. The inspyre inside her seems to dance with surprised joy.

I turn to Lord Allenby. 'You're the last one, sir.'

I close my eyes and shake my head, bringing back my normal vision. Lord Allenby stands before me, looking emotional. Beyond him, Charlie is being welcomed into the group. Rachel is amongst them, as are Bandile, Jin and Easa, and a collection of other lores and knights who I don't yet know by name. The beginning of a team. The beginning of a way to fight back.

Chapter 34

We gather downstairs next to the dungeons, where I explain our plan to the new members of our group.

'You think we're immune to those things?' Bandile says.

'In a way, but it might be dangerous to test it,' Lord Allenby replies. 'After all, they got to most of our knights eventually, even if it took a while. If anyone doesn't want to risk it, we will understand, won't we?'

He casts a challenging glance at me and I nod. I notice that his eyes skate towards Charlie too, and I get the sense that he is half afraid for her, half proud of her when she doesn't join the two thanes – one harker, one reeve – who edge apologetically out of the space.

'Shall we start then?' I say, and nod to Easa as he unlocks the door to the dungeon.

The thorned snakes rear up, hissing and crackling as soon as I enter. They reach towards me, but when Charlie and Bandile enter behind me on Lord Allenby's command, they pause.

'What do I imagine?' Bandile says. 'I can't think of anything right now except how petrified I am.'

'Put your hands on my shoulders and . . .' I think about

what Medraut would hate the most. 'Think about what you want to do with your life. I don't care if it sounds impossible. Just the greatest thing you'd love to do one day if there was nothing in your way, then channel it into me.'

Bandile and Charlie do as I ask, their hands resting firmly on each of my shoulders. The snakes snap towards them both. Nevertheless, I begin to get a sense of their thoughts and dreams. There is a heavy aroma of fear, stifling and musty, but beneath it I can see their ambitions. Charlie's as a biochemist, finding the cures for the world's worst illnesses. Bandile's is softer but not weaker: he wants a family, a partner, a community. Last, I focus on myself. What do *I* want to do with my life? A thousand possibilities flicker through my mind, all glittering with potential. Faces present themselves: Samson, Ollie, Charlie, Natasha . . . all of the people I cannot imagine my life without. I picture gatherings with them in Ithr, a friendship group to last a lifetime, bonded with grief and secrets. But then I think of Annwn, and it is the only solid, permanent ambition that makes any sense to me. That's what I want to do, more than anything: to restore and explore this endless dreamworld. A now-familiar warmth tingles across my limbs.

Holding one hand towards the foremost creature, I pull at the inspyre in Bandile and Charlie, the place where their desires flicker like twin lighthouse beacons, and pass it through my own body, binding our dreams together, then I send it out towards the snake in a beam of blue light. The thing rears its head, and if it had a voice I know that it would be shrieking in pain. It snaps to and fro, trying to escape the light. For an instant I'm reminded of my worst sins: torturing Charlie and Jenny. But I remind myself that this thing is not its own creature with its own purpose – it is part of Medraut, and it must be stopped. No mercy will prevent it from attacking us.

'Is it supposed to hurt?' Charlie says through gritted teeth, although she doesn't let go of my shoulder.

I stop the beam of inspyre immediately, releasing her from the bind of my power. The snake falls to the floor, not defeated but smaller and weaker than it was when we entered the room.

'Are you alright?' I ask Charlie and Bandile.

'Headache,' Bandile says shortly, in a way that tells me he has a migraine. Charlie's eyes are closed, her fists clenched. I can sense that she is in turmoil. The memories of the pain her father inflicted on her are strong.

Without thinking, I grip both of their arms and send a calming pulse from my head to theirs. But to my surprise, Charlie pulls away violently. 'What are you doing?' she says.

'Just pain relief,' I explain.

She stares at me, betrayal emanating from her body in hot waves, before she rushes from the room. Lord Allenby casts me a single, disappointed glare before he turns to follow her.

I don't talk to anyone else that night; not until I get home. In my bedroom, I allow the guilt and confusion to worm its way inside me. I was so sure I'd been doing the right thing. Well, I correct myself, no, I didn't really *think* about it at all. It came so naturally, the nudge to make everything better.

My gaze rests on the pile of Mum's diaries that sit in a box in the corner of my room. A thought comes unbidden to my mind. *Haven't you learned anything from Mum's mistakes?*

Mum created the golden treitre by trying to 'fix' Ellen's fear. Mum helped to cause all the problems between Ollie and me through her attempts to get Immral, and then her decision to give that Immral to me. Why couldn't she just let things be? Why did she have to be the one to find solutions, when she could have worked *with* people to find the right way for them? She was as bad as Medraut – determined that her way was the right way, even when it hurt people. I'm just as bad as Mum, except with me it's worse because I have Immral, and because I've lived long enough beneath Medraut's shadow to know better.

I let myself wallow in self-hatred for most of the morning, but after a while it seems pointless. It's done. I've got Immral, and Sophia's warnings about having to constantly measure my own morality ring through my head. Exhausting though it seems, I'm coming round to that truth now. There's no point in self-pity; I have to do something.

I slip out of the house, not wanting to bump into Ollie and be subjected to a lecture I have already given myself. I make my way along the canal near Victoria Park, where I know Lord Allenby usually sleeps. It feels important to apologise to him, and then on Monday when I'm back in school I will apologise more strongly to Charlie for invading her mind the way her father used to. I hope that Lord Allenby can give me some tips on how to make the apology sincere without using my Immral. Who am I kidding? I'm also hoping he'll reassure me that I'm not irredeemable; that I'm not the monster I could so easily become.

There are a few shopping bags shoved next to a pile of blankets, all full with tatty clothes and energy bars, but Lord Allenby himself is missing. I try to stifle my concern – Ithr was never very safe for the homeless, and now it is even less so.

I loiter there for a while, but it soon becomes clear that Lord Allenby isn't returning any time soon. Disappointed, worried, I make my way back through the Olympic Park, when I hear voices raised in laughter. I recognise both of them. I slow down, edging around a corner so that I can see them without being spotted.

Sure enough, Lionel Allenby is sitting on a bench, looking out towards the river. Beside him sits Charlie. She looks happier than I've ever seen her in Ithr. She tears open a Tupperware box, offering half a sandwich to Lord Allenby and taking half for herself. They are entirely easy with each other, as though this is a Saturday routine. I've been on the periphery of their newfound relationship before, but that was different, that was in Annwn. Ithr was still mine – I have kept Lord Allenby's secret, I have been a good friend, a good thane, a good . . . I can't say the word *daughter*, can I? Not now, when Lord Allenby has found a daughter, and Charlie has found a father. I discovered his secret, but he offered it to Charlie.

I turn back, alone. I desperately want to talk to someone, but I can't face Charlie and Lord Allenby together, and I'm too ashamed of what I did last night to call Samson. That only leaves Ollie, but apologising for misusing the power he so generously gave me is beyond me right now. Then my phone rings. It's Ollie, as if he's heard my thoughts.

'Are you safe?' is the first thing he asks.

'I'm fine. Ollie, I –'

'Where are you? Do you want me to come over? We don't have to talk.'

I'm taken aback. That's not what I was expecting him to say. 'If you like?' I reply.

Within half an hour, he's pacing towards me, hands in pockets, looking out of breath. 'Up there?' he asks, nodding in the direction I have just come from, where Lord Allenby is. I point in the opposite direction, down an overgrown path concealed by low-hanging trees, and we wander along it in silence, towards Wanstead Flats. I can sense Ollie struggling to find the right words.

'All we can do is make amends, right?' he says after a while. 'And do whatever it takes to get our heads straight.'

I look at him curiously. He alluded to misusing his Immral once before. Is this a confession?

'How did you get your head straight?' I ask him.

'I gave you my Immral.'

'You going to tell me what you did?' I ask.

'Nope.'

We cross a road onto the Flats.

'Mum really did a number on us, didn't she?' I say at last. Shame and guilt wash over me. It's the first time I've said out loud that Mum did wrong. Her final fall.

'Maybe,' Ollie replies, 'but she wasn't all bad.'

'I'm sorry, who are you and what have you done with my brother?'

He laughs. 'I really was down on her before, wasn't I?'

'That's an understatement – you hated her. What's changed? It wasn't the letter, because you know I wrote that.'

'Maybe I just grew up,' Ollie says softly, his sadness tangible. I pull him in for a hug. He may not want to tell me what's wrong, but I need him to know that I'm here. He only pulls away when we hear something further down the path. A familiar crackle. A crackle that should be accompanied by blue light. It is the sound of my mirror opening, ready to transport me into Annwn. It is the crackle of a portal. A portal, or a rip.

Chapter 35

We move cautiously down the track, my hand instinctively going to my hip, where my scimitar would rest in Annwn. Ollie's hand is clenched, as though gripping one of his chakrams. As we round the corner, a wisp of blue light wafts past us.

'Ghosts?' Ollie whispers.

This is the place where I was almost burned alive over three years ago, in an accident engineered by my tormentor and aided by my brother. It's strange to think now that that moment marked the death of my old relationship with Ollie, and the start of something new. Something better, kindled from the embers of our enmity.

It's been so long since I gave a thought to the place that once haunted every waking and sleeping breath, that the memory crashes down on me like a confrontation. The trees rear over us.

'Is it me, or is it darker in here than it should be?' I say.

'Don't be silly, it's just the trees blocking the sun,' Ollie says, hesitantly.

I know I'm right – there is a difference between the dark of shadows and the dark of night, and this is definitely the latter. This is no ordinary rip.

'Careful of sluaghs,' Ollie warns. The grey nothingness where Medraut's hybrids live flanks any rip between the worlds.

Faint inspyre plays along the edges of the trees and leaves and along the dry brush floor. Ollie and I step closer to peer through into Annwn. A wild boar roves through the thickets there. I feel the tell-tale pull of my Immral moving through me in Ithr the way it does in Annwn. Inspyre tickles my arm, the hairs there standing on end in response. There's another pull in the back of my head, and a flurry of inspyre leaps from my arms to a nearby tree. Outlined there, faint as a ghost, is myself, tied to the trunk with a dozen ropes and belts.

'Stop it,' Ollie says, a plea rather than a command.

'I don't know how,' I reply. The sight of myself tied up like this throws me. The strong, resilient Fern I've constructed is back to being the terrified victim I was that night. Luckily my brain doesn't construct Jenny and her friends, or I don't know how I would react.

'How is this happening?' Ollie says. 'This is Ithr. It shouldn't be able to . . .'

Then there's another tug at the back of my skull, and inspyre leaps from my hands to the tree in a burst of blue flame. The ghost-Fern screams silently, tugging at her bonds, and once again my hand inches towards my belt where my scimitar should be. The blue flame ripples up the tree trunk, ripples up ghost-Fern. There's another kick in my head, like a signal, then the blue flame morphs from dream to reality, and it is no longer blue. It is white, golden, red. It is real.

The fire takes hold of the copse alarmingly quickly, racing into the branches and leaves overhead. Soon the ground is covered in smoke, and Ollie and I are choking. We pull each other back the way we came, searching for light as we cover our eyes and mouths. The ground is littered with sticks and fallen branches, every one a trip hazard, especially when we can't see clearly and our minds are full of panic and confusion. Eventually, we make our way into the open air, gasping for breath.

'We've got to call the fire brigade,' Ollie says, reaching for his phone.

'Wait,' I say, 'let's get far away first.'

I don't answer him when he asks why, only pull him to the other side of the Flats, running as fast as I can, hoping that no one will spot us given it's broad daylight.

'That fire could spread,' Ollie says as we finally come to a halt. 'What are you thinking?'

'I'm thinking that we don't want to be seen near there,' I reply, 'otherwise the police will think we started it.'

'They wouldn't . . .' Ollie peters out. With our history with that place, and the way I look, and Ollie's known association with Shout Louder, there's no way that police in thrall to Medraut wouldn't try to pin the fire on us. And, in a way, they'd be right to – it was my imagination that made it, wasn't it? Ollie fumbles to call in an anonymous tip-off, but even before he's finished, we can hear the sirens approaching. Someone else must have spotted it. Plumes of smoke rise into the sky, to be seen from miles around.

Afterwards, holed up in my bedroom, Ollie and I talk about what this means. 'I've never heard of inspyre doing that in Ithr before, have you?' Ollie says for the fiftieth time.

'It's Medraut,' I repeat. 'All the experiments he's doing, all the rips he's making – it's mixing up the physics of the worlds.'

'Do you think he meant that to happen?' Ollie says.

I shrug. How could either of us truly fathom Medraut's plans? 'One thing's for sure,' I say, 'I'm not going to underestimate him this time. We've got to assume that he'll find a way to use it to his advantage.'

That night, Lord Allenby agrees with me when we tell him what happened. My actions with Charlie and Bandile may not have been forgotten – I can tell that from the wary glances shot my way – but they have been set aside, for now, in the face of this new information.

'We need to keep an eye on the papers,' Lord Allenby says during one of our castle-wide meetings. 'They might give us a hint about what Medraut is planning. We've been so focused on how he's using Annwn that we took our eyes off Ithr. We've forgotten that the two were always connected.'

'We'll see if Arthur ever did anything like this,' Easa says, and Frankie nods in agreement.

'In the meantime, everyone back to your business, please,' Lord Allenby says, 'and keep a closer eye on those rips.'

As everyone files out, Lord Allenby beckons to me. 'About last night, Fern,' he begins.

'I know, sir,' I say. 'I was wondering if I could take a few days away from those snake things to talk to Jin, if you can spare her?'

Lord Allenby catches my drift. 'Yes. Yes, I think that would be a good idea.'

I meet Jin in one of the treatment rooms that pepper the

apothecary wing. Most hospitals in Ithr are more about healing physical ailments, but in Annwn the bulk of the apothecaries' work is focused on the emotional and mental. I often wonder if we have it the wrong way round in Ithr. How many of mine and Ollie's issues could have been solved years ago by a regular appointment with someone like Jin?

Jin points me at a cosy armchair and produces her notebook and a pen. Despite this being my idea, the sight of the notepad raises my defences. Jin sees me closing up, understands, and puts her notepad and pen to one side – a peace offering.

'Let's try to make this a nicer process than the last time we were here, shall we?' She smiles.

'Well, we weren't friends back then.'

'I'm not your friend now,' Jin says, then seeing my expression, leans in. 'I mean, not in this room, Fern. Not while we're doing this, okay? You can be way more honest with me in here than you can be with your friends and family, understand?'

I had never thought of it like that before: the only people I've ever opened up to are friends, or my brother and dead mother. But I've always held something back. There's always part of me wondering what they're thinking about me, trying to angle my thoughts in a way that's going to get the desired judgement. But Jin has already thought the worst of me. There's no reason to not be totally honest with her. The real question is: do I have it in me, after seventeen years of bottling things up? I dive in at the deep end.

'I'm scared I'm going to turn into him.'

'Medraut?'

I nod.

Jin smiles, looks down at her lap. 'So was I,' she admits, 'but then I got to know you.'

'You saw what I did last night, though? To Bandile and Charlie?'

'I saw. I also know something you don't, Fern.' There's the arrogance again, but I don't hold it against her. Jin leans forward. 'You know how much research I've done into Immral. I can categorically tell you that using your Immral the way you have, to rebuild Tintagel? It's not normal. It's not a natural part of your power. That comes from *you*, not your Immral.'

'It's not as simple as that, though, is it?' I say. 'It's not like, "Oh, make a painting, do something creative and you won't turn into an evil dictator."'

'Of course it's not that simple. It's never simple. But I'm telling you, Fern – it's so rare, what you do.' She pauses. 'It gives me hope.'

'Don't put it all on me again,' I warn. 'We've still got the Grail.'

Momentarily, Jin looks as though she's been caught in headlights. I get a fleeting sense of sadness and compassion, like lavender at the end of a summer day. 'No,' she says at last, 'I don't think we do.'

'What do you mean?'

Jin sighs, and opens one of her desk drawers. She produces a copper box, and opens it. Inside, on a bed of velvet, lies a sword hilt. It is plain, but heavy. The blade is missing.

'This was once Lancelot's sword,' Jin explains. I pick it up, and am immediately assaulted by emotions. Sadness, guilt, anger and, strangest of all, a kind of joyful agony. There are memories mixed up in the hilt, so faint I can barely decipher them.

'Edinburgh's thaneship found this in an abandoned room in their castle. It was with an account of the Grail quest.' Jin is watching me closely as I rifle through the blurry memories.

'What did it say?' I ask. None of the images come into focus, but a feeling grows inside me. A sense of long treks, of patience, of steady sacrifice.

'That the Grail quest didn't take a long time because it was hard,' Jin says. 'It took a long time because it *had* to. Whoever undertakes the quest needs to offer themselves up to it, and prove over a long time that they're worthy.'

I begin to understand the feeling that the hilt is giving me now. Mum copied the idea of tasks from the Grail quest to earn Excalibur, but she did so crudely. For her, it was cut and dry: you passed or you failed. Now, deciphering the sensation of Lancelot's lengthy acceptance and devotion, I understand that the true nature of Annwn's quests are far subtler. If we wanted to find the Grail before Medraut destroys Annwn completely, we should have volunteered months, maybe even years, ago.

'So we've missed our chance to get the Grail anytime soon?' I ask Jin.

'Maybe. Yes, I think so.'

I reach one last time for a clear image – a solid link from me to Lancelot, who lived and died so long ago. As if in answer to my call, one comes to the fore. It is Stonehenge, in Annwn – the circle made of bones under a bright, sunless sky. Except the ground I stand on is bare earth, stripped of grass and root. The henge creaks and groans, as though pleading for its existence. Pieces of bone flake away and dissolve before they hit the ground.

We're almost out of time, a voice intones. *When the henge is gone, there is no coming back*.

And with those words, and what Jin told me, the weight that had landed so heavily on Ollie's shoulders falls squarely on mine. If I can't defeat Medraut before Stonehenge crumbles, then there is no backup, and Stonehenge *was* crumbling when I was last there a few weeks ago. That means there's no time to undertake the Grail quest. I am Annwn's last hope.

Chapter 36

The next morning, I find Dad making pancakes downstairs. He looks so tired – he's been taking on more night shifts lately, so that he can be with Clemmie during the hospital's visiting hours. He spends nearly as much time there as he does at Mum's grave, to the point where I wonder if he loved Clemmie more than I'd given him credit for.

I think about what I learned last night. I hadn't realised how badly I'd been clinging on to the Grail as our get-out-of-jail card – it didn't matter if we got Medraut or not – we'd just find the Grail and *boom*, Annwn restored. Having that possibility snatched away and the responsibility for defeating Medraut falling to me again, makes me feel unbelievably lonely.

'I've decided,' Dad says, 'that I'm going to take you to school now.'

'What?'

'I don't want you going across town on your own.'

He flips a pancake sharply, as though he's been gearing up for the argument he knows I'm about to start.

'I'm not a kid.'

'I know that.' He smiles. 'But I am your dad. I don't mind

walking six feet behind you if that'll make you feel better about it. But I don't want you travelling far on your own any more.'

'You don't have time.'

'Yes, I do.'

I'm not sure how to react. As a seventeen-year-old, I probably should be outraged. That's definitely how I'm going to have to spin it if anyone outside my family finds out that my father's being my bodyguard. But I'm not safe outside the house. Hasn't what happened to Clemmie proven that? Having Dad nearby to step in if I run into trouble is a comfort.

'Ten feet behind me,' I tell him. 'Or I'm disowning you.'

I take my art supplies out to Wanstead Flats to paint in a secluded area. The fire brigade weren't quite quick enough to save the trees in that copse. They stand, like broken sailing masts, lightning-struck and leery, black against the cold spring sky. They sum up my mood: dark, scratchy, violent. I slash my paper with charcoal, burning my imagination into a legacy. I fill the notebook with the same kind of drawings, until I've spent my anger. And then I go home, exhausted, an empty shell. There is no Grail. It's all on me.

I can't be angry tonight in Annwn; I have to be focused on the task at hand.

Tintagel is abuzz with reeves theorising and harkers hunting. Charlie is nowhere to be seen, and when I ask about her, I'm told that she's back in her tower room with Loco, where she feels safe. I climb up there before patrol and pause outside the door. Her desire to be left alone radiates through the wood. I magic up a piece of paper and scrawl an apology onto it, sticking it beside the door, so that she'll see it when she does emerge.

Bandile is easier to speak to.

'It's okay.' He shrugs. 'I get you meant well. And it did make my headache better.'

'Still,' I say.

'Still. Yeah. We're good, though.'

There's something else I need to do. Something I've wanted to do for a long time. Now the urge is too great to ignore. I stop Samson, after patrol notes, before he returns to Ithr. 'Can we talk?' I ask. He must see the desperation in my eyes, because he nods and allows me to lead him to the very top of the dome, higher even than the sentinels who keep watch over London.

'I've never been this high up before,' I tell him as we climb out of a low door that leads out into the open air.

'It's really something,' he replies, placing a hand on my waist as we look out over one of the most stunning views I've ever seen. Annwn's London may be dying, but it still has the power to awe. The sky is mostly grey now – no clouds decorate it, and the moon is fading – but the remnants of the sun cast a golden glow over the city. In the distance, the Thames threads, snake-like, towards the centre of the country. I reach out a hand automatically, wanting to feel the eddies of inspyre that must move beneath the water.

'What did you want to talk about?' Samson asks.

Now we're here, I don't want to talk about how frightened I am. So I settle for a different confession.

'Did I ever tell you what you look like through the eyes of an Immral?'

He shakes his head and settles onto the side of the balustrade.

In Ithr I might have worried that he was too close to the edge, but here we can fly, so we can live dangerously.

'Inspyre flows towards you,' I say, 'like it knows you're trying to save it.'

'Well, I am a dreamer, just not in the way we use the word here.'

I smile. 'You don't understand – I've never seen anyone else who looked like that. The inspyre – it knew you were different.'

'Did the inspyre know, or was it coming to me because it could sense your feelings about me?'

That thought had never occurred to me before. I search my memories. Did I really have that much control over the inspyre that it would act on my emotions like that? I don't know why the thought makes me so uncomfortable. I cover.

'Hang on, that's a bit presumptuous of you to think I had feelings for you all that time ago.'

'Didn't you? Because I know I did.' There's a sparkle in his eyes that makes my stomach swoop. Something stirs further down inside me.

'We might be running out of time,' I say, stepping closer to him.

'We've got all the time we want,' he replies softly, tilting my chin up so that our noses are touching. I breathe in that scent I'd noticed the very first time I met him. We were on the brink of danger then too, in a cramped, grey space in Medraut's fortress. A breeze stirs the hairs on the back of my neck. In the distance, a solitary gull cries out mournfully.

'You don't know that.'

'Even if one of us dies,' Samson says, 'we'll still see each other in here.' He pulls me close, wrapping his arms around my waist, and we look out together over the vastness of Annwn as the sun sets like liquid gold. 'I'll still see you in here.' He presses a hand to my heart.

I reach up to kiss him. 'All those walls I built,' I tell him, 'they've all gone now. It makes me feel . . .' I search for the right word, but the only one that comes to mind makes me blush.

'Afraid. And powerful,' he says, and I nod. Exactly. We hold each other's gaze for what feels like an eternity, asking each other a silent question. Then I press my lips to his once more, but this time there's an urgency behind it. My love's hands slide down my back, and my own reach beneath his tunic. As we tumble to the floor, the sunset keeping watch, I set my thoughts free. I have no need of them now. I am all heart and body and senses and glory.

Chapter 37

Although my body hums with happiness in the days that follow, there is one area of my life that is lacking. I still haven't been able to apologise to Charlie. She isn't ready to talk to me for ages, either in Ithr or Annwn. I lurk – there's no other word for it – at Bosco. The first time I tried to approach her, she got up abruptly and walked away, hiding herself in a toilet. I would find it ironic, given the fact that it used to be me who hid in bathrooms while she lorded it over everyone, but there is no joy to be found in this.

Eventually, I give up and return to spending my lunch breaks in the art room, perfecting the portraits of the Fay, who I still can't restore despite all my efforts. I use different materials for each one: oils, textured and visceral, for Andraste. Watercolour for Nimue and charcoal for Merlin. And on top of them all, the gold leaf that Charlie gifted to me. I flit between them, depending on my mood, choosing whichever one is going to calm the anxiety in my belly that gnaws a little more ferociously each day. My body knows that the reckoning is coming, and it is preparing itself.

Charlie finds me there one lunchtime.

'You've nearly finished,' she says, looking over my shoulder.

'It's weird that you know them,' I reply. 'No one except my brother has ever understood my drawings.'

'Sometimes I wish I didn't understand. Maybe it would be easier to have just done what my father wanted.'

'But you would have lost yourself if you'd done that. Is that really easier?'

Charlie bites her lip, considering. I put my brush down and turn to face her. 'I'm really sorry, Charlie.'

She nods, but doesn't say anything more, and we don't mention it again. Anyway, words are pointless, aren't they? Medraut's shown that – he's full of words, words about *oneness* and *inclusion* and *a happy nation*. But what is he doing? The absolute opposite – making Ithr a place so dangerous for anyone who doesn't fit his narrow ideal that he may as well have stuck a bullseye to our foreheads.

That's the last day I go to Bosco.

When the final bell rings, I file out of school with everyone else, searching for Dad's familiar figure loitering on the pavement opposite. It's become our ritual: I give him a small wave and we walk, as though we're strangers just happening to be going in the same direction, until we get on the tube and drop the pretence. But today, I only get a message from him.

I'm going to be late, love – had a bastard of a customer at the hotel. Wait at school for me. Be there as soon as I can.

I calculate how long he'll take – I'll be waiting for an hour at least, knowing London's public transport. I'm just wondering whether I should run along the road to pick up a drink from the corner shop, when I realise that I'm being followed. A little group of students, moving like a pack, hang back so I don't notice them at first. But my senses tingle. Maybe it's a residual effect of my Immral in Ithr, or maybe when you're used to being bullied you can tell when you're being hunted. You sense eyes lingering on you; you hear the tone of whispers.

There's no way I can wait for Dad. I make a decision to run for the train, hoping that I'll be able to throw them off in the maze of Underground tunnels and escalators. I begin walking, trying to look casual even though my heart is clamouring. I bide my time until I get through the ticket barrier, then dash past commuters, pushing them out of the way as they wind dully across my path. A shout goes up behind me: their prey is getting away. I half slide down one escalator, not even bothering to apologise to those I'm pushing past and squeezing in between. As I reach the bottom, I glance back – half of my classmates are following by escalator, half are tripping down the stairs that run parallel. They're gaining fast, helped by the fact that everyone else is getting out of their way.

I run onwards, praying that there isn't a wait for the next train. The timing in TV shows and movies is always perfect – I'm not going to be so lucky. The crowds will close in, like the rising tide in a cave, and I will drown with a stifled scream. Just as I start to wonder whether I should try to turn back, I pass a shimmer in the tunnel. A wisp of inspyre wafts out from what must be a rip between the worlds. I could use this to my advantage, especially if the rip is wide enough to change the physics of Ithr, as it did on the Flats a few weeks ago.

A train pulls in at the platform beyond. It's packed, and there's an even bigger throng of people waiting to board. I pull at the back of my mind, as I would do in Annwn, and after a moment I feel the tell-tale tug of my Immral.

Move, I command the people ahead. The power is sluggish, maybe because it's working second-hand, as it were, but one more try and the mob parts to let me through.

Get off, I order a man wearing a large backpack who is blocking the carriage. He steps off, looking confusedly at the tube sign. I barrel on board and call to the train driver, trying to tell them to close the doors, but they must be too far away for my Immral to reach.

'There she is!' my pursuers shout, vaulting the other tube-goers with a gymkhana agility to rival Lamb. The train idles.

Block them, I tell those still on the platform. Some people move in front of my bullies, but not enough. Perhaps Medraut's influence is upon them, or perhaps the rip that granted me access to my Immral is already closing.

The buzzer goes to warn us that the train doors are about to close. I might just make it. But as the doors slide shut, one of the students manages to wedge his hands in between and pulls them open.

'You're not getting away,' he hisses through the open door. That seems to work as a siren call to the people around me. They look at me as though they've just noticed the burn scar underneath my make-up, my unusually coloured eyes. Medraut's violet irises are to be admired, but on me they're another cause for suspicion. Some try to help the boy open the door. I have to do something.

I feel anger flood through me, and heat, and that pull at the back of my head. I surge forward. 'Leave. Me. *Alone,*' I say, my voice deeper than usual. My words stab outwards. The boy lets go immediately, and the doors slam shut. The people around me edge backwards.

Just as the man outside with the backpack shouts, 'Hang on, this isn't my stop!', Victoria von Gellert, Charlie's one-time bestie, slams today's newspaper against the glass door. It slides away as the train moves forward, but not before I've read the headline.

Unusuals to be sent to treatment facilities.

'I can't believe it,' Dad says, over and over again, as the TV spreads the word. When I had explained what happened, his anger at getting to Bosco to find me gone dissipated immediately.

The newsreader looks joyous as she narrates. 'In his first major policy shift since taking power, Prime Minister Sebastien Medraut has today advanced a motion through Parliament to remove certain citizens to treatment centres.'

Then Medraut himself appears onscreen, his gaze magnetic. He speaks directly to the camera.

'This isn't about division,' he says, 'this is about the safety of our country. The Christmas protests have shown us that not everyone is as committed to unity as they should be. By removing certain segments of society to safe, purpose-built havens, we will ensure that they cannot contaminate others, and get them the help they so desperately need. This is a policy of compassion.'

As Dad and Ollie rage, I watch with curiosity. Maybe it's a by-product of my own Immral, or a nearby rip, or both, but

I swear I can feel Medraut's power focusing on the camera, and those watching him.

'What are you planning?' I whisper at him.

'Fern can't go back to Bosco,' Ollie says. 'She can't, Dad.'

'You can both stay at home from now on,' Dad says.

'I don't want to hide away,' I say.

'We'll go out together, as a group.' Dad doesn't say, *Where I can protect you*, but it echoes silently around the room. And he does protect us, although it's not because he's older or stronger than us. It's because of Clemmie. Rumours swirl through our community, forgetting that Dad and Clemmie broke up. They believe the propaganda that it was protesters who attacked her, and it makes them sympathetic to her and, by association, us. The lying doesn't sit well with me, but for once I choose cowardice. People are openly attacking anyone who seems different. Crystal Moore's house is regularly graffitied and its windows broken. If I can use Clemmie to stay safe, I will do, and I won't feel guilty about it.

I don't tell anyone in Annwn what has happened apart from Charlie, explaining why she won't be seeing me in Bosco from now on.

'I could talk to them?' she offers. 'Would that help?'

'No offence, but I don't think your friendship is as much of a shield as it used to be.'

She nods and buries her face in Loco's fur.

'I'd much rather have it that way, though,' I add quickly. 'It's no big deal for me to stay at home.'

Although no one says so outright, rumours flow through Tintagel about similar measures taken by the families and friends of the thanes. There is one person who is in danger without anyone else realising, though: Lord Allenby.

'You could come and stay with us, sir,' I tell him. 'Or we could try to get you a bedsit?' I think of my meagre savings – barely enough for a week's protection. But I can't bear the thought that he could be in such danger. The canal is a thoroughfare, and who knows what thugs might pass him and decide to grant Medraut's wishes.

'I can take care of myself, Fern,' Lord Allenby says, smiling.

'But –'

'No more, please. You think about you and yours, and I'll think about me. Annwn first, though.'

Chapter 38

Our patrols are becoming more and more soul-destroying. There are no nightmares any more, only Medraut's dreamers and the dreamers they're attacking. The rips between Annwn and Ithr are becoming more common; some of them stretching widely and growing every day. The Birmingham thaneship report one that stretches across the city from east to west, like some kind of Berlin Wall. With the rips, comes the threat of the sluaghs, who lurk in the space between the worlds.

Lord Allenby puts pressure on the thanes who work in the media to cover up the rips. It's one point where our goals and Medraut's align – no one wants the public to understand what's happening. Or not yet, anyway.

'Would it be so bad to tell the truth?' I ask one night at a Tintagel-wide meeting.

'I agree,' Niamh says. 'Isn't it time that people know what they're facing?'

I stifle a smile. As if she needed permission to tell people.

'It's policy not to,' Lord Allenby counters. 'The heads of the thaneships discuss it regularly, and the decision has been taken to keep it secret, as it has been for hundreds of years.'

'What do you think?' I ask Samson afterwards as we sit in the grounds, nestled in each other's arms.

'I think people will believe what they want to believe,' he replies.

'So even if we told them, some of them wouldn't be having it?'

'And some of them would believe it and turn it into something it isn't. Conspiracy theories. More arguments. I don't think there's a win there for us.'

Nevertheless, the news does start to seep out, even if it isn't the truth. Other countries contact us about their own rips, and some of them make the news. One headline reads, *Ghosts Spotted at the Eiffel Tower*. Countries further afield, who have their own forms of the thanes, ask us to do more, as if we're not already at our limit. 'We can't keep on top of it,' I overhear one of them tell Lord Allenby. 'Medraut's ideas are spreading.'

I can't help but feel guilty – if we'd killed Medraut long before now, maybe his ideas wouldn't be infecting other countries as well as our own.

'Maybe that's not how it works,' Easa says, when I raise this. 'Maybe the ideas were always going to happen and Medraut's just harnessing them for his own purposes. Maybe they didn't start with him at all, but with the rest of the people.'

I don't like that idea. A few years ago I would have accepted it, relished it even – that most people are inherently bigoted. Now, though, I need people to have the potential to be saved, to be good. Otherwise, what will it all have been for? Are they worth the sacrifices we have, and will, make for them?

We might be largely confined to the castle these days, but that doesn't mean we're being idle. The knights spend their time training and theorising, working alongside the reeves and harkers to formulate different plans.

'I want to find a way to use these rips against Medraut,' Lord Allenby tells the assembled thanes and the other lords and ladies. 'There has to be a way. We have to work together to figure it out.'

The atmosphere in the castle is feverish. We all know that we're nearly out of time. Not a night goes by without a thane disappearing, either because they've been snatched by Medraut's sluaghs, or because they've been taken to a 'treatment centre' in Ithr. It tells us everything we need to know about what goes on in those places that when you're inside, you can't dream. And in the back of my head, I can hear the dying groans of a crumbling Stonehenge, far away but somehow ingrained in my Immral-soaked bones.

I spend most of my time performing experiments. We practise opening rips in specific places using my Immral, Maisie and Rachel's work on the Round Table, and Charlie's scientific imagination. Then we go down into the dungeons, where Ellen's snakes are still imprisoned, perfecting our newfound method of protecting ourselves against them.

'It's like a game of Tetris,' Bandile says, wiping his forehead of sweat after one of our sessions. 'I don't hurt nearly as much when I'm with Niamh and Natasha.'

'Dream team,' Niamh says.

He's right, I realise, and Charlie and I share a significant glance. If we can work out the most effective groups, maybe we can start to make a real difference against the sluaghs. She pulls a chewed notebook from Loco's mouth.

'Who wants to go first?' I ask the group.

'Find my match,' Ollie says, grinning. I know exactly who Ollie needs.

'Easa,' I say, beckoning the reeve over. Easa steps forward uneasily, while Ollie glares at me. They stand as far apart from each other as they can in the cramped space down here.

'You know what to do,' I tell them. Reluctantly Easa holds out his hand, and just as hesitantly, Ollie takes it.

'Now think about what you want the most,' I say softly, reaching out to them with one hand, trying not to delve into their minds but allowing them to channel whatever they want to share through me. Still, the onslaught of emotions is almost overpowering. There is hurt and anger from Easa, and fear and guilt from Ollie. But beyond all of that there is mutual longing. A deep desire to see Ollie smile from my friend; wonder at Easa's steady love from my brother. I don't need to combine it in my mind. Those two needs, so aligned already, swirl together of their own accord and burst forth from my outstretched hand, making the sluaghs cringe and shrink.

'Well,' Charlie says breathlessly, 'you two seem like a good pair.'

Ollie and Easa glance at each other, silent, still unsure, but they don't let go of each other's hands.

Within a few days, we have the perfect groups to tackle the sluaghs. Some of them are better in pairs, some of them in threes or fours, but each team is like a finely honed recipe.

'Well done, you two,' Lord Allenby says, as we complete the group that he's in – a pair with Charlie.

'Yours is by far the strongest, sir,' I tell him. 'You two make an excellent team.'

'Not bad for an old man.' Charlie grins at him, and I feel that same stab of jealous-happiness for them.

'Now this is in place, it might be the final piece of the plan we've been forming upstairs,' Lord Allenby says.

We gather in the usual meeting room, Lord Allenby directing me and Charlie to a front pew. Samson and Ollie join us there not long afterwards.

'Having fun in the archives?' I ask, leaning over to kiss Samson.

He grins at me. 'I really should've been a reeve, shouldn't I?'

'I think the fighting-intellectual combination is pretty sexy, to be honest,' I reply.

Lord Allenby clears his throat before Samson can answer. Instead, he pulls me towards him. I rest there, relishing the warmth of his chest against my back.

'We've been wanting to find out what Medraut has planned for some time,' Lord Allenby begins, 'and we think we now have a way to do it.'

Lord Allenby nods to Rachel, who twists her notes in shaking hands. 'We think we can open a rip in Downing Street.'

Murmurs fill the room. Downing Street is the private residence of the prime minister and his closest household. Charlie looks stunned.

'Where?' she asks.

'Not to be weird or anything, but your bedroom,' Rachel replies.

'We think we can use this rip to sneak into Ithr and work out what Medraut has planned. It would be dangerous, obviously. We would be ghosts, and ghosts can't last long in Ithr, but with Fern holding us together, we might stand a chance.'

I nod. It is risky, there's no doubt about that, but we're in as good a shape as we're ever going to be.

'What's the plan?' Niamh asks.

'Tomorrow night,' Lord Allenby says, to general consternation.

'That's not –'

'We're not ready –'

'Enough!' Lord Allenby says. 'I know it's short notice, but Medraut is moving quickly now. You all know what he's doing in Ithr.'

Silence descends. The absence of so many thanes hangs over us. The creaking of Stonehenge echoes in my mind. Lord Allenby is right. We're at the endgame. Medraut's next move will be checkmate, and we've no idea what it will be. We need to do this now.

'How do we stop him from finding the rip?' Easa asks.

'If Charlie locks her bedroom door, we can open the rip inside her room,' Rachel says. 'Unless that would raise suspicion, Charlie?'

Charlie chews her lip. 'Usually I'm not allowed, but I'll think of something.'

'Are you sure?' Lord Allenby asks.

Charlie nods. 'I want to help.'

A lull falls over the room as everyone takes this in. We spend the rest of the night planning, and by morning we're as ready as we'll ever be.

Chapter 39

The next night, we gather in Lord Allenby's office to go over our final plans. Easa has set up a map of Downing Street, which Charlie's been helping to refine, and which now lies on Lord Allenby's desk. Rachel hovers nearby, working out calculations for the rip we're going to open in Charlie's bedroom.

Charlie is more animated than I've ever seen her. 'When I was in my bedroom this morning it was like I could feel Annwn, just out of reach. It made me feel happy, which isn't normal when I'm at home.'

'She's definitely one of us,' Samson jokes. 'You know when you prefer dreamland to reality that you're a true thane.'

Charlie blushes.

'So, Fern,' Easa says, bringing us all back to the matter at hand, 'you're going to wait at the portal's entrance and focus on keeping our roving team intact while they look for information.'

The team in question – Samson, Ollie and Natasha – nod grimly.

'Yep, I'd quite like all my limbs, please,' Natasha says.

Easa continues, 'Lord Allenby, you, sir, and Charlie are going to stay on the Annwn side with Fern, in case the sluaghs find the rip. I'm going to need you to concentrate on that and let Maisie, Rachel and myself coordinate everything else from here, okay?'

Lord Allenby nods.

Maisie takes over, her hand sliding along the map, from inside Downing Street to the street outside it. 'Meanwhile, Niamh and Bandile, our fastest knights, are going to run some misdirection. The aim is to be seen trying to get into Downing Street if we think there's a risk of those inside being discovered, but not be too obvious about it. As soon as you think you've been spotted, get out of there. No heroics.'

'Spoil my fun, why don't you?' Niamh grumbles.

'Hey,' Natasha says, pointing at her, 'I don't want to get what we need just to discover my bestie's gone and got herself killed, okay?'

'We don't want anyone to get themselves killed,' Lord Allenby says. 'This is an undercover operation, not an attack. Ideally, no one will end up –'

'Let's not finish that sentence, please, sir,' Easa says.

Everyone sniggers, a hysterical, nervous laughter. Rachel casts an eye at the sun outside, on its first setting of the night. 'It's time, everyone,' she says, eyes wide but determined.

We say goodbye to Niamh and Bandile, who go to the stables to ride out the long way to Westminster. Then the rest of us line up outside the back door in Lord Allenby's office. He selects a doorknob and fits it, twisting it into place with a satisfying click. He opens it onto an underground passageway that leads far beyond the siege of Tintagel. It will throw us up near Waterloo, and from there it's a quick walk across the river to Downing Street. No one speaks on the way through the tunnels, except to mutter check-ins to the harkers back in the castle and to point out which way we're supposed to go. Charlie's breathing is loud. At one point we stop for a moment, and hear distant tapping in the tunnel behind us.

'What is that?' Ollie says. Images of sluaghs and treitres rear up in my claustrophobic imagination.

'Against the walls,' Lord Allenby growls. We press ourselves to either side, waiting for whatever is following us to show itself. I reach out with my Immral, trying to read beyond the dense inspyre that makes up the tunnel walls.

Tap tap, it goes, *tap tap tap.*

Then it rounds the corner. It's smaller than I was expecting, that's for sure.

'Loco!' Charlie hisses. 'What are you doing?'

Loco wags, oblivious to the fear he just inspired.

'Go back, silly thing,' she says. 'It's not safe.'

But no matter what Charlie says or does, Loco refuses to leave her.

'We're running out of time,' Ollie says impatiently.

'He'll have to come with us,' Lord Allenby says. 'You'll be quiet and stick with your mum, won't you, boy?'

Loco wags his tail agreeably.

So we continue, oddly happy to have the dog with us, despite the increased risk. At least Loco seems to understand the importance of staying quiet. He does no more than pant gently as we move as quickly as possible through the tunnel. Before we come up in Waterloo, we remove our thane tunics and all but a few of us stow away our helmets. Hopefully the simple jumpers and trousers we wear beneath our tunics will be enough not to draw dreamers' attention to us. I project my own Immral over us as well, to form a shield. Nevertheless, we stick close to the walls and move as inconspicuously as we can.

At last, Downing Street comes into view. It's a narrow road, set behind heavily guarded gates that are black and stern, like the slash of a lion's claws. On the other side of the gates, two terraces of tall, porticoed, white stone houses face each other, looming over whoever dares to walk between them. The many windows glint in the light of the rising sun.

The prime minister's house is part way down the street. We know which one it is by the violet sparks that ripple across its facade. Medraut has made it his own. At the front of the building, a smattering of dreamers holding cameras will be gathered. But we're not going in the front. We slip around the back of the street instead. Charlie points to a specific part of the outside wall, and as one we leap up onto the stone, clinging to the vertical surface. I send my Immral into the bricks, and pull a handful away, floating them down to the ground. One by one, we slip through the hole I've created, landing in Charlie's bedroom. On the Annwn side, it is covered in posters. Photos litter the walls and floor: photos of Charlie with Loco, with her mother – a sad, pale woman who I can tell lost any voice she had many decades ago – and with her friends.

Everyone is very quiet.

'In position?' Lord Allenby says into his helmet.

'Yes,' Niamh says.

'You might want to make Loco less conspicuous,' Ben relays.

Of course – a dog hanging outside might seem like nothing to some people, but if Medraut spotted him, he'd know that something was up. I peer out of the makeshift window in the wall. Loco is sitting obediently on the ground below. I reach down to him with my Immral and lift him into the air, sending him a mental command to stay quiet. As soon as he lands in the room he licks me in high excitement. Immediately, the atmosphere lifts. If nothing else, he's good for morale.

'We're activating the rip on the Round Table now,' Maisie says. 'Fern, we could use your help.'

A shimmer appears in the air before me, and I press my hands against it, boosting it with my Immral. Despite all my practising, I still can't get used to the way the inspyre inside me shrinks back, as though cringing away from the violence I'm inflicting on Annwn. I have to try not to gag, as my nausea peaks and the fabrics between the worlds tear apart.

I peel back the rip, revealing a bedroom very different from the one we're standing in. Charlie's room in Ithr is sparse; bare except for a handful of trinkets. She has pushed her desk chair against the door, wedging the back underneath the handle. It wouldn't stop a determined Medraut, but it would give us time to retreat.

'Okay, we're ready,' Ollie says.

'Let's do it,' Natasha agrees.

Samson kisses me quickly on the lips. 'Stay alive,' I tell him.

'Yes, ma'am.' He smiles, and with one smooth movement, he leaps through the rip, and the three of them pass to a different world.

I hover in the doorway, just out of sight, holding the shadowy forms of Samson, Ollie and Natasha in my head. In Annwn, they are clear to me as a blueprint: every crease of skin, every finger and eyelash outlined in a sharp line of inspyre. In Ithr they are fuzzier. The inspyre keeps fading away, and it would take part of them with it were it not for me. The further away they get, the harder it becomes.

Lord Allenby and Charlie stand at my back, steady and humming with imagination, keeping watch for any sluaghs who might ambush us. I can feel the constancy of their minds, always working, always fighting, like props against the quivering of my own.

Samson relays information back to us and the harkers in Tintagel through his helmet. His voice is staticky, but at least the helmets work when he's a ghost in Ithr – our tests had told us that they should, but we'd been prepared for them to cut out entirely on the night. I feel Natasha and Ollie split from Samson to go downstairs. It is deep into the night now and the members of the household should all be asleep. Ghosts do not make noise, but with the physics of the two worlds beginning to merge, they are able to move real objects, like poltergeists, and real objects *can* make noise. They have to be careful.

'I'm in the office,' Natasha whispers. 'The drawers are locked, like Charlie said.'

I reach downstairs and, with a great effort, use my Immral to force each one open. A little glimmer of triumph runs through me. If Medraut had anticipated this side-effect of the rips, I doubt he thought we'd be able to use it against him. Maybe he knew Ollie's Immral wasn't strong enough, and couldn't conceive of Ollie giving up his power to replenish mine.

'I need all of you here,' Natasha whispers. In my mind, I see Ollie and Samson hurrying downstairs to join her.

Natasha and Ollie franticly flick through printed documents, while Samson goes to the desktop and switches it on. I can feel his silent prayer that there's no start-up noise. This is another point where Medraut's own weaknesses work against him – he despises noise, so the computer starts only with a series of gentle clicks.

I send my Immral down into the wiring, translating the binaries I find in there and withdrawing the password from the depths of the technology.

'I love you, Fern,' Samson breathes. My heart thuds with painful joy. That's the first time he's ever outright said that. He couldn't have waited until we were alone and safe? I open my mouth to reply, but then there's movement from somewhere on this floor. The three downstairs hear it too, and freeze.

After an agonising few seconds, the sound stops.

'Hurry,' Rachel whispers over our helmets. 'Just flick through the papers and the computer and we'll record it to look at later.'

'There's a lot of paper,' Ollie says. 'Haven't these guys heard of saving trees?'

For the first time since regaining my Immral, I can feel a headache coming on. Trying to keep my friends and brother whole as ghosts is using much more energy than I'm used to. My skin feels as though it's on fire – as if with every passing moment I am scraping off part of myself to renew their bodies.

'Nearly done,' Natasha says.

I can see her form, dimly outlined, in the office. Then there's another sound – this time from downstairs. I can't see shapes that aren't ghosts, so I'm in the dark as to who – or what – it could be.

'Guard,' Ollie hisses from the door of the office.

The three melt back into the shadows. If they're spotted, any guard not versed in the rules of Annwn might not understand what they were seeing, but three glowing shapes would definitely be enough for them to raise an alarm.

'Niamh, Bandile,' Lord Allenby says quietly. 'Go.'

I reach down with my Immral, wishing there was more I could do, but if I step out into Ithr it will become ten times more difficult for me to keep them alive. I feel their fear, their suspended breaths, as the guard moves closer and closer to the office door. A strange sensation tingles through me as I try to keep my loved ones safe, like threads reaching back across Annwn in one direction and out into Ithr in the other.

Suddenly, I am inside my brother's head. Perhaps it's a trick of the Immral, or maybe it's our twin connection, but I feel his heart thudding as the footsteps approach the office door. There's a pause – the guard is reaching for the doorknob . . .

A distant shout of alarm goes up from outside the building. The guard pauses, deciding whether to continue his round or to investigate the cause of the shout. Curiosity gets the better of him. He moves away, back to the front door. Ollie breathes out, and the breath sends me back to my own body, reeling from the experience of being inside my brother's head.

'Now get out, all of you,' Rachel is whispering into the helmets. 'Now, now, now.'

Ollie and Natasha stuff the papers back into their drawers

and Samson pulls the plug to shut the computer off before plugging it back in again. I mentally re-lock the drawers as they slide up the stairs and back towards the rip.

'Niamh and Bandile are back in Annwn,' Rachel tells us.

Ollie is first up the stairs and I reach out to pull him through. Natasha is next, tumbling across the threshold. Samson is last, racing up the stairs so quickly that he trips on the final one. I gasp, loud enough that I'm sure the whole building must hear. My own hands turn ghostly as I reach through to Ithr, reach for him. He stumbles to his feet and races towards me, closer, closer . . .

Then he's through, in my arms, holding me tightly, his breath hot in my ear as we swing back out of sight of the rip and find the wall of Charlie's bedroom in Annwn, solid and safe.

'We did it,' Natasha says, her eyes bright with tears of relief.

'Let's get out of here, quickly,' Lord Allenby says, and helps Charlie, carrying Loco, back out through the hole in the wall of her bedroom. She and he leap to the ground below, followed by Ollie and Natasha. Samson stays with me as I help Maisie close the rip.

'You said something down there,' I whisper to him. 'Did you realise?'

'I've been saying it in my head for a year,' he replies. 'Thought it was as good a time as any.'

I reach up to kiss him softly. 'Right back atcha, you know?'

'I know. Come on, my love.'

He leads me to the hole and together we jump down, joining the others in the garden of Downing Street. It takes me a second to realise that everyone is frozen, and another before the wave of their terror hits me. For there, flanked by a dozen sluaghs, snakes hissing from their backs and faces, is Sebastien Medraut.

Chapter 40

Without missing a beat, I reach out to Charlie and Lord Allenby, whose hands are already joined, waiting for me to channel their hopes and ambitions and dreams into me. I reach out a hand, moulding their imagination with my own, using it to send out a pulse against the poor, Frankensteined knights. The snakes controlling them hiss and snap, but don't venture closer.

Medraut seems taller here than he is in Ithr. The last time I saw him in Annwn, he was wielding Excalibur, ostentatiously triumphant. I had thought he would be lesser without the sword, but he has only grown in power. Immral crackles around his body, every bit as deadly as the sluaghs beside him. Beneath those crackles, he is dressed in a grey suit, immaculately tailored. He is a man who knows he was born to rule.

If Medraut is taken aback by our ability to defend ourselves against the sluaghs, he doesn't show it. In fact, he ignores all of us except Charlie.

'Lottie,' he says, quietly as usual, 'I've been looking for you.'

Charlie hugs Loco closer, while the dog whines and yips at the man who killed him in Ithr.

Medraut holds out a hand to his daughter, the full force of his charisma directed wholly at her. 'Come here.'

Charlie wavers, and an old expression passes across her face: acceptance, blankness. But before I can intervene, she finds her voice. 'My name is Charlie. I'm never going to follow you again.'

'Whyever not?'

'You killed my dog!' she spits. 'You killed him and blamed it on me!'

Medraut lowers his hand. He looks at her piercingly, then his eyes flick to mine. I read the challenge there. Then he tilts his head at Charlie. 'What dog?'

She scoffs, 'What do you mean, what d–'

She peters out, her arms going lax, so that Loco topples to the ground. He lies there, confused, whining pitifully. Medraut's Immral is directed not just at Charlie, but at all of us.

What dog? What dog? What dog?

What dog indeed? I look at the others, none of whom understand what is happening. Their eyes skate over the creature at Charlie's feet. They cannot see Loco. Medraut is erasing their memories of him. Loco whines again, his tail patting the ground, a little *thud, thud, thud* . . . before it disappears. Loco is vanishing.

'Don't you dare,' I say, and press my hands against Charlie first and then Natasha on my other side. I send my thoughts into them, my own memories of Loco: by the fire in the knights' chamber; in the gardens chasing sticks. I remember what Charlie said about that story from *Peter Pan*. The death of Tinkerbell.

I do believe in fairies.

My friends resist at first. I can taste Medraut's Immral, strong and bloody as iron, bitter and dangerous as petrol, in all of them. Their minds cannot conceive of a world where Loco ever existed.

What dog? What dog? What dog? beats Medraut's mantra.

He's right here, I think, pulling the memories from deep in Charlie's subconscious. Memories of her raising him and training him, walking him along the Thames, letting him bounce all over her. I pull them from her and push them outwards like an expanding dome, sending them rippling across Annwn and out through the rips into Ithr. Dreamers across the country, across the world, suddenly find themselves licked by or throwing toys for or cuddling the silly little creature with black spots on a white fur coat.

The sound of barking echoes across the city: a dawn chorus as the sun rises on its final turn of the night. Locos everywhere. Charlie looks down and sees her dog, renewed tail wagging frantically, and blinks the fog away. Lord Allenby looks fiercely at Medraut, then smiles across at me. Charlie picks up Loco and cradles him, pressing kisses into his warm little body.

'This dog,' she says to her father, her voice strong. 'You won't kill him again.' The snakes hiss, but Lord Allenby and Charlie's combined imaginations keep them at bay.

'A portal's opened up nearby,' Maisie tells us. 'Get there and we'll see if we can close it behind you.'

But I am watching Medraut. His expression never falters, but I can feel his rage boiling. I can hear his thoughts. *The audacity; my own flesh and blood disobeying me. How dare she? HOW DARE SHE?*

I understand what's about to happen before I can stop it.

'Charlie, move!' I shout, but I'm too late. Medraut throws a clenched fist towards his own daughter, a flare of pure Immral, flavoured with hatred, firing straight towards her.

Lord Allenby launches himself in front of Charlie, folding her in his arms, as though she were a child. There's a silent *boom* as Medraut's shot hits his broad, bear-like back, and the life is blasted from him.

Everyone is shouting. Charlie is screaming, clinging to the body of the only man who ever treated her like a daughter. I cradle both of them, and I don't know whether I'm comforting or shielding or collapsing.

'We have to run!' Samson is saying. With Lord Allenby no longer alive, the defences he and Charlie created have fallen, and the sluaghs are advancing. Medraut is balling his fists, ready to take another shot at his disobedient daughter.

'We have to go,' I tell Charlie, and when she doesn't move, I say, more harshly than I should, 'Don't let him die for nothing. Come on!'

She allows me and Ollie to pull her away from Lord Allenby. Loco leaps after us as I pull Charlie into the air, narrowly avoiding another of Medraut's blasts. I push my grief into the back of my mind, focusing only on what Lord Allenby would have wanted us to do – get back to Tintagel safely. Get Charlie out of there. I follow Maisie's directions blindly. And then I see it: the portal. It takes us near enough to Waterloo that we can return to the tunnel that will take us back to Tintagel. No one speaks, the shadows underground are as deep as our grief. I grip Charlie's hand through it all. She may no longer have a father, but for this moment, for now, I will be her guide.

Then the tunnel rises and we tumble out into Lord Allenby's office. Every piece of furniture, every object, reminds me of him: the decanter; the broad, mahogany table; the books set upon shelves in the wall.

I let go of Charlie's hand as Jin and the other apothecaries descend upon us.

'I'm fine,' I say to no one in particular. 'I'm fine.'

I have to get out of here. 'I'll see you tomorrow,' I tell Samson, and rush from the room, towards the portal that will take me back to Ithr.

'Fern?' Samson shouts in a voice high and desolate. 'Fern!'

I can't be there. Samson might need me, but there's someone else who needs me more. I run through the castle, ignoring Rachel and Maisie who call after me, ignoring the huddles of thanes who cling to each other in shock as the news of Lord Allenby's death spreads like a flood, drowning the castle.

When I wake up, mirror still clutched in my hand, my cheeks are wet from tears shed while I was in Annwn. I pull clothes on and dash out into the dawn. The street is silent, pale grey, and wisps of mist drift across the park opposite. The night buses are still running, and I jump on board one before it pulls away. The other passengers stare at me, hostile, but I don't care. All my focus is on a pathway a few miles away. When we're as close as the bus is going to get, I jump off and run into the Olympic Park, making my way towards the canal and bridge where my commander lived.

He's there, bundled in a pile of old blankets and amidst plastic bags full of clothes. He's huddled over himself. From a distance I could imagine him merely asleep – just dozing.

Maybe Medraut's blast was never meant to kill, just stun. After all, he had been aiming for his daughter – surely he hadn't meant to actually murder her? Surely it was just a punishment; a warning, not a death sentence. I cling to the false hope.

I kneel beside the figure.

'Sir?' I whisper. 'Sir, please wake up?'

One of his hands, worn and calloused, lies outside the blankets. Hesitatingly, I place one of my own hands on top of it. His is cold. My throat tight, I inch my fingers up to his wrist, checking for a pulse. There is nothing. I throw my arms around his shoulders and feel the coldness of his bearded cheek against my ear. He's gone. He may have lost his own children in Ithr, but he gained hundreds more in Annwn, and we all of us are lost without him.

Chapter 41

It takes hours before the ambulance responds to my call.

'What's the point?' I hear one of the paramedics saying as they lift Lionel Allenby's body onto a stretcher and lug it to the road where their ambulance idles.

'Have a heart,' his companion says. 'The girl's cut up.' And they both look back at me, considering the riddle of the dead homeless man and the scarred teenager with violet irises.

I'm given a number to call about the funeral, and walk back home through an east London that is stretching to life. I am wrung out. It seems impossible that Tintagel will still be standing when I return to Annwn tonight. Surely it will have crumbled, stone by stone, without its commander?

Ollie is peering out of his window anxiously as I walk, numb, down the street. When he spots me he darts away and rushes out of the door, barrelling into my arms.

'I thought you'd done something stupid,' he murmurs.

'Maybe I did,' I say, and as he leads me back into the house, I tell him everything I know about Lord Allenby's life in Ithr. It's not much, I realise now – I never asked him for more details about the family he left behind because it wasn't my place to ask. But now, as I start to consider the fact that I'm the only person other than Charlie who knows where and who he is, I realise that the funeral will be my responsibility. I feel like an imposter. It shouldn't be me who has this most dreadful and privileged of positions. It should be Charlie or, even better, the wife and children who have no idea he's dead, or why he really left them so long ago. But I don't know if I'll be able to find them, and there's no way I'll be able to reach Charlie in Ithr.

'We have to make it worth something,' Ollie says fiercely as we discuss the mission to Downing Street. 'There's got to be something in those papers that says what he's got planned next.'

'We've got to give people time to grieve,' I say, then add, 'How're Samson and Charlie?'

'Samson was doing his usual strong and silent act. Charlie was hysterical after you left. She was shouting that it was all her fault. We managed to calm her down eventually, but it was difficult. She thought you blamed her.'

It's true that Lord Allenby would still be alive if Charlie hadn't been there, but what good does it do to dwell on that? To apportion blame? All of it belongs to Medraut, who was going to kill his own daughter. Any one of us would have tried to stop him. It just happened to be Lord Allenby who got there first. But that's also not quite true, is it? I spotted what Medraut was going to do before most of the others. But only Lord Allenby acted quickly enough to protect Charlie. It takes a special kind of person to make that sacrifice.

As if conjured from my mind, Dad appears in the doorway, bleary-eyed.

'What are you two doing up so early?' He sees our tear-stained faces. 'What's happened?'

Ollie and I share a look. We can't tell him the truth. 'We lost someone. A friend,' Ollie says eventually.

'Oh, darlings. Sleeping?'

I cringe at the description. *Not* sleeping. Murdered. *Killed*. But outwardly, I nod.

Dad looks puzzled. 'How did you find out so early?'

'His family texted us,' Ollie says without missing a beat.

'Already? I would have thought –'

'Drop it, Dad, okay?' I snap. 'For God's sake, why are you so obsessed with the details when we're clearly upset? Why can't you just comfort us like you're supposed to?'

Ollie grasps my arm and I stop abruptly. Dad looks chastened and busies himself in the kitchen. I stalk upstairs to freshen up. When I come down again, Dad has covered the table in all my favourite breakfast foods. If I had any kind of appetite, I'd be thrilled. I pull up a chair and stare at the spread, wondering if I can force myself to eat anything. Dad hovers over us. 'I'm not very good at any of this, but I can cook,' he says softly. 'I am sorry, Fern. I didn't know this – Lionel, was it? – but Ollie tells me he was a good person. I wish I'd met him.'

I nod silently. The thought of Lord Allenby and Dad in the same room as each other doesn't really compute. One the father I wish I had; one the father I ended up with. For the first time, I find myself wondering whether Mum ever liked Lord Allenby, ever saw him as a prospect? But then I suppose he was married at the time – it was only after Mum was pregnant with us that he left his family, too traumatised to carry on living a normal life in Ithr.

After I've forced down some food, I find myself at a loss. All I know is that I have to stay busy until I can reasonably return to Annwn. I'll need to call the morgue at some point to arrange the funeral, but they'll be closed now since it's the weekend. I consider trying to find Charlie, despite the risk, but as soon as I step out of my front door, I spot a gang on the prowl. They are all dressed in grey – Medraut's colour. I retreat before they can see me, and a few moments later a leaflet is pushed through our letterbox.

Concerned about your neighbour? A family member? A friend? If they've been behaving erratically, let us help them. The government's treatment centres are humane, comfortable residences to help troubled people become helpful members of our great nation.

I scrunch the leaflet up and throw it with force into the kitchen bin. It's clear that it isn't safe for me to venture anywhere near Downing Street. I settle for going for a walk to the same place that Ollie and I visited the day before he gave me his Immral.

'Do you want me to come with you?' Ollie asks as I pull my coat and trainers on.

I shake my head. 'Sorry, I just want to be by myself.'

He nods, but looks lost. My brother has never done well on his own. I, on the other hand, am used to it, and need a regular dose of loneliness to re-centre myself. I go the long way to Epping Forest, keen to avoid busy roads. I've had one too many incidents lately where gangs of people have tried to block my path, jeering and leering at me, making out that they're 'only joking' about marching me to a treatment centre. My route takes me all the way past Wanstead Flats, where the burned tree trunks of a few weeks ago look as broken as my heart.

My phone beeps in my pocket: a message from Samson. *U ok?*

I reply with apologies for rushing off, tell him that I found Lord Allenby's body and promise to explain everything later. Then I turn off my phone. I don't want anyone in my head and heart but me.

Niamh and Natasha's booklet, when I find it, has had more names added since I wrote down Mum's. I read each one before adding *Lionel Allenby* to the bottom. On impulse, I add a five-pointed star beside his name, to distinguish him from the others. Not that their deaths are any less worthy, but Lord Allenby is a special case: he is forgotten by everyone in Ithr, and remembered by everyone in Annwn. A lord who ran a castle, and a man without a home; a father without a family and the patriarch of a community. I need that to be acknowledged, and the star – the most basic sign of the thanes with their five lores – seems the simplest and most enigmatic way of doing that.

Back at home, Ollie is sequestered in his room, talking on the phone. Dad is nowhere to be found. I head up to my bedroom and pull out some drawing paper – a huge piece, fit for a bear. I sketch quickly, trying not to pin down the details of Lord Allenby's features beyond a few that stick out in my mind – the particular way he pressed his chin down to look at you; the way his lord's cloak always fell to the left.

I've never looked at him that way before, but now I see that he must have been rather handsome as a younger man. I wonder again whether Mum ever fancied him. He seems much more her type than Dad. And then I remember something – something I found in her diaries . . .

I flip through them until I find the one I'm looking for. It takes me a while to track it down, buried as it is about halfway through the third of five diaries.

There, written in code: *I have met the man I'm going to marry*.

She only wrote in code when it was something to do with Annwn. That means . . . but it can't have been Lord Allenby she's talking about because she says 'met', and she'd have known Lionel Allenby for two years by that point. I run down the stairs and knock on Ollie's door.

'Hang on,' I hear him say. 'What is it, Fern?'

He's lying on his duvet, eyes still red from fresh tears.

'I'm just talking to Kieran,' he tells me.

I nod. 'When you've finished, can I show you something?'

A few minutes later, Ollie comes up. 'What is it?'

I show him the diary entry. 'I think Mum might have been in love with someone else,' I tell him. 'She wrote this, and it would have been someone she met in Annwn, so . . .'

'It was Dad,' Ollie says shortly.

I falter. I had visions of Mum having a failed romance with some mysterious knight – maybe even one of the Fay, Andraste's brother, perhaps? – and using Dad as a rebound. But Ollie speaks with such certainty that maybe I was wrong.

'How do you know?'

He shifts uncomfortably. 'Do you really want to know, Fern?

I know how much you admire Mum, even if you say you don't . . .'

'Of course I want to know.'

Ollie sinks onto the bed. I cross my legs on the ground in front of him, like a child readying for storytime.

'Do you remember the last time you were going through those diaries? I picked that one up and looked at it?'

I remember that night dimly – Ollie looked disconcerted but wouldn't tell me why.

'Well,' he continues, 'when I read that line I had this . . . vision, I suppose is the best description. Of how she met him, like I was in her head. I didn't understand what was happening at the time, but now –'

'A rip,' I say. 'A rip must have opened up nearby so your Immral worked.'

'Exactly. Anyway, Mum had come across Dad in Annwn and fallen in love with him straight away.' He smiles twistily, and I can't help but smile back – that does sound like the kind of thing our impulsive, ferocious mother would do. Ollie's smile fades. 'Anyway, she decided to use his dreams to make him fall in love with her.'

'*What?*' I gasp.

'I told you you wouldn't like it. Have you never wondered why Dad's still so hung up on her all these years later? How he somehow never has a straight answer for how they met?'

'I just thought he was remembering her through rose-tinted glasses.' I think back over every conversation I've ever had with Dad about Mum. I want to tell Ollie that he's wrong, but now that he's planted the seed, everything starts to make sense. If

Mum had used Dad's imagination to get to know him before she met him in Ithr, then she'd have been able to present herself to him when they *did* meet as his perfect partner. She was quite literally the woman of his dreams.

I feel sick. All this time I've suspected Dad of not understanding Mum, of not giving her credit for being anything more than a pretty face and a loving mother and wife, when all along she was the one who *made* him that way. She got into his head, just like she got into my head and Ollie's, built the impression she wanted and dug her claws into our minds every bit as powerfully as one of Medraut's sluaghs. It's the ultimate betrayal, and its ripples are being felt decades later.

Chapter 42

2002

Una shouldn't have come into Annwn tonight. She realised it as soon as she set foot off the platform. It had only been hours since she'd got the news. She'd been making her favourite dish, a cassoulet recipe she'd charmed off a chef in Paris. Her boyfriend had been helping her simmer the beans while she made breadcrumbs rich with garlic and parsley. They'd been joking about how they wouldn't be able to kiss each other for weeks with the amount of garlic going into this dish, when her phone had rung.

'Darling?' her mother had said weakly. Una was a journalist. She understood how to read a person – their posture, the tone of their voice. So she knew instantly that something terrible had happened. But all of her bad news was confined to her time in Annwn. Her life in Ithr may as well have been charmed in comparison. What on earth could Mum tell her?

'Darling, it's your father . . .'

And she hadn't heard the rest, not really. Una wasn't the kind of person who relied on others for anything, but her father had always been her anchor. She may have left Ireland as soon as she could for the allure of London, but the bond between them had never broken. Maybe it was by virtue of her being an only child, but she was the kind of daughter who called twice a week, sometimes more, even when she had no real news to tell.

And now that thread was severed, and she hadn't even felt it happen. She had been studding an onion with cloves, laughing, working, while her father had been having a stroke, hundreds of miles and a small ocean away. She hadn't felt the cord break, had not been aware of the emptiness.

How could she not have known?

She had cried, of course, but mostly she wanted to fall asleep. It wasn't the normal way of grieving, and her boyfriend had looked at her oddly when she'd told him she was tired, but Una didn't care about appearances. She wanted to lose herself in the knights, pretend that nothing had happened. She wanted to save some people and kill some nightmares. She could think of no better tonic to stave off the despair.

But it wasn't right. Lionel and Ellen could see that as soon as she entered the knights' chamber. She refused to tell them the truth, pleading tiredness and a stressful day at work. But Ellen knew it was more than that. She took Una to one side as they made their way to the stables.

'You shouldn't be here, dearling.'

'I've got nowhere else to go.'

Ellen looked around. The others were distracted.

'I overheard Maisie talking about a rogue portal in Tavistock Square.' She looked at Una meaningfully. 'It would be a shame if someone accidentally walked through it.'

Una smiled for the first time since getting the news. 'That sounds like an adventure.'

'It does, doesn't it?'

Una looked back at Lionel and Clement. Lionel was laughing at something Clement had said. 'What will you tell them?'

'Oh, something,' Ellen said airily. 'You know I'm good at making excuses for you.'

Una hugged her friend, then she was off, springing onto her horse and urging the Arab across the drawbridge, away from Lionel's surprised shout. No doubt the harkers would tell Lord Richards that she was causing trouble again – that was Maisie's usual way, the snitch – but she didn't care. Reprisals could come later. Right now, she needed air.

Tavistock Square was only a short gallop north of Tintagel, although she had to take a detour to avoid running into Gawain's patrol. The last thing she wanted was to be questioned by knight captain Sebastien Medraut – or to have him rooting around in her head and laying bare her grief. She didn't trust him not to use it to his advantage, even if he did it subtly.

Ellen hadn't told her where to find the rogue portal, but she didn't need directions once she entered the square. It would be something circular – it always was. There: a rubbish bin placed next to one of the benches in the little community garden, was pulsing blue. That was it. She dismounted Aethon and made sure the gate to the garden was shut. Hopefully he'd only graze in the square – there was enough greenery around, after all – but he had been known to wander. She supposed it stood to reason, what with him matching with her – they had twin senses of adventure. She briefly considered seeing if he'd go through the portal with her, but no, this she would do alone. She pulled off her knights' tunic at the last minute and stuffed it under a hedge. Tonight, she didn't want to feel like a thane. She didn't want to be herself at all, so the simple blouse she wore beneath her tunic, so unlike anything she'd usually wear in Ithr, was the perfect cover of anonymity.

Still, she couldn't help a thrill of unease as she approached the portal. It could lead anywhere at all if it was rogue. Even into space, or into the midst of a war. On second thoughts, she retrieved the belt and knife from the pile beneath the hedge and clipped them around the blouse. It wouldn't do to be totally unprepared.

She peered into the bin. In Ithr it would be filled with apple cores and dog-poo bags. Here, it cupped a dull blue light; a tunnel inviting her in. She accepted the invitation, legs first.

The light swallowed her, sliding her with a tumble and twist before depositing her on a wet patch of grass on the side of a fast-flowing river. She scrambled to her feet before her bum got too wet, and looked around. She was in a dense wood of Scots pine, and the air was thick with the aftermath of thunder. It wasn't raining, but her face was already coated in cool water. There were so many croaks and chirrups from the branches around her that she could almost imagine the trees themselves were alive.

It was perfect.

At first she thought she was alone. But as she became accustomed to her surroundings, she heard something further down the river. One hand on the knife at her belt, she crept along the bank and peered between the leaves.

A man knelt by the water. He had long hair tied back in a rough bun, a trimmed beard and the hands of a craftsman. He was kneeling over a huge salmon, the blue light around it indicating that it was a dream. The man was untangling the hook from the fish's mouth, and for a moment Una thought he was going to gut it.

Movement on the other side of the river caught her attention: a huge brown bear, also a dream, appeared through the foliage. It spotted the man, then stepped daintily into the stream. The man noticed it when it was only feet away from him. The bear looked at the fish, which flapped uselessly in the man's strong hands.

Una gently moved between the branches, putting herself in a position to intervene should the bear attack.

The man, ever so slowly, lowered the fish back into the river, where it flapped, then sprang off through the water.

'Idiot,' Una whispered. The bear would now come for the man. But the man only pressed his hand to his chest and bowed. The bear bowed too. Una watched as the man clawed at his own chest, sinking his fingers inside his ribcage and tugging. Slowly, he pulled something, scarlet and pulsing, from the cavity. A piece of his heart. The man held it out to the bear, who took it with infinite care, and padded back through the water to eat its meat in private.

Una watched, open-mouthed, as this man who wouldn't sacrifice a make-believe fish, but would give part of himself to nature, collected his fishing tackle and strode back up the slope, away from the river. She followed him. She couldn't not follow him, once she had seen that. He had caught her on a hook far more powerful than any that graced a fishing rod.

The next morning, when she returned to Ithr, she broke up with her boyfriend, and wrote in her knightbook for the first time in many months.

I have met the man I'm going to marry.

Chapter 43

I'm forced to put what I've found out about Mum to the back of my mind for now, although I find myself worrying at it like a loose tooth. It provides a good distraction from the open wound still bleeding from the loss of Lord Allenby, and my fears for Charlie's safety. In Annwn, the thanes react in one of two ways: either they fall to pieces, or they up their game with stalwart stubbornness. A lot don't come back to Tintagel the next night, absconding out of fear. Charlie is one of those who doesn't appear. Medraut must have found her portal. I can't help but picture what revenge Medraut might be taking on the daughter who rebelled against him, and fret about how little I can do to help her. But also, even though I know I'm being horribly unfair, I'm angry that she isn't strong enough to run away in Ithr, or find her way back to Tintagel in Annwn. Lord Allenby deserves better, even if he'd be disappointed in me for thinking so.

There's an emergency council of the other lords, ladies and lieges along with the heads of lore in Tintagel. Ollie and I take the patrol out that night while Samson, as the knight captain, attends. When we get back, a group of thanes has gathered outside Lord Allenby's office, waiting to hear who our new leader will be. I don't join them – I go back to the knights' chamber to wait for news. A lot of our thanes are pushing for Samson to be Lord Allenby's replacement, even if it would make him the youngest Head Thane in Annwn's history. I can't work out how I'll feel if he has been chosen. Proud, obviously, but also worried – I've seen what carrying the weight of hundreds of lives did to Lord Allenby. And while Samson is not Allenby, who knows what the burden would do to the man I love. Selfishly, I wonder if I have the ability to support him through it. I'll have to, I suppose, if I want us to survive.

Survive. I smile grimly to myself. A double-edged word. Full of hope and desperation; a word that could mean a life or a relationship, and who's to say which one matters more?

A few of the other knights wait with me to hear the news, but for the most part we don't talk. In fact, I've barely spoken to anyone since arriving in Annwn: we are all hedgehogs in our grief. When Niamh makes a joke about wanting it to be someone old who takes over so she has a chance at becoming Tintagel's commander before she's forty, Natasha snaps at her for being insensitive. Those two have become so inseparable that the outburst is shocking.

'I'm sorry,' Natasha says after a moment's silence. 'I just can't . . .' She buckles.

'Oh, mate,' Niamh says, stroking Natasha's back, 'I shouldn't have joked about it. Way too soon. I'm sorry.'

I fix my gaze on the door until Samson opens it at last, looking more tired than I've ever seen him.

'It's Maisie,' he tells everyone, taking my outstretched hands. 'Maisie's the new commander.'

The reactions are mixed, but afterwards, when everyone else has gone back to Ithr, I stick with Samson. 'Are you disappointed?' I ask him.

'No,' he replies. 'I want to be commander here, don't get me wrong. But not now, and not like this.'

He looks at me properly for the first time tonight. 'I want to see you again, in Ithr, all the time. I want to make it real between us. Properly real.'

I nod, leaning into him. 'So do I. But not now.'

'When, then? We might not have much time left.'

We both smile, equally aware that Samson was the one reassuring *me* on this front just weeks ago.

'Soon. At the funeral,' I say.

Not going to school any more, and not having anyone particularly bothered about my absence, means that I have plenty of free time to arrange Lord Allenby's funeral. I begin to tell some of the other thanes that Lord Allenby was homeless in Ithr. I feel as though I'm betraying his trust, but it's more important that the people who loved him get to say goodbye. I think he'd understand. Funerals are for the living, not the dead. Ollie and I raid our savings to pay for something simple and, to his credit, Kieran adds his own savings to the pot despite never having met Lord Allenby.

'Hey, he was important to you guys. Dude deserves a decent send off,' he says, when he comes to tell us.

'You're the best friend,' Ollie says.

Kieran glances covertly at Ollie, and I suddenly understand

exactly why he's doing it. I wonder whether I should warn him that Ollie's heart is elsewhere, but then decide it's not my place. It's clear to anyone that Ollie is no longer interested in Kieran; it's up to Kieran if he wants to see that or not.

Besides, there's more important work that needs my attention.

Charlie doesn't turn up at Tintagel the next night either, but we know she's still alive because she's spotted on television with Medraut as he gives an interview outside Downing Street. To my eyes, he looks smugger than usual. Does he really think that without Lord Allenby we'll give up the fight? Well, he's wrong – if anything it's just made me more determined. Charlie hovers behind him, pale as ivory, her smile not reaching to her eyes.

'We have to find her,' Maisie says at our regular thanes meeting.

'She can't be a focus of our plans, my lady,' Easa says gently, 'we have to concentrate on –'

'We can do more than one thing,' Maisie replies. 'I'll remind you who's in charge now, thank you very much.'

Everyone shifts uncomfortably in their seats, avoiding each others' eyes. We're all worried about Charlie, but Easa's right. The best way we can help her now is to bring down her father. I can feel Maisie's insecurity and grief radiating off her. She stares around at us all, eyes hard.

'He knew that every single person was important,' she says, more quietly now. 'He died for that belief. And as long as I'm commander here, I'm going to honour him.'

And suddenly I understand something that I never had before. I understand the deep love Maisie had for Lord Allenby;

deeper than any shallow Immral can determine. Richer than pure romantic love; a love ripened over decades through mutual respect. And then to have that snatched away and the power handed to you – it must be unbearable.

Samson understands too, because he says, 'Have the harkers seen her in Annwn, though?'

'No,' Rachel replies. 'We've been looking, but we can't find her anywhere.'

'I'll help,' I say, 'and if I can't find her I'll see if I can corner her in Ithr.'

Ollie looks at me sharply and Samson shakes his head. I can hear his thoughts: *I don't like that*. I don't like the prospect much either – if I have to find her in Ithr, I'll need to make my way to Chelsea or Westminster – the last time I went there I was hunted by my own classmates. It won't be an easy journey. But maybe Maisie's right – maybe it's enough that it's what Lord Allenby would have wanted.

Maisie nods, grateful, and we move on to the more important matter at hand: the records we stole from Downing Street.

'We haven't found anything directly useful yet,' Easa tells everyone, 'but we're working on it. There are some documents and references to cameras and screens that I'd like more eyes on.' He looks over at me. 'Ideally from someone who understands Medraut.'

I nod, feeling ill. Easa assuming that I would understand Medraut better than anyone else might be true but it's uncomfortable, although I'm not sure that's entirely what's wrong. Something else is happening, although I can't put my finger on it yet.

'You can have your pick of thanes,' Maisie tells Easa. 'I'm suspending the five patrols for now. I know –' she says, holding up her hands to quell the protests – 'I know it seems like overkill but our priority *is* to bring down Medraut, and I'm not risking more than I have to out there with his dreamers on the prowl . . .'

She tapers off. My nausea peaks. And suddenly I understand. Medraut is doing something. There's a distant roaring, so low that it's almost impossible to hear. In fact, it's not something you hear, but something you *feel* in your bones.

'Everyone get out!' I say loudly, trying not to vomit.

'What's happening?' Jin says.

'Do as Fern says,' Maisie shouts, and I throw her a grateful glance for trusting me immediately. 'Get out. Back to Ithr, everyone. Now.'

The roaring is louder – we can hear it with our naked ears. It's the roar of an army. Ollie peers out of the window. 'That's impossible,' he breathes. I follow him, and my heart stops at the sight that greets me. Thousands of dreamers are scaling the walls of Tintagel and swarming into the gardens. Ollie's right – it shouldn't be possible. The power of Tintagel is such that no one who means harm to the thanes should be able to enter. And yet here they are.

'Go!' Maisie shouts. There's a stampede for the door. Easa and Frankie bundle their papers together and stuff them into a hollow panel in one of the walls. Maisie waits for everyone else to leave. She gestures to me. 'Come on, Fern.'

'I can hold them off.'

'No. Tintagel is done. The important thing is to keep enough of us alive. That's an order, knight – get out now.'

I run behind most of the other thanes. Frankie is pulling Ben away from his desk in the cloisters. 'C'mon, Grandad!' she shouts, as he protests at being taken from his job.

Maisie is the only one behind me now. She closes the door to the meeting room and walks briskly after us. She holds her hands out, brushing the walls with her fingers, as if saying goodbye to the castle she has loved and lived in for decades. I run ahead, Ollie in front of me, and out of the wide open doors of the castle. Before me is chaos. The remaining knights are fighting their way to the platform that will take us out of Annwn, huddling in groups with the lores who don't wield weapons.

I look back one more time at the innards of Tintagel. Maisie is standing, alone, next to the Round Table. She runs her hands over its cracked surface, and a waft of inspyre crackles up to meet her touch, like an old friend offering comfort. There's a bang from the other side of the castle: a shattering of glass as one of the windows in the cloisters is smashed in. Dreamers swarm through, polluting the stones with Medraut's purpose.

Maisie looks up at me sadly. 'Go.' I see her mouth, and she presses something on the Round Table. The button she once told Ben not to touch. The outer door slams shut, locking me out. I do not witness her last stand.

Chapter 44

The dreamers in the grounds outside are armed. Their weapons aren't just knives and arrows, but flames. Of course, it would be fire that Medraut sent to Tintagel, as though he's taunting me and my burn scar. The knights are scattered across the gardens, protecting pockets of the other lores as best they can, but there are too few of us and too many of them.

Inside the castle, a rumble begins. Dust eddies into the wind. The angels on the roof take flight as the central dome collapses inwards. Morrigans flit from the windows of their turret as it topples, slow motion, crashing into the cloisters below. Windows splinter. Wooden beams crack. And with one final rush, the castle collapses, sending stone high into the air. Maisie's final act was to take down Tintagel, and the dreamers inside it.

I leap down the steps, away from the rubble, slashing my scimitar left and right like an untrained squire, such is my fury. The dreamers hold their torches to the platform back to Ithr. On it stands Frankie and her grandfather Ben. He sees the oncoming flames before she does, as she is opening her portal. As the dreamers touch their torches to the platform,

Ben shoves Frankie full force from the platform. She lands in the grass at its base, and the platform goes up in flames. Ben's spindly body is engulfed, and his screams of pain are only matched by Frankie's screams of horror.

The platform isn't made of wood, so I can only assume that whatever is powering the dreamers' torches isn't any normal fire. It flicks out, catching anyone within reach. Beyond the platform, dreamers holding torches race towards the stables.

Lamb.

A group of veneurs breaks away from the knights protecting them and rushes towards the stables, anticipating what is going to happen next. More dreamers cut them off, hacking at them mercilessly.

I have to get to Lamb and the other horses, but my fellow thanes are trapped and outnumbered. I reach a hand out to the flames, but Medraut's power is otherworldly, not made of inspyre but of pure hatred. I can't get a purchase on them.

'The marbles, Fern!' Ollie shouts across the crowd, slicing two dreamers at once with his chakrams.

The marbles. Of course. I only have two left – the third was used up in my tournament years ago to save myself from a fire. I scrabble around in my pouch as I run. I leap into the air, over the heads of the dreamers and knights, right over the platform, and drop one into the midst of the flames. There's an unearthly *boom*, and I am suddenly flying through smoke. I emerge the other side and land, looking back only to make sure that the marble has worked. The smoke clears a little, enough for me to see that the fire is extinguished.

Samson rallies the knights. 'Make a pathway!' he shouts. They form a fence, protecting the platform from further dreamers, allowing only the thanes inside to return to Ithr. Easa lifts Frankie onto the platform and activates her portal for her. But a small group follows me as I race towards the stables: Natasha and a handful of veneurs. The stables are already alight, and the sound of panicking horses, screaming in terror, pulls at my heart.

'Domino!' Natasha screams. 'Domino!'

I have the final marble in my hand, but I can't risk it detonating in the wrong place. When we're close enough, I throw it as hard as I can, using my Immral to guide it. Further and further it goes . . . Nearly there . . .

A dreamer – a hyena of a man, small and wiry, leaps into the air and knocks the marble down. It lands short of the stables and blasts a crater in the earth. We stagger, waiting for the ground to stop shaking. The flames from the stables rise higher.

'Come on!' I scream, refusing to give up, and take huge, inhuman leaps towards the sound of screaming horses. The flames are thick now, feeding on wood and fear. I remember my own fear when Jenny set me alight. I remember how useless I felt. And then I remember the nightmares I had afterwards, where Andraste leaped through flames to cut me free.

I must be Andraste now.

I wield my Immral like a shield and leap into my terror, Natasha and the veneurs behind me. Inside the stables is all choking smoke and burning heat. Wooden beams that have stood for thousands of years topple around us. I pull my tunic up over my mouth and dart between the flames, feeling my way along the stable doors, opening every latch I come across. Lamb is at the end.

'Lamb?' I cough out. I can't see her as I fumble at the door. 'Girl, are you there?'

I keep trying to undo the latch but it's stuck; the heat has engorged it. Then I feel her muzzle against my hand. A nuzzle, as if she is reassuring me when it should be the other way around. I will not let another loved one die. Not today. With a surge of Immral I wrench the door of the stable from its hinges, falling with it onto the flame-soaked floor.

'Go!' I tell Lamb. 'Go!'

But the loyal creature whinnies at me, waiting until I'm on my feet. Only then does she join the throng of horses galloping from the burning building. I follow them, stumbling my way out. Natasha is outside already, patting down any horses who are burned, defending them from attacking dreamers.

I throw my arms around Lamb. I look across at the ruins of Tintagel.

'Get to safety,' I whisper.

She nuzzles me again, not understanding. 'I'll find you,' I tell her. 'Now run, my dear.'

Natasha is whispering the same to Domino. Lamb and Domino start trotting towards the walls that once used to keep them safe. The other horses follow them, Balius and Samson's horse catching up with Lamb. Lord Allenby's charger takes the rear, nudging some of the more reticent horses to increase their pace.

'Cover me,' I tell Natasha, and she goes back to back with me, hefting her spear, as I lift my hand, focusing on the herd of horses who have been our companions for so long. As they break into a canter, I reach out to them, holding each one in my mind, and when they reach the wall I push my Immral into their legs, giving them extra height, lifting them over and above the dreamers who wait on the other side. It's all I can do for them now.

'Fern! Natasha! Time to go!' Samson's voice lifts over the fray.

The knights are still defending the platform. Ollie is there, and Easa – the only reeve left – is beside him, inexpertly wielding an iron bar retrieved from the wreckage of Tintagel. Natasha and I race towards them.

'Go!' Ollie shouts at Easa.

'Not until I know you're safe!' Easa replies.

Ollie lowers his weapon and, quick as a heartbeat, presses his lips hungrily to Easa's before pushing him back onto the platform and back to Ithr.

It is now only knights left. As Natasha and I approach, Samson shouts, 'Portals, now!'

We retrieve our portals – mirrors, rings, tokens and coins – and as Natasha and I reach them they step back onto the platform. The dreamers come on, flames ablazing. I open my mirror, and the last thing I hear is Samson's voice, hot next to my ear, saying, 'I'll find you.'

The last thing I see is the platform go up in flames. Tintagel is lost.

Chapter 45

I'm done with crying. I have only fury at the people who did this. Who killed Maisie and the other thanes, who tried to kill Lamb and the horses.

How dare they?

Righteous rage pumps through me. As soon as I reach my bedroom in Ithr I storm downstairs and turn on the TV, keeping the volume low, not wanting to wake Dad, who only got back from his night shift a few hours ago. It's not hard to find Medraut. He's everywhere these days. His face beams out of the screen at me, his words merging into one another until it's impossible to understand what he's saying beyond the usual ideology of *One Voice; a united nation; peace and safety for all.* Words, words, words.

'Turn it off,' Ollie says softly. He too is dry-eyed, but there is no anger in him.

Reluctantly, I reach for the remote, but then something *does* make me take note. A newsreader is saying: 'The prime minister is due to address the nation in a one-of-a-kind speech next month. While it is not yet known what he will say, his advisors promise a revelatory set of plans that seek to unite not just the country, but the world.'

The commentator switches back to the studio as Ollie, now interested, sinks down next to me. The presenters look at each other smilingly. 'One Voice indeed,' one of them jokes, and I wish I could reach through the screen and throttle him.

'What do you think he's going to do?' Ollie says.

'Ostara,' I reply. 'That's when his big speech is. When the walls between Ithr and Annwn are at their thinnest anyway.'

'And even thinner now,' Ollie says.

We both ponder this.

'Do you think the others will have seen?' he says.

'Even if they have, we've got no way of knowing. Even if the portal still works, Tintagel isn't safe. It must be overrun by dreamers now. And the only thane I know in Ithr other than you is Samson. Do you really think he'll have contact details for the rest of them?'

Ollie nods morosely. Still, I message Samson to double-check he got out okay. My mind turns over this news about Ostara in my head. A speech, they said. *Words, words, words*.

'Words!' I say, sitting up.

'Are you just saying random things now, in the hope it'll form a plan?' Ollie asks.

I hit him. 'Irish and Penn's messages. Maybe we can tell people that way.'

'I'm not sure that people are going to be checking those right now, Fern.'

He's right. It's not going to be enough. 'Then we have to take a risk.'

I pull out my phone and begin typing furiously. Ollie looks over my shoulder. 'A memorial?'

'It's the page Ramesh and Sachi's family used when they were telling people about their funerals. People might not check the booklets, but maybe they'll start searching online for each other.'

I show him what I've typed.

Funeral for the homeless

April 2nd, St Jude's Church, 1pm

Our voices won't be silenced.

I hope that I've told enough thanes about Lord Allenby's situation that they'd be able to decipher this. Ollie nods. 'Medraut might know Lord Allenby was homeless. It's a good cover but it's still risky.'

'It's all we've got. Do it?'

'Do it.'

I post the message on every memorial website I can find, and Ollie posts it to his old Shout Louder message boards.

'Now let's step away,' Ollie says, and we both put our phones down and turn off the television. Ollie puts on some music and reads, and I bring my drawing materials downstairs and sketch at the dining table. I'm nearly done with my drawing of Lord Allenby, but it needs a few final touches. At lunchtime, we risk checking our phones.

Nothing.

Everything has been removed. All the messages we posted are gone.

'He found them,' Ollie says dully. 'That's it then.'

I risk trying my portal, even though Ollie tells me not to.

I have to see what's left of Tintagel, to see if there's a chance of finding the rest of my friends again. The light welcomes me as it always used to, and for a moment I think that everything's going to be okay.

But as soon as I climb up out of the dark waters that bridge the worlds, I realise what a mistake I've made. The portal is still standing, although it's scorched and cracked, but everything else has been destroyed. Tintagel is a ruin; not a single wall still stands of its once proud turrets. Pieces of hospital beds and harker desks lie amongst the stone and ashes. The trees have been uprooted and lie beached in what was once the herb gardens. My haven is no more.

But what is even worse is that dreamers, still armed, prowl the grounds, primed for anyone trying to return to the castle. It doesn't take long for them to spot me. They move quickly, but I have remained on the platform, and disappear before they can catch me.

'I told you,' Ollie says.

'Well, at least we know for sure,' I say. 'The real question now is: do we go to sleep tonight or not?'

If we let ourselves fall asleep, we'll be walking through Annwn as dreamers – unconscious, unaware of the mortal danger we face and unable to defend ourselves.

'We can't, can we?' Ollie says. 'Wouldn't Medraut's dreamers spot us and tear us to pieces?'

'But if we don't sleep we won't be able to function. I didn't sleep for a few days after I left the thanes a few years ago, remember? Believe me, it's not easy.'

Ollie ponders this. 'We could sleep during the day. There

are way fewer dreamers then, aren't there? Hopefully we'd be a bit safer.'

It does still feel like a risk, but it's one we're going to have to take.

Someone knocks on the door. Ollie and I are on our feet instantly. What if it's someone from the government, insisting on taking us to a treatment centre? What if Clemmie's latent protection has worn off, and one of our neighbours has reported us? Dad stirs upstairs, still out cold.

The person knocks again.

'Who is it?' I say through the door.

'Fern? It's me.'

I unlock the door hurriedly and throw myself into Samson's arms.

'Sorry it took me so long – Mum and Dad aren't keen to let me out of the house much lately.'

Ollie throws his arms around us both. 'It's good to see you, Captain,' he says.

Ollie busies himself making tea for us all, as I give Samson a three-second tour of downstairs. He pulls me towards him, playing with the bracelet that I never remove. He's wearing glasses that highlight his eyes. It's a good look. A very good look. I kiss him again, resisting the urge to do something that will make Ollie excuse himself.

'Hello,' Dad says from the door. I spring up.

'Dad! This is . . . this is Samson.'

Samson holds his hand out and, after a pause, Dad shakes it. I see the way Samson eyes my dad warily and feel guilty that I've told Samson all about my father's failings, while Dad didn't know of Samson's existence until this moment.

'Are you staying for lunch?' Dad says, trying to look nonchalant at the appearance of a man who could only be his daughter's boyfriend from the way he must have seen me kissing him.

Samson does stay for lunch. An awkward, forced meal. It's hard not to compare it to the dinner when Ollie introduced Kieran, which was so full of joy and acceptance. Is it that Dad's angry about me having a boyfriend? Does he think I'm not ready, not mature enough? Or, even worse, is it Samson he objects to?

'Can we go for a walk?' Samson asks as he takes his plate to the sink and washes it up. 'There's something I want to show you and Ollie.'

I glance at Dad, who merely shrugs.

'Sure,' I say.

As Ollie and Samson don their coats and trainers, I collar Dad.

'Why were you so rude to him?'

Dad looks at me. 'Darling, I didn't mean to be rude, I was just surprised. You could have told me you were seeing someone, you know.'

I stumble. The look of genuine hurt on Dad's face is enough to make me question all my assumptions.

'You don't care that I've got a boyfriend?'

'You're seventeen, of course I don't care. He seems like a lovely chap. I just wish I'd met him when I'd had a chance to take a shower first, that's all.'

Chastened, I hurry to catch up with my brother and

boyfriend, slipping my hand into Samson's as though we've been seeing each other in Ithr for all this time, as if this isn't kind of our first date.

'There,' he says at last, pointing to a building down a side alley.

The wall is covered in graffiti – bad graffiti, the kind that's all tags and no art. But then I see that it's not tags: it's writing. Familiar writing.

Funeral for the homeless

April 2nd, St Jude's Church, 1pm

Our voices won't be silenced.

'It's our message.' Ollie grins. 'Did you do this, Samson?'

'God, no, give me some credit,' Samson replies. 'It's not a sanctioned graffiti wall, it would be illegal.'

I laugh. 'Then who did it, do you think?'

'Does it matter? Someone who saw the message before it was taken down. Come on, there's more.'

Samson drags us across parks and roads, and on nearly every one our message is printed somewhere, sometimes just one sentence, sometimes the whole lot. And sometimes it is accompanied by a star – maybe the symbol I placed next to Lord Allenby's name in the booklet by the lake has caught on, or maybe it's a thane trying to tell us that it's them writing these messages.

Further on, next to Mile End tube station, someone has inscribed a bird next to the message. 'A veneur?' Ollie ponders.

We keep going. In north London, the message is accompanied by an eye; the sign of the harkers. They're everywhere, and the more we walk, the more we notice the quiet words of solidarity that have sprung up overnight between a community whose home has been destroyed but who are determined to find each other. For the first time since Lord Allenby's death, I begin to hope.

Chapter 46

The last time I visited this chapel was for Ramesh's funeral. He was the first friend I laid to rest, but I've lost so many since then. It's hard to believe he died just two years ago. Two years for the world to fall. Two years for me to find so many people to care about, and two years for me to lose so many of them.

It seems fitting for Lord Allenby to be buried here. He won't be far from Ramesh and Sachi, and I'm willing to bet that a few other thanes are in this cemetery somewhere. Ollie is inside, talking to the vicar, telling her about him. 'I don't want her to paint some kind of pity-party picture of him,' he tells me.

I wait outside the church, shifting nervously. I'm keenly aware that Medraut must know about the funeral, since he removed the messages about it, but once the news was shared, there was no backing out. Ollie, Samson and I decided the risk was worth it.

The wind is biting through my black skater dress. I wish I'd thought to bring a coat, but the spring sun had been deceptive, and I hadn't thought about much beyond getting out of bed and getting to the church on time. That, and whether the thanes would actually turn up. Samson is the first to arrive, folding me into his arms.

'You're early,' I tell him.

'And you're surprised?'

'Are you okay?' I ask him. For all my emotions about Lord Allenby, Samson spent far more time with him than I did. He saw him as a father too. I know how much he's hurting.

'You go in,' I tell him, knowing that he needs time alone to pay his respects.

Samson kisses me, then treads heavily towards the church. I wander the graves for a few minutes, veering ever closer to the place where Ramesh and Sachi are laid to rest. The air around me shimmers, and a wisp of inspyre drifts through a rip. It forms a ghost – Ramesh, laughing. I reach for him, but he disintegrates before I can touch him.

There's a crunch of gravel behind me. Someone else has arrived. I hurry back round the cemetery to see who it is.

It's not one person: it's many. I recognise nearly all of them as they trickle through the gate. Leading the way is Niamh, pushing her wheelchair over the stones and swearing profusely. Rachel, far slimmer than she is in Annwn, is arm in arm with Bandile and Nerizan. Behind them comes Miss D, dressed in black tweed and leaning on a cane.

Next, there's a gaggle of reeves and veneurs I don't know the names of, followed by Jin and Easa, and then a series of thanes from other castles: Carys from Cambridge, Asher from Oxford, and Lady Kaur, all the way from Cornwall.

There are two people missing who I had hoped to see, though. One is Charlie, although I hadn't really expected her to come. The other is Natasha.

'Tash isn't coming,' Niamh tells me as she passes. 'She's paying her respects on her own.'

I nod, remembering something Natasha once told me about attending another knight's funeral, and how it only left her with bad memories.

'It's a good turnout,' Easa says quietly, offering his arm. I take it gratefully, and turn away. It's time.

The thought of what is about to happen suddenly hits me, and I have to gulp back a sob. I am saying goodbye. Only this handful of people in Ithr know the best of him. The rest of Ithr thinks of him as a nobody. A bum. A leech. Anger and sorrow battle for dominance in my chest. I want to wrench my arm away from Easa's grip and scream at the unfairness of it.

The service is short, but Ollie has done a good job of conveying to the vicar who Lionel Allenby really was. She seems surprised to see so many people congregated for a homeless man.

I focus on the coffin before me, and the bouquets that have been laid on it. Mine were gathered from the park near our house, surreptitiously taken from the flower beds. I hope the gardeners will forgive me the theft, but I couldn't afford proper flowers and these looked so much better than the wilting articles in the local shop. Where mine are a jumble of colours, Samson has chosen a small wreath of cornflowers and delphiniums – blue to match the colour of the knights. Others have offered slender circles in yellows and pinks, single roses, sprays of freshly cut holly.

Then it comes time for the vicar to step back. 'Would anyone like to say a few words before we lay Lionel to rest?' she asks.

Everyone looks to me, but I nudge Samson. 'You go,' I whisper.

He moves slowly to the podium, surveying the packed pews gravely.

'I didn't like Lionel when I first met him,' he begins. There's nervous laughter around the space. 'I'd spent my whole life being coddled by my parents, and he wasn't having any of it. I *hated* that. I thought he was the kind of person who wouldn't like me if he met me in Ithr. Then one day he decided to ride out on patrol with us, when I was just a squire. I was rude to him, and he took it. But at the end of the patrol he said something. He said, "You've got a lot of potential, Samson. This isn't Ithr. In this castle, you really will get back what you put in. And I think you could put in a lot, if you set your mind to it." I was probably rude to him again, but his words stuck with me. I can hand on heart say that I wouldn't be the same person standing here today if it wasn't for Lionel Allenby. He gave me something beautiful, and I don't know if I ever told him that.'

Samson sits back down, his eyes fixed straight ahead, his jaw set.

Everyone's looking at me, and I realise that I can't get out of this. I'd only known him for a few years, but Lord Allenby's fate has become inextricably linked to my story. To not speak about him would be doing him a disservice. I stand unsteadily.

At the podium, I look over the field of familiar faces. The vicar is looking bewildered by Samson's mentions of Ithr and patrols. I address someone who isn't here, imagining her standing at the back of the church, her eyes closed off, as they were when I last saw her on television. Charlie.

'Lionel was a fighter,' I say, which raises a few smirks. 'He was a warrior and a gentleman. He was an amazing man, and he devoted his life to trying to make what he'd lost worth it. A lot of people would call him a hero for the way he died.

'But I'm not going to call him a hero. I think he'd hate that title. If the last few years have taught us anything, isn't it that heroes are dangerous? If someone's a hero, they can't be wrong. It's harder to question them. We all know where that leads. So no, Lionel Allenby isn't a hero to me. He was a man, flawed and wonderful all at the same time. In the end, he chose a life and a death that meant something. He chose that for himself, and I refuse to take those choices, good and bad, away from him by reducing him to a word as trifling as "hero". He did more good things than bad things, just like all of us. And he tried to learn from the bad things so that he could do more of the good things. And that's what matters in the end, isn't it?'

People around the church are nodding. Ollie is staring at Easa, fighting tears.

'I'm going to miss him so much,' I finish, and step down before my voice breaks completely. The space fills with whispers, warm and approving. The vicar stands. 'Could the pallbearers step forward, please?'

As Samson, Ollie, Carys and the other heads of Tintagel's lores stand up, there's a knock on the church door.

Everyone freezes. We all know that if Medraut wanted to take out a chunk of the thanes in one go, he'd only need to send his followers to this funeral. We'd all been willing to take the risk, but that was when it was hypothetical.

Rachel and I peer out of the stained-glass windows. The patterns and colours make everything too hazy to see in detail, but it's clear that there's a sizeable crowd gathered outside.

'Medraut's people,' Rachel whispers, her face unusually pale.

'He wouldn't set them on us now, would he?' Bandile says.

'You have been around these last few years, haven't you?' Samson says grimly.

The knights amongst us are taking in the candlesticks and the pews, looking for potential weapons with which to defend ourselves.

Another knock.

'Is there a problem?' the vicar says. 'I don't want any trouble.'

'Nor do we, but trouble might have found us,' I tell her.

'Should we call the police?' someone says.

'No,' a dozen voices respond.

'I think we've just got to open the door and try to make a run for it,' Samson says. 'Maybe we can push a path through them to help the others escape.'

'I hate leaving him here,' Carys says, gesturing to Lord Allenby's coffin.

I nod. 'So do I, but we've got to protect ourselves.'

There's another knock on the door. Before we can prepare ourselves, it opens. I push to the front, ready to take the brunt of whatever attack is coming . . . A familiar face peers inside. An older woman wearing a long, black dress. My heart skips. Ramesh and Sachi's mother.

'Are you the knights?' she says in a quiet, nervous voice, so different from her children's.

The others whisper behind me. *How did she know? Who is she? Why is she asking about us?*

'Yes,' I tell her. 'We're the knights, Mrs Hellier. Your son and daughter fought with us.'

She ducks back out to talk to the other people with her. I assume they're Ramesh and Sachi's extended family, although I could never have imagined they'd be quite so sprawling.

The news that our visitors might not be enemies after all spreads through the church. People crowd forward, keen to see what Ramesh and Sachi's parents look like. But when Mrs Hellier returns, she doesn't just bring her husband and their youngest daughter, but a crowd of people who clearly aren't related to each other at all.

'Are Irish and Penn here?' one of them says.

Niamh pushes to the front. 'You found our books?'

'Most of us found you through those books,' the man explains. 'Some of us through the websites, and some because of the graffiti. That's how we found each other.'

'You've all lost someone?' Ollie asks.

Everyone nods. Some of them produce photographs, some of them murmur names. I recognise a few faces. I can tell who some are related to from the family resemblance. I get a jolt when I see a young woman who looks almost identical to Emory, who was killed in the treitres' first attack. This must be her sister.

Most of them are unfamiliar, though – I suppose they're relatives of people who weren't thanes. But they're here. Does that mean they believe?

'We've been researching the knights – the thanes – ever

since you left your message,' Ramesh's mother tells me, 'and we weren't the only ones. A few of us spread the word.'

'Most people think we're crazy, of course,' says Emory's sister, 'but we're not, are we?'

The edge of her voice is desperate. She needs to hold on to this.

'No,' Samson says, 'you're not crazy.'

Some of the group cry silently at Samson's confirmation. Others push to the front.

'We want to help,' Ramesh's father says, 'in whatever way we can. We have very little to lose.'

My heart swells. They're a motley collection, just like the thanes behind me. 'We're definitely going to need your help. But right now we're burying the man who led us. A lot of the people you lost looked up to him. I think they'd have liked it if you joined us.'

And that's how Lionel Allenby, a man who died on his own, is laid to rest in the company of over a hundred people who barely knew him in real life, but who knew that he deserved to be remembered. Memory has power. Compassion has power. As I watch the gathering from the front of the grave, I feel the warmth of their empathy expand across the cemetery. It fashions itself into a shield. Into a weapon.

Chapter 47

Many of us stay on long after the service has ended, exchanging phone numbers and stories, and forming the beginnings of a plan. As the evening grows colder, most of the non-London thanes leave to catch trains or drive back home, and others call it a night. Eventually, only a dozen of us remain, using the light from our phones to illuminate us as we sit on benches or on the grass in the local park. I snuggle into Samson's embrace, and listen to him chat to Jin and Rachel. It's wonderful and strange to see them in Ithr, to match the brave, clever, stubborn thanes I know with their counterparts who go to school or university or have jobs. With a jolt, I realise that I am truly happy in Ithr right now, despite all the tragedy that has happened and that's still to come. I have real friends, and I'm never letting go of them.

On the periphery of the circle, Ollie and Easa sit close together, whispering. Lovebirds. But then I see Ollie's expression, and realise that this isn't a union at all.

'*I'm so sorry,*' I see him whisper, reading his lips. But Easa just shakes his head and rises. He walks away without saying goodbye to anyone. Ollie is left miserable and alone. I disentangle myself from Samson and join my brother.

'Do you want to talk about it?' I ask.

'No,' he says, and lays his head on my shoulder. We sit like that for a while, until the group conversation turns inevitably to Medraut, and how we can defeat him.

'I still think we should try for the Grail,' Niamh says, but the others shake their heads.

'We don't have time,' Jin reminds her. 'Stonehenge is nearly gone. We needed to pursue it months ago.'

'Plus, remember what the tales said about there being a cost to finding it?' Rachel adds, shivering. 'I don't like the sound of that at all. Not after Excalibur.'

Ollie nudges me. 'Do you think we can go home? I don't want to talk about this tonight.'

We say our goodbyes, promising to meet again in a few days. I kiss Samson long and hard, until the others whistle and pretend to vomit.

'Do I get the same when we say hello too?' He smiles at me.

'You get it any time we're off duty, Captain.'

And I sashay away, linking arms with my brother. But my joy is short-lived. There's a sharp, close feel to the air, as though a storm is coming. It's nearly midnight by the time we stumble through our front door. I fall asleep without taking off my dress, too exhausted to worry much about the danger of sleeping.

My dreams are foggy and cold. I walk through an arctic landscape, where the wind is determined to pull me into the ether. I struggle against it, but it whisks my fingers away, one by one. When I have none left, the fog clears to reveal an expanse of ice. A figure sits in the middle of the space, huddled in a chair. As I get closer, I realise that it's an old woman, whose hair is still black and whose hands are still agile. She knits and knits on stubby little needles.

'Are you prepared?' she asks me, without looking up.

'Prepared? For what?'

'For what you must do?'

She holds up her needles. I see that they are not normal needles, but fingers. My fingers.

'Give them back!' I shout, but she laughs and whisks the yarn from my fingers, flinging it at me. It grabs hold of me like a parasite, enveloping my face. I can't breathe.

'*Fern, wake up!*' It's Dad's voice. I struggle with the yarn, desperately trying to pull it from my mouth.

'*Fern, please, love, wake up! For God's sake, wake up.*'

The old woman stabs her needles towards me and I duck, throwing the yarn from my mouth and diving into the deep well that opens up at my feet.

I wake up not in my bedroom, but beneath a crisp night sky. It takes me a moment to orientate myself. I'm sitting on the ground in the little courtyard behind our terraced house. There's a dim sound of shouting from the front of the house. The street lamps flicker unusually. Not street lamps; flames. Another shout goes up, and then there's the sound of smashing glass.

Just as I'm getting to my feet, Dad and Ollie stumble out of the door.

'You're awake, thank God,' Dad says. 'I thought the sound of the riots would have woken you for sure, but you're deep sleepers.'

'It's carnage out there,' Ollie tells me. 'A proper mob.'

I look at the gate that leads out from our back garden to a little, dark alleyway.

'We can get out that way, but where do we go then? And how do we do it without being seen?'

'The car's down the road,' Dad says. 'I've been thinking about an escape plan in case something like this happened, but I didn't think we'd get cut off from the car. I thought we'd have more notice. More fool me.'

'Wait here,' I say, and dash back into the house, against my family's protests. I run up to my room, turning the light off so the mob won't be able to see me. I pull a few things into my pockets and grab a rucksack, filling it as quickly as I can. It can't be more than a few minutes since I went into the house, but Dad is already trying to get inside to fetch me, even with Ollie asking him to trust me.

'Here,' I say, handing Ollie a hoodie and pulling one over my own head. I pass Dad a baseball cap and an old police jacket of Clemmie's that she gave to Ollie and I ages ago, hoping we'd think it was a cool costume item.

'It's a little tight.' Dad smiles thinly. 'But I see what you're doing. Clever girl.'

I show them the other items I've stuffed into the backpack: a few spare clothes, some snacks from the cupboards and some items from Mum, including her diaries. When Dad is looking elsewhere, I hand Ollie his portal.

'Now find some rocks,' Ollie says, scouring the ground.

Five minutes later, we're ready. A thin, unlit pathway divides the gardens of our row of houses and those in the row behind us. The pathway is littered with old cans, paraphernalia, and dog mess, but it follows the back gardens to the end of the street, where it vomits us out onto a main road. We walk as confidently as we can into the light and the chaos. My hoodie is pulled up, my hair pulled over one cheek to mask my burn scar. There's nothing I can do about my violet irises, but the night-time offers a little protection. Hopefully anyone who spots them will think they're just a trick of the flames.

The street has never been so busy. Groups roam up and down, shouting and swearing as though they're at the tail end of a carnival. There's an aggressive jollity to the way they move and talk. More of them are amassed outside our house, and another group is further down the street, outside Crystal Moore's place.

'Shit,' Ollie whispers.

Some people look at us curiously, trying to work out if we're part of their gang.

'Split up,' I mutter. Dad and Ollie break away – if anyone here knows that we're a family of three, hopefully separating might give them pause. I silently point Dad and Ollie towards the Moores' house, and push my way to the front of the mob loitering outside ours.

Someone is spray-painting foul words across our door. The flowers Dad planted out front have been torn up. Someone spits on the remnants of a lavender bush. Then they turn around, and I see who it is. Jenny. The girl who bullied me for years, who is responsible for my burn scar. She is triumphant. Then her eyes land on me. I duck my head, but I'm sure she's recognised me. She jostles through the crowd, wanting to take a closer look. If I run, she'll know it's me for sure.

Instead of running, I move closer to my own home, casually

moving past Jenny at a subtle distance. I take my anger from my chest, roll it up into my fist and raise the stone I took from our back yard. A cheer goes up, hungry. If I do this, hopefully it will convince Jenny that it isn't me, because who would vandalise their own house?

I look at my bedroom window, thinking of the many years I spent there being unhappy, and then the few I spent treasuring the secret of Annwn. That room has seen my blood, my tears, my heartache and my joy. This is the room that was once my mother's office. Am I really strong enough to do this?

Of course I am.

I heft the stone as hard as I can at the second-floor window. It smashes, the glass shattering as though it feels my betrayal. As though I've given them permission, the crowd snatch bricks and rocks and throw them with such violence at my house that within minutes no windows remain unbroken and the render on the wall is pockmarked. My mother's beloved orchids, lined up in a downstairs window, topple from the sill. I slip back, trying to hide my tears. Someone forces the door open, allowing the mob to rampage inside. My home for seventeen years is no longer mine. It has been violated and will never be the same.

I follow Dad and Ollie at a distance as they make their way towards the Moores' house. At first, I fear that my act of vandalism will embolden the people over here. But this lot are still holding back. They confine their violence, so far, to shouting threats and urinating on the front porch. One of the curtains upstairs is twitching. The family are definitely still inside, probably scared out of their senses.

My phone vibrates in my pocket. Samson has messaged me. *Are you safe? x*

I send a quick reply. *Out on the streets disguised as a mobber. It's bad. How about your way? x*

The reply comes almost instantaneously. *We're heading out of town. It's bad here too. x*

Worry gnaws at my chest. Dad joins Ollie and I in a huddle, trying to hide in the shadows.

'The car's round the corner,' Dad says in a low voice.

'What are we going to do about them?' I reply, nodding towards Crystal and her family, stuck inside. 'There's not enough room for us and them.'

'Ah, Fern. Come on, lass, we've got to look after ourselves –'

Ollie virtually spits. 'No, Dad, that's what got everyone into this mess in the first place. Fern and I aren't leaving here until we've worked out how to help them.'

As Dad looks from Ollie to me, sirens sound from the far end of the street. A handful of police cars skid to a halt in front of our house and officers pile out. At first, the mob inside evidently thinks they're in trouble, because they scatter. But then an officer grabs one of them and mutters something in his ear. A cold dread creeps over me. These police aren't here to help us.

'Alright, alright,' Dad says. 'I'll see if I can get in to talk to them.'

'Hang on,' I say, an idea forming. I call Samson, moving deeper into the shadows and keeping my voice low. He answers almost immediately.

'Listen,' I say, 'you've got a lot of space in your cars, right?'

'A bit. Do you need us to pick you up?'

'Not me. Another family.'

Samson doesn't hesitate. 'Where should we meet them?'

I open my mouth, about to give a specific place, and then I glance back at the police. They're looking this way. They arrived a few minutes after I sent Samson the message about being disguised as a rioter. Was it a coincidence? Even if it was, I can't take any chances.

'Meet them where we first met,' I tell him.

'Fern?'

'You remember?'

There's a pause. I know him well enough to know that he understands what I'm worried about. 'Where we first met. Got it.'

I hang up and whisper the plan to Dad. He nods. 'Meet me by the car. Go on, quickly.' He slips something into my hands – the car keys.

I give him a piece of paper and a pen, and walk off as casually as I can with Ollie by my side. Dad holds up the paper, behind the mob, praying that Crystal or one of the kids spots it. On the paper is written the words, *GO BACK. ANGUS.*

The light inside the house goes on and then off again, very quickly. A signal that the message has been understood. Dad lowers the paper. But we might be out of time. The police and the mob from our house are moving this way. Dad darts across the street and disappears down the side alley that joins up with the back gardens.

'Come on,' Ollie murmurs. We amble towards the street where the car's parked, trying to look casual. Ollie slips into the driver's seat while I clamber into the back. We sink down, hoping no one will notice us.

It's an agonising wait, far more tortuous than when we were moving amongst our attackers. We have no idea whether Dad's okay, whether he managed to talk to Crystal or not . . .

The distant sound of the mob grows louder as it makes its way towards us. Then the crowd rounds the corner and its leader looks straight up our road. It's Jenny. Of course it is. She is followed by other rioters and the police.

'Come on, Dad,' I whisper.

'If needs be I can drive us . . .' Ollie says, his voice hitching.

Jenny looks down the other end of the road. They didn't notice us. I breathe out slowly, trying to calm my nerves. It's okay, it's going to be okay.

One of the older rioters fumbles to switch on a torch and hands it to Jenny. She casts it up the street, then swings back our way. The beam slides right across the road and comes to rest on my face. 'It's them!' Jenny shouts.

'Shit,' Ollie says, starting the ignition.

'Come on, Dad. Come on, Dad.'

If we have to leave Dad behind because of our insistence that we try to help Crystal, how could Ollie and I ever forgive ourselves? The mob races towards us, Jenny in the lead. Ollie puts the car into gear and revs the engine, his fingers hovering over the handbrake.

'Come on, Dad . . .'

'Fern . . .' Ollie says. 'I think we have to –'

Then the back door opens and Dad throws himself inside. 'Go!' he orders. Ollie is off before he's even closed the door.

The car jerks forward and I cling on as Ollie swerves across the road. Jenny bangs against the side of the car as we pass, and for a brief moment she and I come face to face, my window the only thing separating us. Then we are past her and she is behind me.

Chapter 48

The mob can't catch us on foot, and the police are too far away from their vehicles to give chase.

'Slow down, drive normally,' Dad says from the back, and Ollie eases off the engine, turning along side streets that force him to drive carefully, as well as avoiding any speed cameras that might pick up our plates.

'Did you get them out?' I ask Dad.

He nods. 'They're meeting your Samson at Royal Arsenal. I made sure they weren't being followed. That's why it took so long.'

'Thanks, Dad.'

'No, thank you. Your mother would never have forgiven me if I'd left them behind.'

Ollie glances at me in the mirror. There's no telling what Mum would have done, quite frankly. She was merciless. She might well have left them behind to protect me, but there's no point in contradicting Dad. Mum did too good a job at making him fall in love with her.

'Now where?' Ollie asks.

'Scotland,' Dad says. 'To my home.'

We drive through the night, stopping only for petrol. Smoke rises from nearly every city and town we pass.

'It's a bloody purge,' Dad says, each time we pass a house with windows smashed in and its belongings strewn across the road. At about two in the morning, Samson messages me.

'He's got the Moores,' I tell Ollie and Dad.

'Thank God. Where are they going next?'

'Wales. He's not saying more than that.'

We all think of the police arriving shortly after Samson and I messaged. Of course my phone is being monitored. *Of course* it is. Other messages begin to come in, from Niamh and Rachel and Nerizan, to say that they managed to get out. It feels strange that only yesterday we were all in the same place in Ithr. Now we're scattered across the country, and with Tintagel overrun it's hard to see how we could ever come together again. But we must, if we're to end this once and for all. I can't do it alone.

It's nearly midday when Dad pulls up at a derelict house on the side of a winding, single track road. My only memories of this place come from photos – the one time I have visited, I was too young to remember. Back then, it was a remote, family-run B&B. It has lain empty the last few years, with Dad's siblings moved abroad and his mum in a care home in Edinburgh. Now it looks forbidding, its double-fronted, stone-frame windows staring down at us with empty eyes.

The smell of damp is thick as we heave open the door.

'First things first – we need to get some firelighters and dry wood,' Dad mumbles.

Ollie and I roam through the house, pulling out old blankets and clothes from the cupboards, while Dad gets back in the car and heads to the nearest supermarket.

'Look at this, Fern,' Ollie calls from another room. He's holding a frame. Pictured there is Mum and Dad, looking so much younger – Dad is stubbled but not bearded. In his arms he carries a little bundle – Ollie, I think, while Mum cradles me. On either side of them are Dad's parents, upright and strict. They stand in front of the house we're now in, although it is better kept: the trees and weeds have been held at bay, the window frames are freshly painted and the lights are on inside. But what I notice is the way Dad looks down at Mum, already lost to her. Mum's look of triumph. And Dad's parents side-eyeing Mum as though they knew, somehow, that she had forced their son to fall in love with her.

'One big happy family from the start, eh?' Ollie says, echoing my thoughts.

'Let's put it on the mantelpiece downstairs. It'll make Dad smile,' I tell him.

When Dad returns a few hours later, the sun is beginning to set, although it's hard to tell through the thickness of the trees surrounding the house. He carries bacon, bread and butter, as well as the means to make fire.

'Have you found the fishing tackle yet?' he asks us. 'It should still be here somewhere, although I might need to get new lines. We don't know how long we're going to be here, so we'd best be as self-sufficient as we can.'

We help Dad light the fire and make bacon sandwiches, then curl up on a mouldy sofa with them, covering our legs in blankets. Outside, a deer ambles past, unaware that humans have once again infringed on its territory. None of what has happened in the last forty-eight hours feels real. This is far more of a dream than some of the things I've experienced in Annwn.

'So,' Dad says, wiping his buttery hands on some kitchen towel, 'are you going to tell me what's been going on? Or am I going to be kept in the dark forever?'

Ollie and I look at each other. 'What do you mean?'

'Come on, now. Secret messages and bleeding eyes. Friends and boyfriends appearing from nowhere when you haven't left the house in weeks. And you two, suddenly thick as thieves. Something's going on, and I'd like to know just how outlandish it is.'

I can't imagine that Dad is going to believe us even if we do tell him. But we're going to have to make plans soon, and I can't see us being able to do that without Dad noticing, now we're all going to be stuck inside this house. Maybe it's time.

I look at Ollie, and he nods in silent acceptance. And together, we tell Dad everything.

'You don't believe us,' I finish, trying to get in there first before Dad can scoff at us.

'It is unbelievable,' he says slowly.

'You dream about Mum,' Ollie says suddenly. 'You dream about finding her, like you did that morning. And you dream about kissing her, only she falls apart in your arms.'

I remember what Ollie's talking about – two years ago we looked for information in our house in Annwn, and saw the traces of Dad's dreams there.

Dad frowns. 'I do dream that, sometimes.'

'You dream it all the time, Dad,' Ollie says softly. We've both heard him thrashing around in his sleep.

'But why wouldn't she tell me?' Dad asks, looking lost.

The one part of the truth we left out, was how Mum manipulated him into loving her. Ollie and I hadn't agreed in advance that we wouldn't tell him. There were many moments when I thought I would, or Ollie would, but it never felt like the right time. It would have been cruel of us. Maybe, just maybe, it's okay for Mum's memory to be pure in this one person's mind. Maybe Dad needs that.

'Maybe she was scared you'd think she was crazy, and leave her,' I suggest.

Dad nods, uncertain. 'I suppose it would explain a lot. Her nightmares. And the way she used to hold that mirror of yours when she was sleeping.' His eyes darken. 'So she didn't pass away naturally? Those marks on her – they were wounds?'

Ollie places a hand on Dad's arm. 'She didn't die for nothing, Dad. It wasn't meaningless.'

Dad almost crumples, and I realise that he's needed to hear that for seventeen years. The same way the Helliers, and all those people who came to Lord Allenby's funeral, needed to hear it. Dad takes a shaky breath. 'So it's been Medraut all along, has it? And he's tried to kill you two as well.'

'He's killed a lot of people. Directly and indirectly,' I say.

Dad nods. 'Well, what are we going to do about it then?'

I'm not sure that Dad truly believes us, or not at first anyway. But him saying that he does allows Ollie and I to communicate freely with the other thanes. Niamh and Natasha set up a network – we pass a message on in code to them over the phone or by email, and they write it on the walls of London, where it spreads across the country by hand and whispered word of mouth. When Dad first sees the messages, and that there are hundreds of people working alongside us, his uncertainty melts away into wonder.

Ostara is approaching fast, and we know that Medraut is planning something big for then. It's Easa who calls Ollie late one night with a breakthrough. Ollie blearily puts him on speaker.

'I've been writing down everything I can remember from those records you pulled from Downing Street,' Easa says. 'It was bugging me for the longest time, but I think, combined with that announcement –'

'What do you think he's going to do?' I interrupt, tiredness making me rude.

'I think he's going to use the cameras to break the worlds once and for all.'

'The cameras?' Ollie says. 'How would he even do that?'

I think about the times when Medraut has used the media to spread his message, even though no one could tell you what he said. Then I remember the feeling I had when he made the announcement about the treatment facilities – the sense that he was broadcasting his Immral through the screens.

'The physics of Ithr and Annwn are combining, aren't they?' I point out. 'And he's made sure that his announcement is going to be broadcast all over the world, wherever there's a screen. What if he creates a rip where he's going to make the announcement, and uses his Immral from Annwn to reach out to every single person watching the broadcast?'

'And if he reached enough people,' Easa continues, 'if he used his Immral to convince enough people to join him, then the impact on Annwn would be devastating. Nearly all the remaining inspyre would be wiped out.'

Dad appears in the doorway, listening closely

'Do you think it would work?' Ollie says.

'Unfortunately, yes,' Easa replies. 'It would be game over.'

'Not if you use it against him,' Dad pipes up.

'What do you mean?'

Dad joins Ollie and I around the phone. 'Everything you've told me about what he's done says that he thinks that he has the most power over this – Immral, was it? Well, now Fern has it, and she has you lot. What if you used it against him?'

'What, use the cameras to *fix* Annwn?' I say.

'Exactly. You've got Immral, same as him. If he's going to use this broadcast to brainwash all of us, why shouldn't you use it to give everyone their thoughts back?'

I imagine it: me, the woman who never voluntarily talks to anyone she doesn't know, standing in front of dozens of cameras, addressing the world. Giving them back their voices. It has a certain poetry, I suppose.

'But the last time we tried something like that, Medraut ended up stealing Excalibur from us and becoming prime minister,' Ollie says.

'Point taken,' Dad says, 'but I'll put two things to you. First, what have we got to lose? And second – he thinks he's got you beaten. He thinks you're scattered, and that there aren't enough of you to pose a real threat to him any more.'

'He's right,' I say.

'No. He's not. Because it's not just the knights or the thanes he's got to deal with.' Dad looks more determined than I've ever seen him. 'You've got dreamers on your side. Maybe not all of them. Maybe not even a majority. But you've got those of us who've lost someone, who've lost family or friends or freedom because of that man. We're on your side. And in my experience – something you've taught me, both of you – lots of voices will always be more powerful than one, no matter how insidious that one is.'

There's a pause as everyone absorbs this.

'You should be a public speaker, sir,' Easa says on the phone.

Dad laughs self-consciously. But he's lit a fire inside me. A memory of Nimue's belt and the power it imbued in all of us.

When you are ready, it will find you. Here, beneath the dome.

'You're right, Dad,' I say, 'and I have a plan. But first of all, there's something I'm going to need to fetch.'

I am, at last, ready.

Chapter 49

Planning takes up most of our time over the next few days. That and foraging for food in the local woodland and in the river that runs along the bottom of the garden. Dad doesn't want to risk heading into town again where CCTV might recognise him. With Ostara in just a few days, we're counting on Medraut being too busy and too triumphant to spend much effort trying to find me. None of us have been back to Tintagel since the night after it fell, other than a few of the knights who wanted to confirm that it was still being defended by Medraut's dreamers. We take to sleeping in shifts during the day, checking on each other for signs of distress. At one point, Ollie started shouting in his sleep and when I woke him, swore that a mob had descended on him, egged on by a woman with snakes coming out of her back. It took him hours to calm down, and all of us days to let ourselves sleep once more, knowing that the danger was very real.

On the night before Ostara, we hold our final meeting to go over our plans. We've been talking and messaging in code until now, in case Medraut's people are still tracing us, but this call is too important. We have all bought burner phones for the purpose.

'Rachel, you're still coordinating from Ithr, okay? The speech is at four p.m., so we need to be ready before then,' I say.

Niamh chimes in, 'God, I'm looking forward to seeing you all again. Natasha's got a decent face but there's only so long I can look at the same person.'

'I resent that,' Natasha's voice comes over the phone. 'I have a lovely face and I've been making you cornbread every night.'

'Stop it,' I say. It's not that I don't love hearing my friends' voices, but I need to keep us focused. 'We can't mess this up, and there's a lot we could mess up if we're not careful.'

'Fern's right,' Samson says. 'We've got to make Tintagel safe again, storm the most secure building in the UK, probably have to deal with more sluaghs, take down Medraut then use his own idea against him.'

'That's the part I'm most worried about,' I say. 'There's going to be fighting – probably a lot of fighting – wherever Medraut is. It's going to get messy. But we cannot damage those cameras. I need them working if we're going to reverse what he's done. He'll have set them up to help him broadcast his Immral, and we won't have enough time once we're in Ithr to repair them. We have to keep the cameras safe.'

'We *know*, Fern. Honestly, you can trust us,' Bandile says.

'I do trust you. But this is everything. Annwn's survival depends on this.'

'It's okay, we can always fall back on the Grail,' Ollie jokes.

'Stop it,' Jin says. 'The Grail isn't an option, okay? Get that out of your head.'

Jin's always been snappy, but never like this.

'Jin? You okay?' I say.

'Yes. Yes, I'm fine. Sorry. I'm just stressed. I'll see you tomorrow.' There's a beep as she disconnects, and a murmur of anxious laughter as everyone comments on how very *Jin* that was. Eventually, though, we descend into silence once more.

'Okay,' Samson says, 'last preparations. Those of us who need to be on the road better get going.'

'See you all soon,' I say, feeling the nerves bouncing across the country between us long after we've all hung up.

We say goodbye to the house early the next morning and begin the long drive back to London. Not everyone has to be back in the capital, but for Dad to play his part, we need to be there. I wind down the window and drink in the crisp morning air, while Ollie dozes in the back seat.

Dad is quiet for much of the journey, and I allow the landscape of the Lake District, unbearably beautiful even in Ithr, to soak into my soul. Every time we round a bend in the road a new vista opens up before us: wide valleys plunging into lakes that stretch into fog. When we reach the motorway, I check that Ollie's still sleeping and look over at Dad.

'I'll make sure he gets back safely,' I say.

'What?' Dad pulls himself out of his daze.

'Ollie. I'll make sure he's okay.'

Dad looks at me with another of those hurt expressions. 'Make sure *you* come back safely, Ferny. Both of you.'

Suddenly, he pulls the car into a lay-by and cries silently, his hands still on the steering wheel. 'I messed it all up, didn't I? Your mum would be so angry with me. I got it all wrong.'

My shame is excruciating. I've made Dad feel this way,

all because I wanted him to know that I knew Ollie was his favourite. Then he pulls me in towards him, one-handed, and gives me the most bone-crushing side-hug. 'I love *you*, Ferny. Always have done. You and Ollie are the only people who kept me going. I couldn't bear to lose one of you. Please come back. Promise me you'll come back.'

I cling on to him, crying too. We stay that way, the gearstick digging into my ribs, until Ollie wakes up. While Dad wanders off to check the car over, Ollie and I eat sandwiches on the verge.

'There's something I've been thinking about for a while,' I say to my brother.

'What's that?'

'You weren't mad at me for using my Immral on Charlie all those months ago. And you pulled away from Easa right after you learned about Mum manipulating Dad into loving her.'

Ollie has stopped eating.

'You did something to Easa, didn't you? You made him fall for you?'

Ollie's eyes are fixed on the road. 'Do you hate me?'

'Hey.' I kick him gently. 'Don't do that. You told Easa the night of Allenby's funeral, didn't you?'

Ollie nods. 'He's never going to forgive me.'

'But why did you do it in the first place? Easa liked you to begin with.'

'But not as much as I liked him,' Ollie says. 'I just wanted to even the score.'

'You idiot,' I say softly.

'I know.'

Dad ambles over. 'Ready to go? I think we've got enough petrol to get us there.'

We get as close as we can to central London and park in a little side street. I pull my hoodie over my face one last time and Ollie and I peel off from Dad with a final hug. 'Be safe,' he whispers to both of us. 'I'll see you soon.'

Ollie and I walk towards St Paul's Cathedral, still proudly standing in Ithr where it is nothing but a pile of rocks in Annwn. The cathedral is nearly empty, which is unusual for a Sunday – but no doubt everyone is staying at home, glued to their televisions and phones to see what Medraut is about to announce. A few stragglers sit in pews or roam the grounds. I spot some familiar faces: Rachel in the cloisters, fiddling with her bag; Bandile sitting quietly on a bench at the back; Samson leaning over the gallery, watching me intently. I blow him the softest kiss, then turn my attention to the task at hand. And there, in the cloisters, a group of familiar faces: Emory's sister, Crystal Moore, Brandon's brother and uncle, Kieran and a few others from Shout Louder. They might not be able to meet us in Annwn, they might not even understand what is happening, but they are with us, and they can defend a little collection of sleeping bodies from those who might want to hurt us.

The clocks strike two. It's time.

All across the country, people set off fireworks, bang pots and pans and beep their car horns – a flurry of noise to signal the start of a revolution, and to wake up anyone who might still be sleeping. I can hear it from inside the cathedral, followed shortly by the wail of police sirens as they rush to do Medraut's bidding. This will certainly be *too loud* for his liking. It's the signal for Ollie and me. As one, we take out our portals and open them, allowing the light of Annwn to swallow us in the middle of St Paul's Cathedral, beneath its great dome.

I swim up to the platform of Tintagel. The grounds are mercifully empty – the noise let off by hundreds of thanes and their allies has worked. Ollie appears next to me. It might not be long before people start falling asleep again, especially those on night shifts, so we have to be quick.

I leap off the platform and run towards the pile of rubble that was once Tintagel. I thrust my arm forward, feeling the welcome pull of Immral there and using it to throw aside the stones, to forge a path between them to the central circle. The multi-coloured marble is cracked in places, but still beautiful as I clear it of debris. I plunge my hands into it, feeling the inspyre glimmering deep inside it, the ancient power that helped to create it, and I say, 'I'm ready now.'

At first, there is nothing but a tingling across my fingers. Then the ground stretches, as if a great beast were awakening from below. The pressure in my head builds and builds until it pops. When I open my eyes, something is protruding from the centre of the circle. A hilt, many-coloured, a familiar object full of desire and terrible memories.

The last time I pulled Excalibur from its resting place, I handed power to Medraut and drained myself of my Immral. I caused the death of Andraste. But I had a warning then – my whole body was telling me to flee the temptation; that I wouldn't be equal to it. Not this time. This time my body is telling me to claim what is mine.

'You can do it, Fern,' Ollie says.

'I know,' I reply. I take hold of the sword's hilt and weigh it in my hands, absorbing the power I can feel inside it, waiting to be unleashed. I look over at Ollie. 'Give me your hand,' I say.

'What? No, it'll hurt me.'

'It won't,' I say. 'I won't let it.'

I take one side of the hilt, and he takes the other, and together, as it always should have been, we pull the sword from the stone like a knife from honey.

Chapter 50

As the power of Excalibur flows through my arm, I wrestle it into submission. Arthur's Immral fights me, desperate to wield the sword for a darker purpose. But this time, instead of leaching my strength, I'm able to use the sword's energy for my own ends. Just as I did last year with the Round Tables, I harness it, lashing its teeth and limbs until it bends to my will. I've never felt the full strength of my completed Immral until this moment. It's as though I've placed my Immral in a scale against Arthur's, and found it, for the first time, sufficient to tip the balance in my favour. It's intoxicating.

I harness Excalibur, sending my command deep into its metal. The sword's power pulses through me, creating tidal waves of Immral that crackle like lightning onto the rubble. Grasping the hilt with both hands, I imagine a Tintagel renewed, its walls strong against enemy invasion. I imagine the stables and the Round Table whole again. The sword obeys, but it asks a price. The inspyre inside me weaves around the Immral; a cord of imagination and power. I send my memories into the sword, feeding it with a diet it has never before known. This is a sword created for destruction, like all weapons. At first, it fights my commands; it's rusty and clumsy. But as I awaken the long dormant Fay powers deep in the metal, it begins to warm to its task. There I pluck on Puck's daring; here Nimue's patience.

'Look,' Ollie breathes next to me, his eyes on the sword's blade. 'It's so beautiful.'

I can sense every part of the sword as though it were part of my own body. The colours inside the metal are alive and moving.

Build, I command, and the sword sends out a great beam of light. The energy builds like a storm, whirling around us, recrafting the stones that were dust, replanting the trees that were fallen, until at last, Tintagel is whole again, and Ollie and I are standing beneath the vast and splendid dome of a castle renewed. The walls surrounding Tintagel are once more impenetrable. No one who means us harm can enter while I wield Excalibur; not even Medraut. But my skin is prickling. It has flaked away in places, as though the price of rebuilding was my own body. Asher's words come back to me. *It would come at a great cost*.

On the platform outside, I feel the cracks of the other thanes appearing, tentatively at first but then like popcorn in a pan. The doors open and they flood in: Jin and Easa, Rachel, Niamh, Nerizan and Natasha, Samson and Bandile.

'You did it!' they shout, as they run to their stations. Jin approaches me, her smile more contained than the others'. She spots my flaked skin and runs a hand over it gently, sadly.

'Jin?' I say, and when she meets my eyes I see the truth there. The reason she was so terse yesterday; the reason she watched me so carefully when she gave me the hilt of Lancelot's sword. She's known all this time.

'We'll use the cameras,' she says. 'That's all we need to do.'

I nod, pulling myself together. My task isn't over yet. I delve into the fabric of Excalibur. I feel the many flavours of the Fay who created it. The floral scent of Nimue and the iron of Merlin. And there, wound so thoroughly into the sword that it is the subtlest, basest note – the treacle of Andraste.

Bring them back. All of them, I tell the sword, and point it straight ahead, at the portal where Tintagel meets the rest of Annwn. With a flick of my mind, so simple, so painless, the portal activates. Blinding light shoots down from the top of the dome, far brighter than on any tournament day.

Patterns move behind the light. Shapes that begin fuzzily and then take more concrete form. Then the light dims, and the shapes emerge.

First come the animals, some of them pets, some of them mythological creatures who could never have walked through Ithr. I have forged them from the memories of every dreamer I can feel flowing through my veins.

Behind them, larger shapes step through the light. These are harder to create. Here are the imaginary friends, the playmates and the gods and goddesses of yore. Merlin and Nimue and Puck. Even as I focus my energy on my final task, I search for her amongst them. I know she's here. I know I succeeded. There. The wild bird's-nest hair; the ill-fitting armour.

Andraste strides towards me, her face as scarred as ever. I could have mended the scars, I suppose, but why would I do that? They're part of her and she is proud of them, as I am proud of mine. It is one of the many connections that bind us together.

'Nearly there,' she says softly, and I nod, throwing my energy into this hardest of tasks.

More shapes move behind the light. So many of them, all pulled from my memories, from my heart, and from the minds and hearts of the thanes around me and the dreamers who once more roam beyond the castle bounds. And when at last they are ready, I command the shapes to reveal themselves.

First through the light are two people, hand in hand. Seen next to each other, the similarities in their features are striking. Ramesh and Sachi, happier than I ever saw them in Annwn or Ithr. A rose-tinted version, but I don't regret that.

Next is Phoebe, and behind her Rafe and Emory, all a little hazy because it's been a while since I saw them. Brandon is behind them, jovial, although I can't quite erase the mark at his throat. Some memories don't go away. With him walk Vien, Milosz and Linnea, Maisie and Ben, and behind them all strides Lord Allenby.

There are more. So many more, some of them knights, some of them from other lores. And some who were once dreamers, mined from the memories of others. Because I can feel those other memories now, like an onslaught of images and emotions. The names in that notebook in Epping Forest leap from their pages and take form. Constantine Hale emerges, and every person killed by Medraut's followers.

At last, when Tintagel is full of ghosts, I create one final memory. I shape her as best I can from the photographs I have seen and from the memories I have glimpsed. But I can't help but add my own touches – a lightness to her mouth that makes her seem always about to smile; a warmth that I'm not at all sure was there in real life. But this is my gift to myself. I'm allowed to build the mother I always wanted.

I can hear Ollie's intake of breath as she approaches. She bows to Andraste and then she puts one hand each on mine and Ollie's cheeks.

'You've done it, both of you,' she says, her voice just as balsamic as I remember from the recorded snippets we have.

She opens her arms to us, but neither Ollie nor I can step into her embrace. I have spent so long imagining this moment. I have spent so long wanting to make her proud, wanting to follow in her footsteps. But I have come to know my mother, and now that she's here, I can't let everything I've discovered about her just fall away. The things she's done matter. She paid for some of them with her life, but she's made others pay too. She's made my father and brother pay, and that's something she's never had to reckon with.

Andraste is watching me intently. A deep pain, a deep weight in my heart – is holding me apart from everyone else. I have to ask her.

'If this doesn't work,' I say to her, 'do you think . . . Am I . . . ?'

Andraste's eyes are nothing but compassion. 'Only if you want to be.'

I nod, the weight settling deeper. 'I suppose we'd better win then.'

Rachel approaches. 'Fern, we're ready. We've primed the Round Table. We're just waiting for you.'

'There's one more thing,' I say. I close my eyes and send out a call across Annwn. I can sense them, on a distant plain, but they hear me. They hear me and they come with the speed granted them by Excalibur itself. The doors to Tintagel bang open once more and a dozen horses gallop in, skating on the stone floors. At their head is my Lamb, her ears flopping in every direction as she slides to a halt in front of me.

'Hello, girl,' I whisper into her mane. 'Shall we have one last ride?'

All around me, knights are mounting their steeds: Ollie on Balius, Samson on his mare and Natasha on Domino. Loco dances around our legs. Andraste raises her arms and from the dome drops a golden chariot, its bejewelled wheels pulled by two huge lions. She springs into the carriage, hefting her sword in one hand and the reins in the other.

'Are we ready?' I say.

'Not yet,' a voice calls from the entrance. Miss D strides in and vaults onto the back of one of the riderless horses. 'Someone find me a weapon, please,' she says to a reeve.

'I thought you had paid your dues,' I remark.

'It turns out I had a little left on account.'

A hush falls upon the hall, brimming though it is with life and memory and imagination. I realise that everyone's waiting for me to make a speech. It's as if they don't know me at all.

'Why are you still looking at me?' I ask them all, smiling. 'I'm not your leader. I'm not your Chosen One. The only reason I'm here now is because my mother persuaded someone to give me their Immral, and my brother chose to give me his.'

I look across at Ollie, my gratitude for him springing up like water from a well. 'I am special, but no more than all of you. The thing that makes us powerful isn't my Immral, not really. It's that every single one of us has *chosen* to be here. We're not fighting because we've been brainwashed. We're not fighting because of hatred or fear. We're fighting for our freedom, and the freedom of the people and the world that we love. *That's* what's going to help us win this.'

All around the castle, people are nodding, arming themselves, embracing each other. Ollie starts it: he places a hand on my shoulder, and I reach across to grab Samson's hand. It spreads from thane to thane, from god to dream, as everyone in the building takes hold of a friend, a lover, a soulmate, until we are all connected. The chains that bind us spiral out like a flower opening its petals to the sun. As one, we take a moment. Then I heft my sword, and the chain breaks, although the spell of our bond lingers in the air.

Samson leans across and kisses me. 'See you on the other side?'

Easa approaches Ollie, and looks up at him, gripping his leg. 'You come back to me, okay?' Easa says. 'I don't care what you did. Make sure you come back, and then we can talk.'

Rachel nods at me from her place at the Round Table. 'We've connected the dome with portals in the other thaneships,' she says. 'We're good to go.'

'It's time!' I shout. 'Everyone to their places.'

Rachel begins the countdown. 'Rips activating in five, four, three –'

I raise Excalibur, pointing it directly at the dome above us.

'Two –'

I send a silent prayer to keep my loved ones safe.

'One –'

And I send my Immral through the sword and into the air, and tear great holes in the fabric of Annwn.

Chapter 51

Light pours through the rip in Annwn as it grows wider and wider, tearing across the dome of Tintagel and down to the marble floor. Castle gives way to cathedral, and as one we burst through the rip into Ithr. I feel the pull of the ghosts on my Immral, but I fix them all in my mind, holding their ephemeral bodies together with inspyre. We charge out into the daylight of Ithr, hundreds of ghosts flooding the courtyard and streets around St Paul's.

I turn Lamb to the west, but others spread far and wide. Kieran's sister goes east, to find her family. Amina's memory looks to the mountains of Wales. Some of them fly to the outreaches of Scotland; some across the sea to Ireland. Imaginary friends go in search of the adults who once played with them. Long dead pets dash to find their old owners. And the dead touch ghostly foreheads with the ones who still remember them. I can feel them all, stretching out and out across Ithr like a spider's web on a dewy morning, glittering with memory.

Across the country, other rips blast through Annwn, a chain reaction set off from the one in Tintagel, designed by Rachel when she connected every thaneship's portal to ours. Carys leads her knights out into Ithr's Cambridge; Lady Kaur gallops across the Cornish moors with her regiments behind her. I can feel them all, their energies pulsing through me. Something sparks, across the country, in the dulled minds of those who witness the ghosts. Wonder and awe, the most powerful emotions of all. The only emotions that can truly combat Medraut's fear. As we race past, some people scream and run, but more reach out to try to touch us.

Lamb and I lead the group of knights and memories that charges towards Westminster, skirting the shining Thames as it slides us along its curves. Up ahead, Big Ben chimes four o'clock. Time for Medraut's speech, and his reckoning.

The Houses of Parliament is a stately, ribbed building that sits on the river, its many windows glinting in the afternoon sun. The security guards at its perimeter back away from the ghostly army I'm leading, trying to barricade the doors when it becomes clear that we're heading their way.

But we ghosts do not care for doors.

I urge Lamb up, and she leaps like a gazelle through one of the windows, landing in a shower of glass inside Parliament. My fellow knights land around me. Samson leaps off his horse and calls to his team, 'Find Medraut! Find him!' Nerizan and Bandile follow him. I ignore the people cowering away from us. My task is elsewhere. I push Lamb into a canter through the hallways. The security team inside the entrance try to stand their ground, but they are no match for Ollie and me. Balius kicks one of them aside, while Ollie rips the guns from the others' hands with his chakrams. I focus on the main doors, pushing my Immral inside the locks. It doesn't want to obey me, even though I now wield Excalibur.

Then a voice rings out. Medraut's voice. It doesn't come through any speaker. It drills into my head, quiet but inescapable.

'Citizens of the world,' it says, 'it is time to unite our countries, our continents, beneath one banner. No more war, no more territories. Only one people, and one voice.' I can feel the power behind his words, but more than that – I can feel what it does to the already fragile walls that keep Annwn and Ithr separate. Another rip opens behind me, one that slices across the worlds – Annwn, Ithr and the grey in-between. I feel more opening across the land, each one a draw on the inspyre that I am using to sustain myself and the other ghosts.

But with more rips comes more Immral, and when I now command the doors to open, they obey. The lock slides back and the hinges burst from their mounts. Ollie pushes the doors apart. Behind them, a crowd is waiting. At its head: our father, and Ramesh and Sachi's parents. They rush in, urging the security guards to join us.

In the middle of the chaos, my father stops and gapes. My mother comes to him, runs her hands over his features. It is the image of true love.

'Fern, we've found him!' Samson shouts from one of the doors. I leap from Lamb's back and run after him, calling to the others to follow. We race through tunnel-like corridors where the paintings and wallpaper shimmer and warp as the barriers between the worlds crumble. And behind us, from the grey in-between world, comes the hiss and click of the sluaghs.

'There's too many of them,' Ollie says. There are – far more than we've ever encountered. Medraut has summoned them all to this place: hundreds of tortured, broken knights. An army of our own friends, used against us.

'Keep going, we'll hold them off!' Niamh shouts. She and Natasha join hands, throwing their hopes and dreams towards the advancing creatures. I can feel them flowing through me – their friendship, true and pure, and the hopes they hold for each other to live a safe and joyful life. Their undeclared love, and the plans they each had to admit it when this is all over. But there are too many sluaghs. Too many for even the most beautiful dream. Niamh and Natasha's hopes bloom so, so brightly inside me for a brief, blinding moment, and then the sluaghs advance, and I feel their souls blink out as one.

The corridors open out into a wide chamber that I have seen many times on television. Galleries look down upon two sets of ramped benches that face each other across a wide pathway. In the centre of that pathway, Sebastien Medraut stands in front of a film crew, repeating his mantra, *One Voice*, as his sharp suit crackles with violet Immral. The chamber shimmers and the green leather that lines the benches fades to grey.

Behind him stand his advisors and there, right at the back, are Charlie and her mother, neat and cowed.

Medraut smiles, and I hear his voice in my head, one Immral to another. *You're too late.*

A cry goes up behind me, and I don't need to turn to know that the sluaghs have caught up with us. I can feel them as an absence of inspyre, each one a coiling mess of Immral attached to the beating, soulless heart of a former knight. The snakes snap and stab at humans and ghosts alike.

'Remember!' I shout, using Excalibur to take out two sluaghs in a single stroke. 'Don't forget!'

The knights take up the chant, and the people with us call out the names of their lost, until the space is a cacophony of names. The creatures are everywhere, though, blocking my path to Medraut. There is one thing that might give us an edge. With a thought, I send him across the chamber: Lord Allenby's ghost, offering a hand to Charlie, willing her to come back to her true family.

Medraut doesn't see what's happening until Charlie, ever so slowly, pulls away from her mother, walks past the sluaghs, and looks up at Lord Allenby in wonder. 'We need your help,' he tells her. 'Ready?' She nods silently, and I can feel the imagination that refuses to lie dormant for long inside her sparkle to life.

'Lottie!' Medraut says, his voice high and clear above the roar of the fight. 'Lottie, what are you doing?'

As if waking from a trance, Lottie turns to him. 'I've only ever had one father,' she tells Medraut. 'And it was never you.'

She joins hands with Lord Allenby's ghost, and throws her dreams towards me; dreams that are coloured in curiosity and freedom and deep grief. I take them and mould them into a shield; one that is strong enough to stretch across the knights and our little army, and to push back the sluaghs for a moment.

Medraut snarls, and sends balls of Immral shooting towards us. I raise Excalibur and knock them away. We advance.

'Be careful,' Ollie warns, as we pass the filming set up, the cameras still rolling.

Medraut backs up, all the way to the podium where he gave

so many of the speeches that wrought division under the guise of unity. He remains upright and proud to the last.

'It's time,' I say softly, so that only he and I can hear. Still crackling with Immral, he raises both his hands and tries to push me away, but even though I feel the strain, I withstand the attempt. Then Andraste descends upon him, pulling back his arms and exposing his chest.

'Do it, Fern,' she says, her voice dark and wild.

I raise Excalibur. I have waited so long to do this – to kill the man who killed my mother, my friends, who tried to kill me. I have imagined this moment, wondered whether I have it in me to kill a person like this – not in the chaos of battle but in cold blood. Now he's in front of me, I know that this has to happen, even though I don't relish the execution. I can read his thoughts, and there is no remorse or doubt there. His purpose is pure and deadly and unstoppable.

I press the sword towards him, but with the last of his strength, he withstands me and the sword, as I thought he would.

You're not strong enough, he taunts me. *You never were.*

'I never had to be,' I say, smiling at him for the first time. I call upon Excalibur to expand, its hilt lengthening until it is as long as the chamber; as long as London; as long as Ithr. The power of Annwn is here, and, as one, every ghost and human who yearns for discovery and beauty and revenge is able to take hold of the sword. Their thousands of imaginations, combined with mine, are stronger than any amount of Immral that Medraut can concoct. For they, like me, were not born with the mantle of Chosen One; they decided to wear it. Medraut's eyes widen as he realises that together we are stronger than him. His eyes flick to Charlie, both her hands firmly on the hilt; and to Ramesh and Sachi's parents; and to Mum's ghost, the ghost of the woman who toppled him from power seventeen years ago; and finally to me and Ollie, side by side, as the blade sinks into his chest.

He whispers something. At first I think he's begging for mercy. It is only when the last of his Immral crackles from his final breath that I realise what he's doing.

'Someone stop the sluaghs!' I call, but I'm too late. Medraut's last command to them was to destroy the rolling cameras, the ones that I was going to use to heal Ithr, as he had used them to break it. The snakes descend on the equipment, crushing the plastic and ripping the wires from their casing.

Medraut's lifeless body folds to the floor, the wound that killed him no more than a red mark on his chest. Excalibur is heavy in my grip. The sluaghs begin to disintegrate, wisping into the air with a final hiss. I run to the cameras, pointing Excalibur at them desperately, commanding it to fix them. But the power of Annwn is fading. The rips are closing. I can't mend the cameras, the final pieces of the plan.

'Fern?' Nerizan says. She holds up a hand. It disappears before our eyes. I focus my Immral, put her back together again, but I'm nearly spent.

'You have to get back to Annwn,' Andraste says.

'But the cameras –' I say.

'It's too late, Fern. Run, now!'

Mum's ghost stays with Dad as Ollie and I rush down the corridors. I look back to see them entwined in each other's arms. There's a pull on my mind as I sense one rip closing after another. The strength of my Immral is fading. All around me, ghosts flicker in and out of existence, and each one is a weight in my head, clamouring for attention. We vault onto our horses and gallop back out into London, racing for the biggest rip of all: the one that will take us back to Tintagel.

Across the country, ghosts flow back to the safety of Annwn, but my power here is waning, and I can't save them all. Some fall, some disintegrate as they run, and *forgive me, forgive me* is all I can think because I know that in some deep-down place I'm choosing to sacrifice them over the ones I know and love.

'Nearly there!' Ollie cries out, his voice distant. He's fading, even as we cross the courtyard and clatter up the cathedral's steps. I reach for him, and he for me. He flickers . . . We are at the rip . . .

I throw myself through the closing rip, dragging Ollie with me. We land, tangled at our horses' feet – a panting, heart-hammering mess. The rip closes, and we are in Tintagel once more, the remnants of our army pooled around us, and the harkers and reeves who stayed in Annwn cheering and checking on us.

Jin runs over. 'Did you do it?' she asks.

'We killed Medraut,' I tell her. She reads my face to understand that I couldn't use the cameras to reverse what he had done.

'Oh, Fern,' she whispers.

The thanes pour out into the sunlight of Annwn, out onto Tintagel's lawns. The rips have caused untold destruction: London is barren, its buildings crumbled. The Thames runs dry.

'But we killed him,' Rachel says. 'It'll reverse, won't it? It has to.'

'Any moment now,' Ollie says, looking up at the bare branches of an oak tree. The others are craning their necks to see if the sky fills with birds, or climbing the walls of the castle to glimpse the rejuvenation of Annwn beyond Tintagel's bounds. There is not a piece of me that isn't pounding heart.

'Come on, come on,' Samson murmurs.

It's going to happen, I tell myself. All it needs is a spark. A blossoming of inspyre, to replenish all that we've lost. Like a flame, starting somewhere innocuous and spreading slowly. Maybe it's already begun far away, in the places where Medraut struggled to reach. That would make sense. That's what's happening. It will take time to get here, that's all.

But I know, deep down, that my hope is unfounded. I can feel Annwn through my veins, through the sword I still hold loosely in one hand. I'm connected to this world in a way that none of the others are. There isn't enough inspyre left to make Annwn whole again. We were too late.

The murmurs of distress start as the truth sinks in for the others. I can't be with them, not right now.

I know what I have to do.

Chapter 52

The knights Lancelot, Bedevere, Palomides, Dagonet and Gawain assembled in the tower of Avalon to debate the matter of the Grail. The sword Excalibur lay in the centre of the table, wrapped in sack cloth. None of them spoke of the guilt they felt at what they had done. It was a coward's murder: ambushing their own king in Ithr, where his power could not help him. But it had been done in the name of Annwn, and in the name of the vows they took, when they believed that they were pledging to protect this land, not destroy it.

It had not been enough to undo Arthur's devastation. The tower of Avalon was the only structure that had survived.

'We have no choice but to choose the Grail,' Bedevere said. 'That's the only way of restoring this land now.'

'But who?' Gawain said. 'Each one of us has bonded with Annwn. Any one of us could be the Grail.'

The knights couldn't meet each others' eyes.

'I have a wife and three children,' Palomides said. 'I cannot leave them destitute.'

'My castle and land provide jobs,' Dagonet said.

'I must care for my mother,' said Gawain.

Lancelot and Bedevere looked at each other silently, struggling with what they must do. The grey land beyond the tower seemed to shimmer in anticipation.

'I will be the Grail,' Lancelot said at last.

'There must be another way. It's asking too much,' Bedevere said.

'No, it is not.' He looked at them all steadily. 'It's not asking too much, my lords. One life, given freely, to save a whole world. A life full of joy. Is that not what Annwn has given to us, time and time again? Who are any of us to resent sacrificing ourselves for the chance to save such beauty?'

One by one, the knights excused themselves, until only two remained. Lancelot bowed his head in acceptance.

'You do not need to do this,' Bedevere told him.

'No,' said Lancelot, 'but I will, for the land that I love.'

Chapter 53

I push past the other thanes and walk, unseeing, back into Tintagel. I don't return to the knights' chamber, or greet the cheers of the reeves who pass me.

'Fern?' Samson's voice is the only one that stops me. I turn, fixing a smile on my face. He hugs me and I cling to him, his warmth, his love.

'You did it,' he whispers.

'Not exactly.'

'We'll work it out,' he says, kissing me again and again. 'We'll find the Grail, even if it takes months. A new mission for us. What do you say?'

'Definitely.' I reach up and kiss him deeply. 'I've got to go and do something. Meet you in the knights' chamber?'

He nods, bemused, but is carried onwards by the other thanes. Bandile is clutching a bottle of something in one hand. Nerizan is dancing with Rachel, tears and laughter mixing. Ollie and Easa are whispering to each other, clasping hands.

I unlock Lord Allenby's office door with my Immral, and pass inside. The light coming through the stained-glass windows coats the room in a melancholy glaze. Lord Allenby's desk stands, empty and abandoned. The wooden panel that hides the doorknobs is open. I look for a specific one: smooth ivory, as pale and sun-cleaned as the place where it will take me.

Stonehenge greets me like an old friend, but it is so different from when I was last here. Only one henge stone still stands, teetering. The rest of the circle has vanished, or lies in pitiful piles of teeth and finger bones on the grass.

The bones call to me, groaning and creaking with the desperation of holding on to existence. I sit on the sacrificial slab, turn my face up to the empty sky, and feel the grass beneath my boots crumple and stretch. I take a deep breath of the empty air. But nothing can relieve the crushing weight on my chest.

'Fern? What are you doing here?'

Ollie has followed me through, as I somehow knew he would. I see a flash of memory: Jin telling him to find me. She knew what I had come to do, and she knew I'd need to say goodbye.

'We need a new game plan,' Ollie's saying. 'We've got to find the Grail, right? That can –'

'I know where the Grail is,' I tell him.

He stares at me. 'You . . . That's great! Why didn't you say before? Where . . .' He trails off. He sees the truth in my eyes. He understands without me having to say anything. Because he's my twin, my soulmate.

'No,' he whispers. 'No, you can't. You can't be.'

Andraste appears behind him, vibrant and beautiful, with the grime of battle still on her skin. I don't know if she followed me through the doorway from Tintagel or whether I called to her, as I always used to do when I was desperate.

As Andraste speaks, I dig my fingers into the soil, trying to come to terms with what I have to do. Trying to tell myself that it isn't just that it must be done, but that it will be worth it. One life to re-make a world. One life to return the voices of the silent. One little life to spark a new Renaissance. That's cheap. That's nothing.

'The path of the Grail is a choice,' Andraste is saying, and as she explains, the warmth that has flowed through me every time I've vowed to protect Annwn over the last year flows through me once more. Only now I understand that it is the deepest power of Annwn, acknowledging my promise to it.

'There has to be another way,' Ollie says, his voice cracking.

'I'm sorry,' Andraste says. 'There is no other way. Fern chose to be the Grail a long time ago, even though she didn't know it.'

'When *did* you realise?' Ollie says.

'Just before the battle. But I think, deep down, part of me's known for months. I just didn't want to face it.'

The story of the Immral who turned his arm into a waterfall. Every time I repaired something with my power and my skin flaked away – the beginnings of the *great cost* of the Grail. The way Sophia told me that my fixing Tintagel was nothing to do with my Immral. It was all leading to this realisation.

'But what if *I* want to be the Grail?' Ollie says, shaking me. '*I* choose it, okay?'

'It doesn't work like that, Ols. It's not a split-second sacrifice. It's not something I can give you, like you gave me Immral.'

I suddenly see how I have been built, layer upon layer of yearning and loss and effort, to become the woman I am now.

The woman who sees that if Annwn is to be saved, she cannot be.

'This wasn't how it was supposed to end,' Ollie whispers. '*I* was supposed to be the one who died. I thought that was how it was going to go.'

'I'd never have let that happen.'

The unfairness of all of this bears down upon me, and I crumple into his arms. We clutch each other, our chests heaving. I can't bear it, any of it. For so long, I had no interest in living. I didn't want friends, I didn't want Ithr at all – it had no use for me and I had no love for it. But now – now I have friends there. Rachel and Jin and Samson . . . Oh God, Samson. Part of me is relieved that he isn't here, that he's celebrating with the others, unaware of what is about to happen. Part of me wishes I could kiss him, lose myself in him and have him lose himself inside me, one last time and forever.

But Ollie, my brother, is the one I will miss the most. I have to make this bearable for him. I don't want him to make guilt his companion.

'You have to pack my life into yours now,' I murmur into his ear. 'You have to live for both of us, okay? If you think you're going to honour me by just giving up, I'll never forgive you.'

He half laughs, half cries.

'I mean it, Ollie. Don't you dare fade away. We've hated each other for so long. And we've just turned that into something wonderful. Please don't make us about sadness again. You're the one who has to do that for us now. And you have to make sure Dad does it too. He has to learn to remember Mum and me without letting us imprison him. We're not his gaolers.'

Ollie nods. 'I know. I know.'

I take his hands again. I want to say something I haven't said in five years. I want to say it so badly, but it's too loaded now.

Andraste is hovering in the background, gazing up at the empty sky. The dying henge creaks and cracks, a ticking clock reminding me that I must do it now, or even my sacrifice will not be enough.

I stand, brush myself down, breathe deeply, try to control my emotions.

'Will you stay with me?' I ask Ollie and Andraste, the two who have been by my side from the very beginning.

'I will always be with you, and you will always be with me,' Andraste says, laying a hand on my shoulder. 'You are a warrior woman, Fern. You are one of my stories now, if you want to be. You have all of Annwn to explore, you know.'

I think of my ambition, the one I used to combat the sluaghs. My dream of discovering all there is to find in this beautiful, mercurial world. Maybe death won't be so bad.

Ollie takes my hand. 'I'll always look for you in my dreams.'

I push Excalibur into the earth, and make it sink deep beneath Stonehenge. The Fay will know what to do with it. Then it is time. I sit cross-legged on the stone slab, close my eyes, and sink inside myself.

I'm not dying, not really. I'm becoming one with the world that I love so much. Art, science and creation is all about giving something of yourself. All my dreams, gifted to all the dreamers. It's up to them what they do with them.

It only hurts as much as I let it. I take the inspyre that holds my body together and break it apart, in sand-like fragments at first, then bigger pieces. They whirl in the breeze of Annwn, whisked away to a far-off place. Ollie and Andraste never leave my side, but this journey is one I must take alone.

Suddenly, there is no pain, only the sweet melancholy of a dying flower. My lifeblood, my flesh, my bones, transform into inspyre. My head fills with all the stories that ever were, and all the stories that ever will be.

There is a moment where I hold on to the image of my brother, smiling through his tears, trying to tell me it's okay. He'll be okay. It's hard to say goodbye, but I have to.

We say the words at the same time, a final whisper that marks the passing of my mortal body. 'I love you.'

I smile

I break apart

And I

s c a t t e r

m y s e l f

across a multitude

an era

a universe

of dreams.

Acknowledgements

Well, that's it. The trilogy is done, and it's time to say goodbye to Fern and Ollie and Annwn. Writing this book has involved an odd, potent mixture of heartache and joy and finally-I-can-write-this-scene moments. What has kept me going through all of it are the readers and booksellers who have so kindly and generously messaged me to say nice things about the first two books and to anxiously check whether Ollie would survive (well . . . I hope you're happy!). My first thanks have to go to you all – while the very thought of anyone reading my work is absolutely terrifying, I have to admit that it is necessary in order to make any kind of living from this book-writing business. Thank you, to my readers, for taking ownership of these stories through your own imaginations; and to the booksellers who have seen fit to give my books some space in your shops, when there are so many incredible novels out there to choose from.

The team at Hot Key, once again, have done the most amazing job of shepherding this book into existence. Thank you to Georgia Murray, the editor of dreams, for not letting me get away with all the plot and character holes I was trying to get away with; to my copy editors Melissa Hyder and Jenny

Jacoby for picking up on every tiny inconsistency; and to my proofreader Jane Burnard. Thanks also to the marketing and publicity teams, in particular Emma Quick and Molly Holt, who have borne with my scattergun ideas with endless patience. I think we can also agree that Sophie McDonnell and Gavin Reece have excelled themselves yet again on the cover. It's almost enough to make me want to write a fourth book just to see if they could make something even more gorgeous. Thanks also to the audio team, especially Marina Stavropolou at Hot Key and the amazing Billie Fulford-Brown, who brings the characters' voices to life so perfectly.

Thank you to my agenting team – Anna Dixon, who is just the best at pep talks and who I know will always be on my side – and James Munro and Erin Bradshaw at WME.

Thanks are also due to my dear friends, whose support and laughter is sustenance. Special shout-outs are due to Chris, Simon, Mat, Lizzie D and Lizzie C, Rosie, Greg, Nat and Gez; to fellow authors Kat Ellis, Bex Hogan, Menna van Praag and Gytha Lodge; and to my little band of screenwriting-authors, James Bailey, Anna Bell, Lorraine Brown, Katharine Corr, Ava Eldred, Clare Harlow, Gillian Perdue and Tina Orr-Munro, for *Ted Lasso* arguments and impromptu group therapy.

Last but not least, thank you to my family – my darling husband Alex and our darling daughter Ada, and my parents, Louette and Bob. I believed in magic, and I found it, thanks to you.

Holly Race

Holly worked as a development executive in the film and TV industry for nearly a decade. These days, when she isn't writing, she can usually be found either script editing or baking. She is a Faber Academy graduate, and the first book in this trilogy, *Midnight's Twins*, was her debut novel. Holly used to live in Fern and Ollie's neck of the woods, but now resides in Cambridge with her husband and daughter.

You can find out more about her and keep up to date with her book news at www.hollyrace.com